BASIC
English
Grammar

FOURTH EDITION
WORKBOOK

Betty S. Azar
Stacy A. Hagen

Basic English Grammar, Fourth Edition
Workbook

Copyright © 2014, 2006, 1996 by Betty Schrampfer Azar
All rights reserved.

Azar Associates: Shelley Hartle, Editor, and Sue Van Etten, Manager

Pearson Education, 10 Bank Street, White Plains, NY 10606

Staff credits: The people who made up the **Basic English Grammar, Fourth Edition, Workbook** team, representing editorial, production, design, and manufacturing, are Dave Dickey, Nancy Flaggman, Amy McCormick, Robert Ruvo, and Marian Wassner.

Text composition: S4Carlisle Publishing Services

Illustrations: Don Martinetti and Chris Pavely

Printed in the United States of America
ISBN 10: 0-13-294227-5
ISBN 13: 978-0-13-294227-0

38 2022

For Julianna

-S. H.

Contents

The titles listed below, for example, *Singular pronouns + **be**,* refer to section names, not practice titles. In general, one section has multiple exercises.
The chart numbers refer to the grammar explanations in the *Basic English Grammar* **Student Book.**

Preface

The *Basic English Grammar Workbook* is a self-study textbook. It is keyed to the explanatory grammar charts found in *Basic English Grammar, Fourth Edition,* a classroom teaching text for English language learners. Students can use the *Workbook* independently to enhance their understanding of English structures. Practice ranges from the basic to the more challenging so students can choose from a variety of exercises that will help them use English meaningfully and correctly.

This *Workbook* is also a resource for teachers who need exercise material for additional classwork, homework, testing, or individualized instruction.

The answers to the practices can be found in the *Answer Key* in the back of the *Workbook.* Its pages are perforated so that they can be detached to make a separate booklet. However, if teachers want to use the *Workbook* as a classroom teaching text, the *Answer Key* can be removed at the beginning of the term.

Chapter 1
Using Be

▶ **Practice 1. Using *he*, *she*, or *it*.** (Chart 1-1)
Rewrite each sentence using the correct pronoun: *he*, *she*, or *it*.

1. The bus is here. _It is here._

2. Sara is late. _She is late_

3. English is difficult. _It is difficult_

4. Mr. Jefferson is sick. _It is sick_

5. Mrs. Jefferson is also sick. _It is sick_

6. Henry is ready. _He is Ready_

7. The weather is cold. _It is cold_

8. Ms. Hogan is single. _It is single_

▶ **Practice 2. Using *am*, *is*, or *are*.** (Chart 1-1)
Complete each sentence with *am*, *is*, or *are*.

1. She ___is___ hungry.

2. I ___am___ sick.

3. You ___are___ nice.

4. The weather ___is___ hot.

5. Mr. Kimura ___is___ old.

6. Julianna ___is___ young.

7. It ___is___ cold.

8. You ___are___ early.

9. Ms. Rossi ___is___ here.

10. She ___is___ nervous.

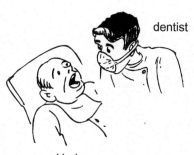

dentist

He is nervous.

► **Practice 3. Singular and plural pronouns.** (Charts 1-1 and 1-2)
Choose the correct picture.

A   **B**

1. I am here. _____A_____

2. You are sick. _____A, B_____

3. They are ready. _____A, B_____

4. We are tired. _____A, B_____

5. She is from Canada. _____A_____

6. You are late. _____A, B_____

► **Practice 4. Pronoun + be.** (Charts 1-1 and 1-2)
Create your own chart by completing the sentences with a form of **be**.

1. I _____am_____ cold.   6. You (two) _____are_____ cold.

2. You (one) _____are_____ cold.   7. We _____are_____ cold.

3. He _____is_____ cold.   8. You and I _____am_____ cold.

4. She _____is_____ cold.   9. They _____are_____ cold.

5. It _____is_____ cold.   10. You and they _____are_____ cold.

► **Practice 5. Pronoun + be.** (Charts 1-1 and 1-2)
Complete the sentences with the correct pronouns.

1. Jack and Bruno are homesick. _____They_____ are homesick.

2. Bruno is homesick. _____He_____ is homesick.

3. Julia is homesick. _____she_____ is homesick.

4. Mr. Rivas is homesick. _____He_____ is homesick.

5. Mrs. Rivas is homesick. _____she_____ is homesick.

6. Mrs. Rivas and Mr. Rivas are homesick. _____they_____ are homesick.

7. Mr. Rivas and I are homesick. _____We_____ are homesick.

8. You and I are homesick. _____We_____ are homesick.

9. Jenna is happy. _____she_____ is happy.

10. You and Jenna are happy. ___they___ are happy.

11. The children are happy. ___is___ are happy.

12. Dr. Chen is ready. Dr. Greco is ready. ___they___ are ready.

13. Ella is ready. ___she___ is ready.

14. Brian is ready. ___he___ is ready.

15. Ella, Brian, and I are ready. ___they___ are ready.

▶ **Practice 6. A or an.** (Chart 1-3)
Write **a** or **an** before each word.

1. ___an___ office   6. ___an___ animal

2. ___a___ boy   7. ___an___ ear

3. ___a___ desk   8. ___a___ letter

4. ___an___ apple   9. ___a___ table

5. ___a___ city   10. ___an___ insect

INSECTS

a bee   a fly

an ant   a mosquito

▶ **Practice 7. A or an.** (Chart 1-3)
Complete the sentences with **a** or **an**. Then choose *yes* or *no*.

1. Chinese is ___a___ language.   (yes)   no

2. Paris is ___a___ city.   (yes)   no

3. Canada is ___a___ continent.   yes   (no)

4. Hawaii is ___an___ island.   (yes)   no

5. Africa is ___a___ place.   (yes)   no

6. English is ___a___ country.   yes   (no)

7. French is ___a___ language.   (yes)   no

8. Asia is ___a___ continent.   (yes)   no

► **Practice 8. Plural nouns.** (Chart 1-4)
Write the plural forms for the given nouns.

Singular		Plural
1. a city	→	_cities_
2. a dog	→	dogs
3. a language	→	languages
4. a machine	→	machines
5. a country	→	contries
6. a season	→	seasons
7. a dictionary	→	dictionaries

► **Practice 9. _A, an,_ or _Ø._** (Charts 1-3 and 1-4)
Write complete sentences using _is/are_ and _a/an/Ø_ (nothing).

1. A bee \ insect
   A bee is an insect.
2. Ant \ insect
   Ants are insects.
3. Russian and Spanish \ language
   Russian and spanis are language
4. China \ country
   china is a. Country
5. South America \ continent
   south America is a. Continent
6. Dogs \ animal
   Dogs are animals
7. Bangkok \ city
   Bangkok is a City
8. Thailand \ country
   thailand is a country

► **Practice 10. Singular and plural nouns.** (Charts 1-3 and 1-4)
Complete the words with _-s_ or Ø.

1. A lion _Ø_ is an animal _Ø_ .
2. Lion _s_ are animals _s_ .
3. Korean _Ø_ is a language _Ø_ .
4. An air conditioner _Ø_ is a machine _Ø_ .
5. Tulip _s_ are flower _s_ .
6. A fly _Ø_ is an insect _Ø_ .
7. Flies _s_ are insect _s_ .
8. Spring _Ø_ and summer _Ø_ are season _s_ .

a lion

a tulip

9. Soccer _*o*_ and tennis _*o*_ are sport _*s*_.

► **Practice 11. *Be* with singular and plural nouns.** (Charts 1-3 and 1-4)
Choose the correct verb.

1. Mosquitos (*is* / (*are*)) insects.

2. A chicken ((*is*) / *are*) an animal.

3. Chinese and Russian (*is* / (*are*)) languages.

4. December and January (*is* / (*are*)) months.

5. A refrigerator ((*is*) / *are*) a machine.

6. Refrigerators (*is* / (*are*)) machines.

7. Bali ((*is*) / *are*) an island.

8. Indonesia and Malaysia (*is* / (*are*)) countries.

9. Carrots (*is* / (*are*)) vegetables.

10. Winter ((*is*) / *are*) a season.

11. Horses (*is* / (*are*)) animals.

a refrigerator

a horse

► **Practice 12. Pronoun + *be*.** (Charts 1-3 and 1-4)
Complete the sentences. Use a verb (***am*, *is*,** or ***are***) and a noun (***a student*** or ***students***).

1. She ___*is a student*___.

2. I ___am a student___.

3. You (one person) ___You are one person.___.

4. You (two persons) ___You are two persons.___.

5. They ___they are students.___.

6. He ___He is student.___.

7. We ___We are students___.

8. Carlos and you ___Carlos and you are students___.

9. He and I ___are students___.

10. Mia and I ___are students.___.

▶ **Practice 13.** *Be* **with singular and plural nouns.** (Charts 1-3 and 1-4)
Write complete sentences. Use a verb (*is* or *are*). Use the singular or plural form of the noun.

1. Asia \ continent   *Asia is a continent.*

2. Africa \ continent   *Africa is a continent*

3. Asia and Africa \ continent   *Asia and africa are continent*

4. Paris \ city   *Paris is a city.*

5. Cairo \ city   *Cairo is a city*

6. Paris and Cairo \ city   *Paris and Cairo are city*

7. Malaysia \ country   *Malaysia is a country*

8. Japan and Malaysia \ country   *Japan and Malaysia are a contry*

▶ **Practice 14.** *Be* **with singular and plural.** (Charts 1-3 and 1-4)
Complete the sentences with *is* or *are* and one of the nouns from the box. Use the correct singular form of the noun (with *a* or *an*) or the correct plural form.

animal	country	language
city	insect	machine

1. A dog   *is an animal* .

2. Dogs   *are animals* .

3. Spanish   *Spanish is a language* .

4. Spanish and Chinese   *spanish and chinese are languages*

5. Thailand and Vietnam   *thailand and vietnam are countries*

6. Thailand   *thailand is a country* .

7. A butterfly   *butterfly is an animal* .

8. Butterflies   *Butterlies are a animal* .

9. A car   *Car is an machine* .

10. Cars   *Cars is a machine* .

11. Berlin   *Berlin is a city* .

12. Berlin and Baghdad   *Berlin and Baghdad are a city*

a butterfly

► **Practice 15. Contractions with *be*.** (Chart 1-5)
Write the contraction.

1. I am _____I'm_____
2. you are _____You're_____
3. he is _____He's_____
4. we are _____We're_____

5. it is _____It's_____
6. they are _____they're_____
7. she is _____she's_____

► **Practice 16. Negative forms of *be*.** (Chart 1-6)
Complete the sentences with the negative form of *be*.

1. I ___am not___ sick.
2. You ___are not___ sick.
3. He ___is not___ sick.
4. She ___is not___ sick.
5. The cat ___is not___ sick.
6. It ___it's___ sick.

7. We ___are not___ sick.
8. They ___are not___ sick.
9. The students ___are not___ sick.
10. Katie and I ___are not___ sick.
11. The teacher ___is not___ sick.
12. The teachers ___is not___ sick.

► **Practice 17. Negative forms of *be* and contractions.** (Chart 1-6)
Complete the sentences with the negative form of *be*. Then write the contracted form. Give both forms where possible.

	Be: Negative		Contraction
1. You	are not	late.	aren't OR you're not
2. She	is not	late.	isn't or is not
3. I	am not	late.	I'm not or I am not
4. He	is not	late.	He's not or He isn't
5. The bus	is not	late.	s'nt or isnt
6. It	is not	late.	It's not or itsnt
7. We	are not	late.	We're not or we arent
8. You	are not	late.	arent or you're not
9. They	are not	late.	arent or they're not

► **Practice 18. Using *is*, *isn't*, *are*, or *aren't*.** (Charts 1-5 and 1-6)
Complete the sentences with *is*, *isn't*, *are*, or *aren't*.

1. Canada and Sweden _____aren't_____ continents.

2. Japan _____isn't_____ a language.

3. A computer _____is_____ a machine.

4. Tennis _____isn't_____ a season.

5. Bees _____isn't_____ insects.

6. Carrots _____isn't_____ animals.

7. A rabbit _____is_____ an animal.

8. Seoul and Beijing _____are_____ cities.

9. Refrigerators _____isn't_____ continents.

10. Greenland _____is_____ a city.

a rabbit

► **Practice 19. Using *be*.** (Charts 1-5 and 1-6)
Complete the sentences with the correct information. Use a form of *be* with a contraction.

1. Korea _____isn't_____ a city. It _'s a country_____.

2. Computers _____isn't_____ insects. They _are machine_____.

3. Asia _____isn't_____ a continent. It _'s a country_____ a country.

4. Spring and summer _____aren't_____ sports. They _are a season_____.

5. Arabic _____isnot_____ a country. It _s a continent_____.

6. I _____am_____ an English teacher. I'_m an English_. _teacher_

7. We _____are_____ students. We _____are_____ English students.

► **Practice 20. *Be* + adjective.** (Chart 1-7)
Complete the sentences with the correct information. Use *is*, *isn't*, *are*, or *aren't*.

1. A mouse _____isn't_____ big.

2. A diamond _____isn't_____ cheap.

3. Diamonds _____is_____ expensive.

4. Bananas _____isn't_____ expensive.

5. The earth _____is_____ flat. It _____is_____ round.

6. English grammar _____isn't_____ hard. It _____is_____ easy.

7. This exercise _____isn't_____ difficult. It _____is_____ easy.

8. Flowers __isn't__ ugly. They __are__ beautiful.

9. Traffic at rush hour __are__ noisy. It __isn't__ quiet.

10. Ice cream and candy __are__ sour. They __are__ sweet.

▶ **Practice 21. *Be* + adjective.** (Charts 1-5 → 1-7)
Write complete sentences using ***is/isn't*** or ***are/aren't*** and the given words.

1. apples . . . blue / red

    Apples aren't blue. They're red.

2. a circle . . . round / square

    Square isnt around a circle

3. a piano . . . heavy / light

    a piano isnt heavy is light

4. potato chips . . . sweet / salty

    Potato ships are sweet and salty

5. the Sahara Desert . . . large / small

    the sahara Desert isnt small is large

6. the Nile River . . . short / long

    the Nile River isnt short is long

7. this exercise . . . easy / difficult

    this exercise isnt difficult

8. my grammar book . . . new / old

    My gramma book isnt new is old.

9. electric cars . . . expensive / cheap

    electric Cars arent cheap are expensive

a piano

► **Practice 22. Identifying prepositions.** (Chart 1-8)
Write the preposition in the blank. <u>Underline</u> the prepositional phrase in each sentence.

Preposition

1. _____*in*_____ David is <u>in his office.</u>

2. _____at_____ Mr. Han is at <u>the train station.</u>

3. _____FROM_____ Karim is from <u>Kuwait.</u>

4. _____ON_____ My book is on <u>my desk.</u>

5. _____iN_____ Lily's wallet is in <u>her purse.</u>

6. _____ON_____ The post office is on <u>First Street.</u>

7. _____Next to_____ The post office is next to <u>the bank.</u>

8. _____are_____ My feet are under <u>my desk.</u>

9. _____between_____ My nose is between <u>my cheeks.</u>

10. _____on_____ My apartment is on <u>the third floor.</u>

11. _____It's_____ It is above <u>Mr. Kwan's apartment.</u>

► **Practice 23. Understanding prepositions.** (Chart 1-8)
Follow the instructions.

Put an "X" . . .

1. above circle A.

2. under circle B.

3. in circle A.

4. between circles A and B.

5. next to circle A.

► **Practice 24. Review: nouns, adjectives, and prepositions.** (Chart 1-9)
Write the words in the correct columns on the next page.

✓ at	✓ easy	next to	single
between	empty	on	sister
✓ city	– happy	outside	– teacher
country	hungry	parents	

Nouns	Adjectives	Prepositions (of Place)
city	*easy*	*at*
parent	Happy	next to
sixter	hungry	on
Contry	Empty	Between
teacher	single	outside

▶ **Practice 25. Sentence review.** (Chart 1-9)
Complete the sentences using the given structure.

1. Dr. John Brown is (*noun*) _____ a dentist / a doctor, etc. _____.

   (*place*) _____ here / at home, etc. _____.

   (*adjective*) _____ friendly / nice, etc. _____.

2. Anna is (*noun*) a teacher _____.

   (*place*) at school _____.

   (*adjective*) happy, _____.

3. Russia is (*adjective*) is big _____.

   (*place*) in EuroPa _____.

   (*noun*) Russa _____.

4. *Basic English Grammar Workbook* is (*place*) is at the lbrary _____.

   (*adjective*) is easy _____.

   (*noun*) is a Book _____.

▶ **Practice 26. Sentence review.** (Chart 1-9)
Make true sentences using the given words and a form of *be*.

1. Canada \ a city

   _____ Canada isn't a city. _____

2. Canada \ in North America

   Canada ist in north America

3. France \ next to \ Germany

   France is nex to Germany

4. The downstairs of a building \ above \ the upstairs

the downstair of a building isnt above the upstairs

5. Ice \ hot

Ice isnt Hot

6. apples and oranges \ vegetables

apples and oranges are vegetables

7. airplanes \ fast

airplanes are fast

8. vegetables \ healthy

vegetables are healthy

9. an alligator \ dangerous

an alligator is dangerous

10. alligators \ friendly

alligators are friendly

an alligator

▶ **Practice 27. Review of be.** (Chapter 1)
Complete the sentences with the correct form of **be**.

Kara and Tia ___are___ from Greece. They ___are___ new students. Mrs. Kemper
                    1   2
___she___ the teacher. She ___is___ very nice. Fifteen students ___are___ in the class.
    3   4   5
They ___are___ friendly. Kara and Tia ___they're___ happy in this class.
         6   7

▶ **Practice 28. Review of be.** (Chapter 1)
Complete the sentences with the correct form of **be**.

MR. QUINN: Hi, I ___am___ Mr. Quinn. Mrs. Kemper ___she is___ not here.
                    1   2
             She ___is___ sick. I ___M___ your teacher today.
                    3   4

KARA: Hi, my name ___is___ Kara.
                              5

MR. QUINN: Hi, Kara. It ___'s___ nice to meet you.
                             6

KARA: I ___M___ happy to meet you too. This ___is___ my sister, Tia.
                  7   8

MR. QUINN: Hi, Tia. I ___M___ glad* to meet you too.
                            9

glad = happy.

Chapter 2
Using Be and Have

▶ **Practice 1. Yes/no questions with be.** (Chart 2-1)
Choose the correct completion.

1. _____ you happy?
   a. Am   b. Is   (c.) Are

2. _____ they here?
   a. Am   b. Is   (c.) Are

3. _____ he absent?
   a. Am   b. (Is)   c. Are

4. _____ she a teacher?
   a. Am   b. (Is)   c. Are

5. _____ I late?
   (a.) Am   b. Is   c. Are

6. _____ we ready?
   a. Am   b. Is   (c.) Are

7. _____ you and Paul ready?
   a. Am   b. Is   c. (Are)

8. _____ Roberto and Elena at home?
   a. Am   b. Is   c. (Are)

9. _____ Emily here?
   a. Am   b. (Is)   c. Are

10. _____ you from Canada?
    a. Am   b. Is   c. (Are)

▶ **Practice 2. Yes/no questions with be.** (Chart 2-1)
Make yes/no questions with the given words and a form of **be**.

1. you \ a student ___*Are you a student?*___

2. he \ a student ___he a student___

3. they \ students ___they're students___

4. she \ from New Zealand ___she is from new zealand___

5. you \ ready ___You are reddy___

6. we \ ready ___We are ready___

7. it \ ready ___It is Ready___

8. I \ ready ___I'm Ready___

▶ Practice 3. Yes/no questions with *be*. (Chart 2-1)
Make questions for the given answers.

1. A: ___*Are you a doctor?*___
   B: Yes, I am a doctor.

2. A: are bananas healthy?
   B: Yes, bananas are healthy.

3. A: Is Taka a nurse
   B: Yes, Taka is a nurse.

4. A: Are the kids at school
   B: Yes, the kids are at school.

5. A: Are we ready for the test
   B: Yes, we are ready for the test.

6. A: Is Liz at school
   B: Yes, Liz is at school.

7. A: are you tired
   B: Yes, I am tired.

▶ Practice 4. Short answers with *be*. (Chart 2-2)
Complete the sentences with short answers.

1. Is Paris a city?   Yes, ___*it is*___ .

2. Are Paris and Tokyo cities?   Yes, they're .

3. Are dogs animals?   Yes, they're .

4. Is Carlos sick today?   Yes, he's .

5. Are apples fruits?   Yes, they're .

6. Is the sun hot?   Yes, it's .

7. Is Jane a teacher?   Yes, she's .

8. Are you a student?   Yes, I'm .

9. Are you students?   Yes, we've .

10. Am I early?   Yes, I'm .

Complete the questions and answers.

Anna
an English teacher

Mr. Sanchez
an English student

Susan
a photographer

Mrs. Brown
a police officer

Joe
a college student

1. ___Is___ Mr. Sanchez a student? Yes, he ___is___.

2. ___is___ Anna a teacher? Yes, she ___is___.

3. ___is___ Joe a student? Yes, he ___is___.

4. ___is___ Susan a photographer? Yes, she ___is___.

5. ___Are___ Joe and Mr. Sanchez students? Yes, they ___are___.

6. ___is___ Mrs. Brown a police officer? Yes, she ___is___.

7. ___Are___ Anna and Susan women? Yes, they ___are___.

8. ___Are___ Mr. Sanchez and Joe men? Yes, they ___are___.

9. ___Are___ you a student? Yes, I ___is___.

10. ___Are___ you and Mr. Sanchez students? Yes, we ___are___.

▶ **Practice 6. Capitalization and punctuation.** (Charts 2-2)
Rewrite the sentences. Add capitals letters and the correct punctuation.

1. is Paris a country   no it isn't

   Paris isn't a country (Paris is a city

2. are October and November months   yes they are

   Are october and november months? Yes they are

3. is soccer a season   no it isn't

Soccer It isn't a season. Soccer is a sport.

4. are fall and winter seasons   yes they are

Are fall and winter seasons? Yes they are

▶ **Practice 7. Questions and short answers with *be*.** (Chart 2-2)
Make questions and give short answers. Use contractions where possible.

NEW STUDENT INFORMATION	NEW STUDENT INFORMATION
Name: Rosa Gonzalez	Name: Dong Vuong
Country: Spain	Country: Vietnam
Age: 22	Age: 24
___ male X female	X male ___ female

1. ____*Is*_____ Rosa a student?   Yes, she ____*is*____.

2. ____*Is Dong*_____ a teacher?   No, he ____*isn't*____.

3. *Are Rosa and Dong* students?   Yes, *they are*.

4. ____*Is Rosa*_____ from Mexico?   No, she *isn't*.

5. ____*Is Dong*_____ from Vietnam?   Yes, *he is*.

6. ____*Is Rosa*_____ 22?   Yes, *she is*.

7. ____*Is Dong*_____ 25?   No, he *he isn't*.

8. *Are Rosa and Dong* 23?   No, they *aren't*.

▶ **Practice 8. Questions and short answers with *be*.** (Chart 2-2)
Complete the conversations. Use contractions where possible.

1. A: _____*Is*_____ Gloria a student?

   B: Yes, ____*she is*____.

   A: *Are you* a student?

   B: No, I'm not.

2. A: *Are you* students?

   B: No, we *aren't*. We *re* teachers.

   A: Is Mr. Ito a teacher?

   B: No, *he isn't*. He *'s* a student.

*aren't weren't   we are not
                  rent*

► **Practice 9. Understanding *where*.** (Chart 2-3)
Choose the correct question for each response.

Question	Response

1. a. Where is Toshi?
    (b.) Is Toshi at work?

Yes, he is.

2. a. Are the students in the cafeteria?
    (b.) Where are the students?

— They are in the cafeteria.

3. (a.) Is my grammar book at home?
    b. Where is my grammar book?

Yes, it is.

4. a. Where are the dictionaries?
    (b.) Are the dictionaries in the classroom?

Yes, they are.

5. (a.) Where are you?
    b. Are you at home?

I am at home.

6. a. Is the teacher in her office?
    (b.) Where is the teacher?

She is in her office.

► **Practice 10. Questions with *be* and *where*.** (Chart 2-3)
Make questions.

1. A: _____*Where is the teacher?*_____
    B: In the classroom. (The teacher is in the classroom.)

2. A: ___Where is the teacher in the classroom___
    B: Yes, she is. (The teacher is in the classroom.)

3. A: ___Where are Pablo and Diana?___
    B: At home. (Pablo and Dina are at home.)

4. A: ___Are Pablo and Diana at Home?___
    B: Yes, they are. (Pablo and Dina are at home.)

5. A: ___Is the map in the car?___
    B: Yes, it is. (The map is in the car.)

6. A: ___Where is the store?___
    B: On First Avenue. (The store is on First Avenue.)

7. A: ___Are you outside?___
    B: Yes, we are. (We are outside.)

8. A: ___Where are you?___
    B: Outside. (We are outside.)

► **Practice 11. Using _have_ and _has._** (Chart 2-4)
Complete the sentences with the correct form of _have_.

1. I _____have_____ a book.

2. You _____have_____ a book.

3. She _____has_____ a book.

4. He _____has_____ a book.

5. Mr. Marks _____has_____ a book.

6. The dog _____has_____ a book.

7. It _____has_____ a book.

8. Mrs. Hong _____has_____ a book.

9. They _____have_____ books.

10. The students _____have_____ books.

11. You _____have_____ books.

► **Practice 12. Using _have_ and _has._** (Chart 2-4)
Complete the sentences with _have_ or _has_.

1. You _____have_____ a ruler on your desk.

2. Eric _____has_____ an eraser on his chair.

3. We _____have_____ grammar books.

4. I _____have_____ a grammar book. It _____has_____ a red cover.

5. Lucy _____has_____ a blue pen. She _____has_____ a blue notebook too.

6. Stella and Dave _____has_____ notebooks. They _____have_____ pencils too.

7. Samir is a student in our class. He _____has_____ a laptop computer.

8. You and I are students. We _____have_____ laptops on our desks.

9. Mike _____has_____ a wallet in his pocket. Mira _____has_____ a wallet in her purse.

10. Nadia isn't in class today because she _____has_____ the flu.

11. Mr. and Mrs. Collins _____have_____ two teenagers.

► **Practice 13. Be and have.** (Chapter 1 and Chart 2-4)
Complete each sentence with the correct form of *be* or *have.*

1. My apartment . . .

   a. _____has_____ five rooms.

   b. _____is_____ comfortable.

   c. _____is_____ in the city.

   d. _____is_____ twenty years old.

   e. _____has_____ a new kitchen.

   f. _____is_____ expensive.

   g. _____is_____ on the fourth floor.

   h. _____has_____ many windows.

   i. _____is_____ a view of downtown.

2. My neighbor . . .

   a. _____is_____ thirty years old.

   b. _____has_____ brown eyes and brown hair.

   c. _____is_____ tall.

   d. _____has_____ two children.

   e. _____has_____ a small apartment.

   f. _____is_____ friendly.

   g. _____is_____ a student at the university.

   h. _____is_____ very busy.

   i. _____has_____ a busy life.

► **Practice 14. Be and have.** (Chapter 1 and Chart 2-4)
Complete each sentence with the correct form of *be* or *have.*

a toothache

1. Jean _____has_____ a toothache. She _____is_____ at the dentist.
2. Several students _____are_____ absent. They _____have_____ colds.
3. I _____M_____ not at school. I _____have_____ a stomachache.
4. My parents _____are_____ sick. They _____have_____ fevers.
5. Mr. Paul _____is_____ a backache. He _____is_____ at home.

a backache

▶ **Practice 15. _Be_ and _have_.** (Chart 2-4)
Complete the sentences with **has**, **have**, **is**, or **are**.

The people in Dr. Lin's waiting room _____are_____ sick. Billy _____has_____ a cold.
1   2

Thomas _____has_____ a stomachache. Mr. and Mrs. Gleason _____has_____ fevers.
3   4

Mrs. Martinez _____has_____ a headache.
5

The construction workers _____have_____ backaches.
6

Nicole _____has_____ a sore throat.
7

Dr. Lin _____has_____ very busy.
8

▶ **Practice 16. Possessive adjectives.** (Chart 2-5)
Complete the sentences. Use **my**, **your**, **her**, **his**, **our**, or **their**.

a backpack

1. He has a backpack. _____His_____ backpack is heavy.

2. You have a backpack. _____You_____ backpack is heavy.

3. I have a backpack. _____My_____ backpack is heavy.

4. We have backpacks. _____our_____ backpacks are heavy.

5. You have backpacks. _____My_____ backpacks are heavy.

6. They have backpacks. _____their_____ backpacks are heavy.

7. The students have backpacks. _____their_____ backpacks are heavy.

8. Tom has a backpack. _____his_____ backpack is heavy.

9. Kate has a backpack. _____her_____ backpack is heavy.

10. Tom and Kate have backpacks. _____their_____ backpacks are heavy.

11. Kate and I have backpacks. _____Our_____ backpacks are heavy.

12. You and I have backpacks. _____Our_____ backpacks are heavy.

▶ **Practice 17. Possessive adjectives.** (Chart 2-5)
Use the information in the chart to complete the sentences about the after-school activities of Jenny, Bill, Karen, and Kathy. Use *his*, *her*, or *their*.

Jenny   Bill   Karen   Kathy   Bill

	Jenny	**Bill**	**Karen and Kathy**
Monday	dance class	soccer practice	baseball game
Tuesday			
Wednesday	piano lesson		soccer practice
Thursday		piano lesson	

1. _____His_____ soccer practice is on Monday.

2. _____her_____ dance class is on Monday.

3. _____his_____ piano lesson is on Thursday.

4. _____their_____ soccer practice is on Wednesday.

5. _____her_____ piano lesson is on Wednesday.

6. _____their_____ baseball game is on Monday.

▶ **Practice 18. *Have* and possessive adjectives.** (Chart 2-5)
Complete the sentences. Use *have* or *has* and *my*, *your*, *her*, *his*, *our*, or *their*.

1. I _____have_____ a teenage daughter. _____My_____ daughter is busy.

2. You _____have_____ homework. _____Your_____ homework is easy.

3. Peter and Ellen _____have_____ new cell phones. _____their_____ cell phones are inexpensive.

4. We _____have_____ an old car. _____our_____ car is slow.

5. Hector _____has_____ a mustache. _____his_____ mustache is black.

6. Maria *has* two grandchildren. *her* grandchildren are friendly.

7. Nathan *has* a motorcycle. *his* motorcycle is slow.

a motorcycle

8. Mr. and Mrs. Brown *have* an apartment. *their* apartment is on the top floor.

9. I *have* a dictionary. *My* dictionary is English-Japanese.

10. The workers *have* boots. *their* boots are heavy.

▶ **Practice 19. *This* or *that*.** (Chart 2-6)
Complete the sentences with *this* or *that*.

1. _____*This*_____ is my house key.

2. _____*that*_____ is your phone card.

3. _____*that*_____ is your checkbook.

4. _____*this*_____ is my credit card.

5. _____*this*_____ is my briefcase.

6. _____*that*_____ is your bag.

7. _____*this*_____ is your baseball cap.

8. _____*that*_____ is my wallet.

► **Practice 20. These or those.** (Chart 2-7)
Complete the sentences with *these* or *those*.

1. ___These___ are apples.

2. ___these___ are oranges.

3. ___those___ are pears.

4. ___those___ are lemons.

5. ___these___ are bananas.

6. ___those___ are carrots.

► **Practice 21. This, that, these, and those.** (Charts 2-6 and 2-7)
Choose the correct completion.

1. (*This* / *These*) keys are your house keys.
2. (*That* / *Those*) keys are my car keys.
3. (*This* / *These*) thumb drive is cheap.
4. (*That* / *Those*) thumb drives are expensive.
5. (*That* / *Those*) computer is new.
6. (*This* / *These*) computers are slow.
7. (*This* / *These*) computer is fast.

a thumb drive

► **Practice 22. This, that, these, and those.** (Charts 2-6 and 2-7)
Complete each sentence with *this*, *that*, *these*, or *those*.

1. (*This* / *These*) ___This___ book is inexpensive. (*That* / *Those*) ___Those___
   books are expensive.

2. (*This* / *These*) ___these___ chairs are comfortable. (*That* / *Those*) ___those___
   chairs are uncomfortable.

3. (*This* / *These*) ___this___ car is fast. (*That* / *Those*) ___that___ car is slow.

4. (*This* / *These*) ___these___ cats are friendly. (*That* / *Those*) ___that___ cat is
   unfriendly.

5. (*This / These*) _this_ library card is new. (*That / Those*) _that_ library card is old.

6. (*This / These*) _____ shoes are comfortable. (*That / Those*) _____ shoes are uncomfortable.

7. (*This / These*) _this_ exercise is easy. (*That / Those*) _those_ exercises are hard.

▶ **Practice 23. Understanding *who* and *what*.** (Chart 2-8)
Choose the correct response for each question.

1. Who is that?
   ⓐ That is Rita.   b. That is a toy.

2. What is that?
   ⓐ That is an electric car.   b. That is Tom.

3. Who are they?
   a. They are flowers.   ⓑ They are new students.

4. What are they?
   ⓐ They are small insects.   b. They are Dick and Mira.

5. Who is this?
   a. This is my new car.   ⓑ This is Kenny.

6. What are they?
   a. They are my children.   ⓑ They are batteries.

batteries

▶ **Practice 24. *Who* and *what* + *be*.** (Chart 2-8)
Make a question with *who* or *what* for each answer.

1. A: _Who is that?_
   B: That is the teacher.

2. A: _What is that?_
   B: That is medicine.

3. A: _What is that?_
   B: These are DVDs.

4. A: _Who are they?_
   B: They are visitors.

5. A: _What is that?_
   B: Those are aspirin.

6. A: _Who is that?_
   B: That is Dr. Benson.

Aspirin

▶ **Practice 25. Review: questions and short answers.** (Chapter 2)
Answer the questions. Choose from the responses in the box.

Yes, it is.	This is Donna.	Yes, I am.
It's in Norway.	Yes, they are.	No, it isn't.
Yes, he is.	This is an insect.	Yes, she is.

1. Are the students smart? _____Yes, they are._____

2. Who is this? _This is Donna._

3. Is Oslo a city? _Yes, it is._

4. Is Megan a dentist? _Yes, she is._

5. Is Canada a continent? _No, it isn't_

6. Is Charles a teenager? _Yes, it is._

7. Where is Oslo? _It's in Norway_

8. Are you sick? _Yes, I am_

9. What is this? _This is an insect._

▶ **Practice 26. *Be* and possessive adjectives.** (Chapters 1 and 2)
Complete the sentences. Use the correct form of *be* and the appropriate possessive adjective.

Pat   Bob

Karen   Joe   Bonnie

Tom

  This is the Jackson family. Pat is the mother. Bob is ___her___ husband. They have
                                                            1
two children. _their_ children are Karen and Joe. Karen is Joe's sister. Joe is _her_
              2   3
brother. Joe and Bonnie are married. They have one child. Tom is _their_ son. _his_
                                                                  4   5
grandparents are Pat and Bob.

► **Practice 27. Be and have.** (Chapters 1 and 2)
Complete the sentences with the correct forms of **be** and **have**.

I __have__ one brother and one sister. My brother __is__ a nurse. He __has__ a
good job at a medical clinic. His name __is__ Daniel. He __is__ 30 years old. My
sister __is__ a doctor. She __is__ very busy. She __has__ many patients. Her name
__is__ Monica. She __is__ 35 years old. My name __is__ Martha. I __am__
28 years old. I __am__ an English teacher. We all __have__ good jobs. We __are__
happy with our work.

► **Practice 28. Be and have.** (Chapters 1 and 2)
Complete the sentences with information about your life.

1. My name __is Kevin A. Johnson Almonte._____.
2. I __am__ from __Dominican Republic._____.
3. __I'am__ a student.
4. My classes are __Very smart._____.
5. _____ and _____ are two of my friends.
6. My family is __beautifull_____.
7. My father is __Tall and_____.
8. My mother is __Cute_____.
9. I __am_____ (single/married).
10. I have __roommate_____ (an apartment/a house/a dorm room/a roommate).

Chapter 3
Using the Simple Present

▶ **Practice 1. Form of the simple present tense.** (Chart 3-1)
Complete the sentences with the correct form of **wake up**.

1. I _____*wake*_____ up early every day.

2. We _____wake_____ up early every day.

3. They _____wake_____ up early every day.

4. He _____wakes_____ up early every day.

5. You _____wake_____ up early every day.

6. She _____wakes_____ up early every day.

7. The dog _____wakes_____ up early every day.

8. It _____wakes_____ up early every day.

9. Mr. and Mrs. Ito _____wake_____ up early every day.

10. Mr. Ito _____wakes_____ up early every day.

11. The teacher _____wakes_____ up early every day.

12. The students _____wake_____ up early every day.

▶ **Practice 2. The simple present tense.** (Chart 3-1)
<u>Underline</u> the simple present verbs.

Spiro <u>works</u> at night. He teaches auto mechanics at a school in his town. He leaves his apartment at 5:00. He catches the bus near his home. The bus comes at 5:15. It takes him 40 minutes to get to work. His classes begin at 6:30. He teaches until 10:30. He stays at school until 11:15. A friend drives him home. He gets home around midnight.

▶ **Practice 3. Form of the simple present tense.** (Chart 3-1)
Complete the sentences with the correct form of the verb in parentheses.

1. My alarm clock (ring) _____*rings*_____ at 5:00 every morning.

2. I (get) _____*get*_____ out of bed slowly.

3. My husband (make) _____*makes*_____ breakfast for us.

4. He (cook) _____*cooks*_____ a hot breakfast every morning.

5. We (leave) _____*leave*_____ for work at 6:00.

6. I (drive) _____*drive*_____ us to work.

7. We (listen to) _____*listen to*_____ the morning news.

8. My husband and I (work) _____*work*_____ at the same company.

9. We (arrive) _____*arrive*_____ at work early.

10. Our two co-workers (come) _____*come*_____ later.

11. They (take) _____*take*_____ the same bus to the office.

▶ **Practice 4. Form of the simple present tense.** (Chart 3-1)
Complete the sentences with the correct form of the verb in parentheses.

Joan and I are roommates. We are very different. Joan (wakes / wake) _____*wakes*_____ (1)
up early. I (wakes / wake) _____*wake*_____ (2) up at 11:00. I (eats / eat) _____*eat*_____ (3)
breakfast at lunchtime. Joan (eats / eat) _____*eats*_____ (4) breakfast at 7:30. She (leaves /
leave) _____*leaves*_____ (5) for school at 8:00. I (takes / take) _____*take*_____ (6) evening
classes, so I go to school at 5:00. Joan (cooks / cook) _____*cooks*_____ (7) an early dinner
and (falls / fall) _____*fall*_____ (8) asleep around 9:00. I (eats / eat) _____*eat*_____ (9)
at midnight and (falls / fall) _____*falls*_____ (10) asleep in the early morning. We (sees / see)
_____*see*_____ (11) each other on weekends. We (has / have) _____*have*_____ (12) very
different lives, but we are good friends.

► **Practice 5. Frequency adverbs.** (Chart 3-2)
Rewrite each sentence using the given frequency adverb.

1. Olga has cream in her coffee. (*always*)

   Olga always has cream in her coffee.

2. I eat breakfast. (*rarely*)

   I rarely eat breakfast.

3. The students buy their lunch at school. (*seldom*)

   The students seldom buy their lunch at schoo[l]

4. They bring lunch from home. (*usually*)

   usually they bring lunch from home.

5. My husband and I go out to a restaurant for dinner. (*often*)

   Often my husband and I go to a restaurant for dinner.

6. My husband drinks coffee with dinner. (*sometimes*)

   sometime my husband drinks coffee with dinner.

7. We have dessert. (*never*)

   We never have dessert.

► **Practice 6. Frequency adverbs.** (Chart 3-2)
Rewrite the sentences using an appropriate frequency adverb.

1. Beth has fish for lunch. (50% of the time)

   Beth sometimes has fish for lunch.

2. Roger gets up late. (10% of the time)

   Roger seldom/rarely get up late

3. Mr. and Mrs. Phillips go to the movies on weekends. (90% of the time)

   Mr. and Mrs. phillips usually go to the Movies on weekends.

4. I clean my apartment. (75% of the time)

I often clean my apartment.

5. My roommate cleans our apartment. (0% of the time)

My roommate never cleans our apartament

6. The students do their homework. (100% of the time)

the students alway do their Homework

7. The teacher corrects papers on weekends. (50% of the time)

The teacher sometime corrects papers on weekends.

▶ **Practice 7. Frequency adverbs.** (Chart 3-2)
Agree or disagree with the sentences about your morning activities. If the answer is *no*, write the correct frequency adverb.

1. I always wake up early.   (yes)   no

2. I sometimes sleep late on weekends.   (yes)   no

3. I seldom eat a hot breakfast.   yes   (no)

4. I often listen to the radio in the morning.   yes   (no)

5. I usually watch TV during breakfast.   yes   (no)

6. I rarely study English at home in the morning.   yes   (no)

7. I never exercise in the morning.   yes   (no)

▶ **Practice 8. Frequency adverbs.** (Chart 3-2)
Complete the sentences about yourself in the evening.

1. I always *get early at work.*

2. I never *get late at work*

3. I sometimes *Canceled appoinment*

4. I often _____

5. I seldom _____

6. I rarely _____

► **Practice 9. Other frequency expressions.** (Chart 3-2)
Rewrite the sentences using the expressions from the box.

once a day	✓ three times a week
once a month	twice a month
once a year	twice a week
three times a day	twice a year

1. I have classes on Mondays, Wednesdays, and Fridays.

   I have classes three times a week.

2. I pay my phone bill on the first day of every month.

   I PAy My Phone bill once a month

3. I exercise from 10:00 to 11:00 A.M. every day.

   I exercise once a day.

4. I visit my cousins in December and June every year.

   I Visit my cousins twice-a Year.

5. Dr. Williams checks her email at 6:00 A.M., noon, and 10:00 P.M. every day.

   Dr. williams checks her email three time a dy.

6. The Browns take a long vacation in August.

   The Browns take a long vacation once a Year

7. Cyndi gives dinner parties at the beginning and end of each month.

   Cyndy gives dinner Parties twice a month

8. Sam buys vegetables at the farmers' market on Mondays and Fridays.

   Sam buys vegetables twice a week

▶ **Practice 10. Position of frequency adverbs.** (Chart 3-3)
Complete the sentences with the given frequency adverb.

1. *often*   Joan _____Ø_____ is _____often_____ sick.

2. *often*   Joan __often__ feels __Ø__ sick.

3. *sometimes*   Carly __Ø__ is __Sometime__ hungry.

4. *rarely*   It __Ø__ is __rarely__ cold in the summer.

5. *rarely*   It __rarely__ rains __Ø__ in the summer.

6. *usually*   I __Ø__ am __usually__ in bed at 9:00.

7. *usually*   I __usually__ go __Ø__ to bed at 9:00.

8. *never*   I __never__ sleep __Ø__ late.

9. *never*   I __never__ wake up __Ø__ late.

10. *always*   I __Ø__ am __always__ up early.

▶ **Practice 11. Frequency adverbs.** (Charts 3-2 and 3-3)
Make sentences using the given words.

1. The teacher \ clean up the classroom \ usually

   _____The teacher usually cleans up the classroom._____

2. The students \ help the teacher \ often

   The students often help the teacher.

3. The classroom \ be clean \ always

   The classroom is always clean.

4. The parents \ visit the class \ usually

   The parents usually visit the class.

5. The parents \ help the students with their work \ sometimes

   The parents sometime help the student with their work.

6. The parents \ be helpful \ always

   The parents are always helpful.

7. The classroom \ be quiet \ seldom

   The classroom is seldom quiet.

▶ **Practice 12. Spelling of verbs ending in -s/-es.** (Chart 3-4)
Write the correct form of the verb in the appropriate column.

✓ call	⌐eat	⌐ fix	– listen	talk
✓ catch	– finish	kiss	sleep	wish

-s

he _____ *calls* _____

he _____ *eat* _____

he _____ *litens* _____

he _____ *sleeps* _____

he _____ *talks* _____

-es

she _____ *catches* _____

she _____ *finishes* _____

she _____ *fixes* _____

she _____ *kisses* _____

she _____ *wishes* _____

▶ **Practice 13. Final -s/-es.** (Charts 3-1 and 3-4)
Write the forms of the given verbs.

1. I (teach) _____ *teach* _____ English.

2. She (teach) _____ *teach* _____ English.

3. You (mix) _____ *mix* _____ the salad.

4. He (mix) _____ *mixes* _____ the salad.

5. Sara (miss) _____ *mixes* _____ her friends.

6. They (miss) _____ *miss* _____ their friends.

7. I (brush) _____ *brush* _____ my hair.

8. The girl (brush) _____ *brushes* _____ her hair.

9. She and I (wash) _____ *wash* _____ the dishes.

10. He (wash) _____ *washes* _____ the dishes.

11. He (cook) _____ *cooks* _____ dinner.

12. She (read) _____ *reads* _____ magazines.

13. Richard (watch) _____ *watches* _____ movies.

14. Class (begin) _____ *begins* _____ early.

15. Many students (come) _____ *come* _____ late.

16. The teacher always (come) _____ *comes* _____ on time.

▶ **Practice 14. Spelling of verbs ending in -y.** (Chart 3-5)
Complete each sentence with the correct form of **study**.

1. The students _____ *study* _____ hard.

2. One student ___ studies ___ hard.

3. I ___ study ___ hard.

4. My friend ___ studies ___ hard.

5. You ___ study ___ hard.

6. We ___ studyes ___ hard.

7. She ___ studies ___ hard.

8. They ___ study ___ hard.

9. He ___ studies ___ hard.

10. My friends ___ studys ___ hard.

▶ **Practice 15. Spelling of verbs ending in -y.** (Chart 3-5)
Write the correct form of each verb in the appropriate column.

✓ buy	enjoy	pay	say	try
✓ cry	fly	play	study	worry

-ies

he _____ *cries* _____

he ___ Flies ___

he ___ studies ___

he ___ tries ___

he ___ worries ___

-s

she _____ *buys* _____

she ___ enjoys ___

she ___ pays ___

she ___ plays ___

she ___ says ___

▶ **Practice 16. Simple present tense: spelling.** (Charts 3-1, 3-4, and 3-5)
Complete each sentence with the correct form of a verb from the box. You will use a verb more than one time.

brush	close	fly	✓ start	study
call	fix	help	stop	

1. Dr. Lee _____ *starts* _____ work at 6:00 every day.

2. Sara ___ brushes ___ her teeth after every meal.

3. The grocery store ___ closes ___ at 11:00 every night.

4. Birds _Fly_ south in the winter.

5. An airplane often _Flies_ over my house.

6. I'm lucky. The bus _stops_ in front of my apartment building.

7. Martha is a mechanic. She _Fixes_ cars.

8. I talk to my mother on the phone every day. I _Call_ her, or she _calls_ me.

9. Inga _studies_ in the library every afternoon.

10. John is a teacher's assistant. He _helps_ the teacher with her work.

▶ **Practice 17. *Has, Does, and Goes.*** (Chart 3-6)
Make sentences about the people in the chart. Use the correct form of *have class at*, *do homework at*, and *go to work at*.

	Jimi	Marta	Susan	Paul
9:00	class		homework	homework
10:00	homework	class		
11:00	work	homework	class	class
1:00			work	work
2:00		work		

1. Jimi

   a. He ___has class at 9:00.___

   b. He ___has Homework at 10:00___

   c. He ___go to work at 11:00___

2. Marta

   a. She ___has class at 10:00___

   b. She ___has Homewor at 11:00___

   c. She ___go to work at 2:00___

3. Susan and Paul

   a. They ___have homework at 9:00___

   b. They ___have class at 11:00___

   c. They ___go to work at 2:00___

► **Practice 18. Simple present tense.** (Charts 3-1 → 3-6)
Complete the sentences with the words in parentheses.

Ricardo (*leave*) _____*leaves*_____ his house at 4:30 every morning. He (*catch*)
_____*catches*_____ the bus near his house. He (*get*) __*gets*__ to work at 5:00. He
(*work*) __*works*__ in a restaurant. He (*fix*) __*fixes*__ wonderful dishes from his
country. Many people (*come*) __*come*__ to the restaurant for his food. He (*finish*)
__*finishes*__ work at 3:00. Then he (*meet, often*) __*often meets*__

with students from his country and (*help*) __*helps*__ them with English. They (*have,
usually*) __*usually have*__ dinner together. After dinner he (*go*) __*goes*__ home.
Sometimes he (*have*) __*has*__ a snack. He (*be, often*) __*is often*__ tired at the
end of the day, but he (*enjoy*) __*enjoys*__ his work and the time with the students from his
country.

► **Practice 19. Simple present tense.** (Charts 3-1 → 3-6)
Add *-s/-es* or Ø (nothing) where necessary.

Sam enjoy _*s*_ cooking. He and his wife like _*Ø*_ to have company for dinner. They
ask _*Ø*_ me to dinner about once a month. When I arrive, his wife greet _*s*_ me. She
invite _*s*_ me into the kitchen, and we talk _*Ø*_ to Sam while he cook _*s*_. The
kitchen always smell _*s*_ wonderful. I get _*Ø*_ very hungry when I sit _*Ø*_ and talk
to Sam. Sometimes he give _*s*_ me a few bites of food from the pots. When dinner is
ready, we take _*Ø*_ a long time to eat it. It taste _*s*_ delicious. After dinner, Sam clear
_*s*_ the table, and his wife serve _*s*_ dessert. These meals are wonderful, and I always
enjoy _*Ø*_ myself with Sam and his wife.

► **Practice 20. *Need/want*** (Chart 3-7)
Think about what most people ***need*** for life in the 21st century and what many people ***want*** to have. Write the words from the list in the correct column.

✓ air	electricity	a leather coat	a smartphone
– diamond jewelry	an expensive house	money	a sports car
a digital camera	food	a place to live	water

need	***want***
air	diamond jewelry
food	an expensive house
electricity	a smartphone
a place to live	a sports car
water	a digital camera
money	a leather coat

► **Practice 21. *Want to* and *need to*** (Chart 3-7)
Part I. Read the story. Underline the infinitives with ***want*** and ***need***.

Pierre is a high school student. It is his first year of high school. He is very smart, and his classes are very easy. Pierre wants more in-class work. He wants to have more homework too. His math skills are excellent. He needs to have more difficult work. He wants to do college-level math.

His high school says he needs to take French. But Pierre speaks fluent French because his dad is from France. He likes the French teacher, but he wants to skip the class.

Pierre likes the social part of high school, but he wants to have more difficult academics.

Part II. Choose all the correct answers.

1. Pierre wants . . .
    a. to do homework.
    b. more homework.
    c. easy math.
    d. a new French teacher.
    e. a new high school.

2. Pierre wants to . . .

    (a.) study more.

    b. do more homework.

    c. learn advanced math.

    d. skip high school.

    e. learn to speak fluent French.

3. Pierre doesn't need . . .

    a. to do homework.

    (b.) to speak French.

    c. college math.

    d. easy classes.

    e. to take easy classes.

▶ **Practice 22. *Like to, need to, want to.*** (Chart 3-7)
Use the words from the list or your own words to complete the sentences. Use an infinitive (***to*** + verb) in each sentence. Some words can be used more than once.

buy	✓ go	→ play	┐watch
─ eat	─ listen to	take	swim
┐ cash	─ marry	─ talk to	
⌐ do	pay	┐ wash	

1. Anna is sleepy. She wants _____*to go*_____ to bed.

2. Mike wants _____*to watch*_____ TV. There's a good program on Channel 5.

3. Do you want _____*to play*_____ soccer with us at the park this afternoon?

4. I need _____*to talk to*_____ Jennifer in person, not on the phone.

5. I want _____*to go*_____ to the bank because I need _____*to cash*_____ a check.

6. James doesn't want _____*to do*_____ his homework tonight.

7. My clothes are dirty. I need _____*to wash*_____ them.

8. I want _____*to go to*_____ downtown today because I need _____*to buy*_____ a new coat.

9. John loves Mary. He wants _____*to marry*_____ her.

10. Helen needs _____*to take*_____ an English course.

11. Where do you want _____*to eat*_____ lunch?

12. Do you want _____*to listen to*_____ some music on the radio?

13. Jens goes to the beach often. He likes ___to swim___ in the sea for exercise.

14. David's desk is full of overdue bills. He needs ___to pay___ his bills.

▶ **Practice 23. Simple present tense: negative.** (Charts 1-6 and 3-8)
Write the correct form of the verb. Use the negative.

	have	*eat*	*be*
1. I	don't have		am not
2. You	don't have	don't eat	arn't
3. He	doesn't have	doosn't eat	isn't
4. She			
5. It			
6. We			
7. They	don't have	don't eat	arn't

▶ **Practice 24. Simple present tense: negative.** (Chart 3-8)
Rewrite the sentences using the negative form.

1. I have time. ___I don't have time.___

2. You need more time. ___You don't need more time___

3. They eat breakfast. _____

4. Yoshi likes bananas. _____

5. Susan does her homework. _____

6. We save our money. _____

7. The printer works. _____

8. The coffee tastes good. _____

9. Mr. and Mrs. Costa drive to work. _____

Use the given words to make true sentences.

1. *wear* Cows _____ *don't wear* _____ shirts.

2. *be* Fruit _____ *is* _____ healthy.

3. *have* A child _____ gray hair.

4. *break* Glass _____ .

5. *grow* Apples _____ on grass.

6. *walk* A newborn baby _____ .

7. *cry* A newborn baby _____ .

8. *fly* Cars _____ .

9. *have* People _____ twenty fingers.

10. *help* A doctor _____ sick people.

11. *fix* A dentist _____ broken legs.

12. *fix* A dentist _____ broken teeth.

13. *like* Mice _____ cats.

14. *chase* Cats _____ mice.

15. *be* The sun _____ cold.

16. *rain* It _____ a lot in London.

17. *rain* It _____ often in Algeria.

18. *wash* Washing machines _____ dishes.

19. *wash* A washing machine _____ clothes.

► **Practice 26. Simple present tense: negative.** (Chart 3-8)
Part I. Below is information about the activities Tom, Janet, and Mark do every day. Write sentences using the given words.

	Tom	Janet	Mark
drink coffee	x	x	
watch TV			x
walk to school	x		
study grammar	x	x	x
go shopping		x	
take the bus		x	x
skip lunch	x	x	
eat dinner at home	x		x
eat dinner out*		x	

*eat dinner out = eat dinner at a restaurant.

1. (*drink coffee*) _____ Tom and Janet drink coffee. _____

2. (*watch TV*) _____

3. (*walk to school*) _____

4. (*study grammar*) _____

5. (*go shopping*) _____

Part II. What don't Tom, Janet, or Mark do every day? Write sentences using the given words.

6. (*take the bus*) _____ Tom doesn't take the bus. _____

7. (*watch TV*) _____

8. (*skip lunch*) _____

9. (*eat dinner at home*) _____

10. (*eat dinner out*) _____

► **Practice 27. Simple present tense: negative.** (Chart 3-8)
Complete the sentences. Use the words in parentheses. Use the simple present tense.

1. Alex (*like*) _____ likes _____ tea, but he (*like, not*) _____ doesn't like _____ coffee.

2. Sara (*know*) _____ Ali, but she (*know, not*) _____ Hiroshi.

3. Pablo and Maria (*want*) _____ to stay home tonight. They (*want, not*) _____ to go to a movie.

4. Robert (*be, not*) _____ hungry. He (*want, not*) _____ a sandwich.

5. Mr. Smith (*drink, not*) _____ coffee, but Mr. Jones (*drink*) _____ twelve cups every day.

6. I (*be, not*) _____ rich. I (*have, not*) _____ a lot of money.

7. This pen (*belong, not*) _____ to me. It (*belong*) _____ to Pierre.

8. My friends (*live, not*) _____ in the dorm. They (*have*) _____ an apartment.

9. It (*be*) _____ a nice day today. It (*be, not*) _____ cold. You (*need, not*) _____ your coat.

10. Today (*be*) _____ a holiday. We (*have, not*) _____ class today.

11. Abby (*eat, not*) _____ breakfast. She (*be, not*) _____ hungry in the mornings.

12. I (*read*) _____ the newspaper. I (*watch, not*) _____ TV news.

13. My roommate (*read, not*) _____ the newspaper. She (*watch*) _____ news online.

▶ **Practice 28. Yes/no questions.** (Chart 3-9)
Make questions with the given words.

1. she \ study ___*Does she study?*_____

2. they \ study _____

3. he \ know _____

4. the doctor \ know _____

5. we \ know _____

6. I \ understand _____

7. you \ understand _____

8. the manager \ understand _____

9. your roommate \ work _____

10. the car \ work _____

11. it \ work _____

12. I \ care _____

13. She \ care _____

▶ **Practice 29. Yes/no questions.** (Chart 3-9)
Below is information about four people and the activities they do. Make questions for the given answers.

	Tom	**Roger**	**Renee**	**Lisa**
swim	x			
run		x		
play soccer	x		x	x
lift weights		x		x

1. Tom

   a. _____Does he swim?_____ Yes, he does.

   b. _____ Yes, he does.

   c. _____Does he run?_____ No, he doesn't.

   d. _____ No, he doesn't.

2. Roger

   a. _____ Yes, he does.

   b. _____ No, he doesn't.

   c. _____ Yes, he does.

3. Renee and Lisa

   a. _____ Yes, they do.

   b. _____ No, they don't.

   c. _____ No, they don't.

Choose the correct response for each question.

1. Do you like fish?
   (a.) Yes, I do.   b. Yes, I like.

2. Does your husband like fish?
   a. Yes, he does.   b. Yes, he likes.

3. Do you want to go out to dinner?
   a. Yes, I want.   b. Yes, I do.

4. Do you have a question?
   a. Yes, I have.   b. Yes, I do.

5. Do you need help?
   a. Yes, I do.   b. Yes, I need.

6. Does your friend need help?
   a. Yes, she needs.   b. Yes, she does.

7. Do your friends go to school?
   a. Yes, they do.   b. Yes, they go.

8. Does your husband teach English?
   a. Yes, he teaches.   b. Yes, he does.

▶ **Practice 31. Yes/no questions and answers.** (Chart 3-9)
Make questions. Give short answers.

1. Ann is a doctor. She examines children.

   _____*Does she examine*_____ adults? No, _____*she doesn't*_____ .

2. Tom is a mechanic. He fixes cars.

   _____ boats? No, _____ .

3. I am a pilot. I fly small planes.

   _____ jets? No, _____ .

4. We are teachers. We teach teenagers.

   _____ young children? No, _____ .

5. My sister and I are janitors. We clean office buildings.

   _____ schools? No, _____ .

6. Lynn and Doug are architects. They design houses.

   _____ offices? No, _____ .

7. Mrs. Adams is a writer. She writes for a magazine.

_____ for a book company? No, _____.

8. I am a nurse. I work at a hospital.

_____ at a clinic? No, _____.

9. They are construction workers. They build hotels.

_____ office buildings? No, _____.

10. Mr. Smith is a musician. He plays for a symphony.

_____ for a rock band? No, _____.

▶ **Practice 32. Be and do in questions.** (Chart 3-9)
Complete the questions with a form of **be** or **do**.

1. ____Are____ you ready?

2. _____ the bus here?

3. _____ the bus usually come on time?

4. _____ you often ride the bus?

5. _____ the bus comfortable?

6. _____ you do your work on the bus?

7. _____ you read books on the bus?

8. _____ you enjoy the ride?

9. _____ you drive to work sometimes?

10. _____ you tired of my questions?

▶ **Practice 33. Be and do in questions.** (Chart 3-9)
Complete the questions and answers. Use a form of **be** or **do**.

1. A: _____Are_____ you sick?

   B: No, I __am__ not.

   A: ___Are___ you tired?

   B: Yes, I __am__.

   A: ___Do___ you want to go to bed?

   B: No, I __don't__.

2. A: ___Do___ you know the time?

   B: Yes, I __do__. It __is__ 5:55.

3. A: __are you__ you hungry?

   B: Yes, I __am__.

   A: __Do__ you want some chocolate?

   B: Sure. Mmm.

   A: __Do__ you like it?

   B: No, I __don't__. I love it!!

4. A: __Are__ you students?

   B: Not exactly.

   A: __Are__ you teachers?

   B: Not exactly.

   A: What __are__ you?

   B: We __are__ student teachers.

5. A: __is__ Mr. Jones here?

   B: No, he __isn't__.

   A: Where __is__ he?

   B: I have no idea.

   A: __Is__ his wife here?

   B: No, she __isn't__.

   A: Where __is__ she?

   B: With Mr. Jones.

6. A: Where __Are__ my glasses? __Do__ you know?

    B: No. __are__ they in your purse?

    A: No, they __aren't__.

    B: __are__ they in your pocket?

    A: No.

    B: Oh, I see them! They __are__ on your head.

▶ **Practice 34. Questions with *where* and *what*.** (Chart 3-10)
Complete the questions with *where* or *what*.

1. _____ does Gino live? He lives in Rome.

2. _____ does Albert work? He works at Valley Hospital.

3. _____ do the kids play after school? They play soccer.

4. _____ do you want for breakfast? I just want toast and coffee.

5. _____ do you want to sit? I want to sit at the table by the window.

6. _____ does Helene like to do for vacation? She likes to travel.

7. _____ does Helene like to go? She likes to go to Hawaii.

8. _____ do you need? I need a vacation.

▶ **Practice 35. Questions with *where* and *what*.** (Chart 3-10)
Make questions for the given answers.

1. A: ____*Where does David live?*_____

   B: In Miami. (David lives in Miami.)

2. A: Where does the teacher want?

   B: Our email addresses. (The teacher wants our email addresses.)

3. A: Where does Dr. Varma stay?

   B: At the Plaza Hotel. (Dr. Varma stays at the Plaza Hotel.)

4. A: Where do you catch the bus?

   B: On First Street. (I catch the bus on First Street.)

5. A: What does Lillian need?

   B: A new job. (Lillian needs a new job.)

6. A: What do the children want?

   B: A baby brother. (The children want a baby brother.)

7. A: Where does the construction workes eat lunch

   B: In the park. (The construction workers eat lunch in the park.)

8. A: _____
   B: Downstairs. (Victoria and Franco are downstairs.)

9. A: _____
   B: Flowers. (Mark brings his wife flowers every week.)

10. A: _____
    B: The flight number. (I need the flight number.)

▶ **Practice 36. Questions with *where* and *what*.** (Chart 3-10)
Read the story. Make questions about Paulo for the given answers.
Use ***where*** and ***what***.

Paulo enjoys his work. He spends most of his time outdoors. He has two jobs, one for the summer and one for the winter. In the summer, he works in the forest. He looks for forest fires. He stays in a lookout tower. In the winter, he works in the mountains. He is a ski instructor. He teaches skiing to young children. He lives in a small ski hut with other teachers. Paulo loves both jobs. He is happy to be outdoors.

a lookout tower

1. A: ___*Where does Paulo spend most of his time?*___
   B: Outdoors.

2. A: _____
   B: In the forest.

3. A: _____
   B: Forest fires.

4. A: _____
   B: In a lookout tower.

5. A: _____
   B: In the mountains.

6. A: _____
   B: Skiing.

7. A: _____
   B: In a small ski hut.

8. A: _____
   B: Both jobs.

a ski hut

▶ **Practice 37. *Where, what,* and *when* in questions.** (Charts 3-10 and 3-11)
Complete the questions with *where, what,* or *when.*

1. _____Where_____ does Tom work?   At the bank.

2. _____When_____ does he leave for work?   At 7:00.

3. _____ does he eat lunch?   At noon.

4. _____ does he eat for lunch?   A sandwich.

5. _____ does he go after work?   To the gym.

6. _____ does he go home?   At 8:00.

7. _____ does he have for dinner?   Chicken or fish.

8. _____ does he do after dinner?   He watches TV.

9. _____ does he get ready for bed?   After dinner.

10. _____ does he sleep?   On his sofa.

▶ **Practice 38. Review: yes/no and information questions.** (Charts 3-9 → 3-11)
Make questions for the given answers.

1. A: _____*When do you go to bed?*_____
   B: Around 9:00. (I go to bed around 9:00.)

2. A: _____
   B: Yes, I do. (I get up early.)

3. A: _____
   B: At 5:30. (The bus comes at 5:30.)

4. A: _____
   B: Yes, it does. (The bus comes on time.)

5. A: _____
   B: At a hospital. (I work at a hospital.)

6. A: _____
   B: At 6:00. (I start work at 6:00.)

7. A: _____
   B: At 7:00. (I leave work at 7:00.)

8. A: _____
   B: Yes, I do. (I like my job.)

9. A: _____
   B: Yes, it is. (It is interesting work.)

10. A: _____
    B: Yes, I am. (I'm a doctor.)

► **Practice 39. Review: yes/no and information questions.** (Charts 3-9 → 3-11)
Read the note. Then make questions and answers about Dr. Ramos and his schedule.

1. be \ a science teacher?

   Is he a teacher?

   Yes, he is.

2. what \ teach?

   What does he teach?
   He teachs biology and
   chemistry.

3. where \ teach \ chemistry?

   Where does he teach?
   He teach chemistry
   in the chemistry

4. when \ be \ in the chemistry lab?

   When is he in the chemistry
   He's in the chemistry lab at 12:: o'clock.

5. where \ teach \ biology?

   Where does he teach biology?
   He teachs biology in the biology.

6. be \ in his office \ every day?

   Is he in his office every day?
   No, he isn't.

7. be \ in his office \ at 1:00?

   Is he in his office at 1:00?
   Yes, he is.

8. teach \ at 8:00?

   Does he teach at 8:00?
   No, he, doesn't.

9. when \ teach?

   When does he teach?
   he teachs at 9:00, 10:00 and 12:00

Dr. Ramos

Schedule Change
My new office hours
are from 1:00 to
2:00, Monday,
Wednesday, and
Friday. I teach
biology at 9:00
and 10:00 in the
biology lab. I teach
chemistry at 12:00
in the chemistry lab.

► **Practice 40. Review: simple present tense.** (Chapter 3)
Complete the sentences with the correct form of the verb in parentheses. Some sentences are negative, and some are not.

1. Mario likes to talk. He (*be*) _____ isn't _____ quiet.

2. Janna isn't quiet. She (*love*) _____ loves _____ to talk.

3. Susan is a good student. She (*study*) _____ studies _____ a lot.

4. The nurses are very busy. They (*have*) _____ don't have _____ time for lunch.

5. John's bedroom is messy. He (*clean*) _____ doesn't clean _____ it often.

6. This soup is delicious. It (*taste*) _____ tastes _____ wonderful.

7. A new car is expensive. It (*cost*) _____ costs _____ a lot of money.

8. Several students want to answer the question. They (*know*) _____ know _____ the answer.

9. Several students don't know the answer. They (*want*) _____ don't want _____ to answer the question.

10. A: Your eyes are red. You (*look*) _____ look _____ tired.

    B: Actually, I'm sad. I (*be*) _____ am not _____ tired.

► **Practice 41. Question review.** (Chapters 2 and 3)
Make questions using the information in the note.

1. A: _____ Is Jane at home? _____
   B: No, she isn't. (Jane isn't home.)

2. A: _____ Where is she? _____
   B: At work. (She is at work.)

3. A: _____ Are Susie and Johnny at Home? _____
   B: No, they aren't. (Susie and Johnny aren't home.)

4. A: _____ where are they? _____
   B: At school. (They are at school.)

5. A: _____ what time is the Dinner / when is dinner _____
   B: At 6:00. (Dinner is at 6:00.)

6. A: _____ what does Jane have for dinner? _____
   B: A pizza. (Jane has a pizza for dinner.)

> Ron,
> I'm at work. Susie and Johnny are at school. You need to pick them up. Dinner is at 6:00. I have a pizza in the fridge.*
> See you soon!
>   Jane

*fridge = refrigerator.

Choose the correct completion for each sentence.

1. Alex _____ know French.
   a. isn't   (b.) doesn't   c. don't

2. _____ Alex speak Russian?
   a. Is   (b.) Does   c. Do

3. _____ Alex from Canada?
   (a.) Is   b. Does   c. Do

4. When _____ you usually check your email?
   a. are   b. does   (c.) do

5. Anita _____ a job.
   a. no have   b. no has   (c.) doesn't have

6. Omar _____ his new car every Saturday.
   a. wash   b. washs   (c.) washes

7. Where does Tina _____ to school?
   (a.) go   b. goes   c. to go

8. Fumiko _____ English at this school.
   a. study   (b.) studies   c. studys

9. Fumiko and Omar _____ students at this school.
   a. is   (b.) are   c. be

10. They _____ speak the same language.
    a. aren't   b. doesn't   (c.) don't

Chapter 4

Using the Present Progressive

▶ **Practice 1. The present progressive.** (Chart 4-1)
Which sentences are true for you?

Right now

1. The sun is shining.   yes   no

2. It is snowing outside.   yes   no

3. I am sitting at a desk.   yes   no

4. I am checking text messages.   yes   no

5. Music is playing.   yes   no

6. Friends are talking to me.   yes   no

7. People are calling me on my phone.   yes   no

▶ **Practice 2. The present progressive.** (Chart 4-1)
Complete each sentence with **am**, **is**, or **are**.

Right now

1. Some students __*are*__ waiting for the bus.

2. Their teacher __is__ correcting their homework.

3. I __am__ doing my homework.

4. Mark __is__ doing his homework.

5. Sandra __is__ shopping at the mall.

6. Her friends __are__ shopping with her.

7. Mr. and Mrs. Brown __are__ watching TV.

8. Their daughter __is__ reading a book.

9. You __are__ reading this exercise.

10. We __are__ learning English.

11. My friend and I __are__ learning English.

12. Dr. John __is__ looking for medical information on the Internet.

13. A nurse __is__ talking to a patient.

14. Several patients __are__ waiting in the waiting room.

▶ **Practice 3. Spelling of *-ing*.** (Chart 4-2)
Write the *-ing* form of each verb.

1. shine ___shining___
2. win ___winning___
3. join ___joing___
4. sign ___signing___
5. fly ___flying___

6. pay ___paying___
7. study ___studying___
8. get ___getting___
9. wait ___waiting___
10. write ___writing___

▶ **Practice 4. Spelling of *-ing*.** (Chart 4-2)
Write the *-ing* form of each verb.

1. dream ___dreaming___
2. come ___coming___
3. look ___looking___
4. take ___taking___
5. bite ___biting___

6. hit ___hitting___
7. hurt ___hurting___
8. clap ___clapping___
9. keep ___keeping___
10. camp ___camping___

► **Practice 5. The present progressive.** (Charts 4-1 and 4-2)
Complete each sentence with the correct form of a verb from the box. Use the present progressive.

come ✓	go	read –	talk
do ✓	kick	sit ✓	✓ wait

It's 3:00 and the classroom is empty. Some students are outside. They
_____*are waiting*_____ for the city bus. A few students _____*are sitting*_____
        1   2
on the ground under a tree. They _____*are talking*_____ about their plans for the
                                          3
weekend. A girl on a bench _____*is doing*_____ her homework. The boy next to her
                                    4
_____*is reading*_____ a book. A few students _____*are kicking*_____ a soccer
        5   6
ball. The bus _____*is coming*_____ now. The students _____*are going*_____
                      7   8
home.

► **Practice 6. The present progressive: affirmative and negative.** (Chart 4-3)

Part I. Tony is an engineer. Right now he is in his office. Check (✓) the activities he is doing. Make possible sentences for all the given phrases.

__✓__ meet with his manager   ____ talk on the phone

____ repair his car   ____ ride a horse

____ work at his computer   ____ buy food for dinner

1. _____*He is meeting with his manager.*_____

2. _____*He isn't repairing his car.*_____

3. _____

4. _____

5. _____

6. _____

Part II. Anita and Ben are nurses. Right now they are at the hospital. Check (✓) the activities they are doing. Make possible sentences for all the given phrases.

_____ talk to patients   _____ work with doctors

_____ wash cars   _____ give medicine to patients

_____ watch movies

1. _____

2. _____

3. _____

4. _____

5. _____

Part III. What are you doing right now? Check (✓) the activities and make true sentences for all the given phrases.

_____ listen to music   _____ study in the library

_____ sit at a desk   _____ wait for a friend

_____ work at home   _____ ride on a bus

1. _____

2. _____

3. _____

4. _____

5. _____

6. _____

▶ **Practice 7. The present progressive: affirmative and negative.** (Chart 4-3)
Use the verb in each sentence to make a true sentence.

1. I (*think*) _am thinking / am not thinking_ about my family right now.

2. I (*write*) _____ in a classroom right now.

3. I (*listen*) _____ to music right now.

4. I (*travel*) _____ in another country today.

5. A cat (*sit*) _____ beside me right now.

6. A bird (sing) _____ outside my window.

7. My phone (ring) _____ at this moment.

8. A computer printer in the room (make) _____ noise right now.

▶ **Practice 8. The present progressive: questions.** (Chart 4-4)
Make questions with the given words. Use the present progressive.

1. he \ study English? _____*Is he studying English?*_____

2. you \ work? _____

3. they \ leave? _____

4. she \ stay home? _____

5. we \ go to school? _____

6. the computer \ work? _____

7. it \ work? _____

8. I \ drive? _____

9. your friend \ come? _____

10. the students \ laugh? _____

11. Mr. Kim \ sleep? _____

12. Monica \ dream? _____

▶ **Practice 9. The present progressive: questions and negatives.** (Chart 4-4)
Use the verbs in parentheses to make logical questions and answers.

1. Anna is in the kitchen. (*cook, sleep*)

A: _____*Is she sleeping*_____?

B: No, _____*she isn't*_____. She _____*is cooking*_____.

2. Pablo is in the car. (*drive, run*)

A: _____?

B: No, _____. He _____.

3. Terry and Tony are in the swimming pool. (*swim, study*)

A: _____?

B: No, _____. They _____.

4. Mrs. Ramirez is at the supermarket. (*teach, shop*)

A: _____?

B: No, _____. She _____.

5. Marta is in her bedroom. (*sleep, fish*)

A: _____?

B: No, _____. She _____.

6. Some teenagers are in the park with their soccer ball. (*play, work*)

A: _____?

B: No, _____. They _____.

7. I am on a plane. (*wash dishes, read a book*)

A: _____?

B: No, _____. I _____.

▶ **Practice 10. The present progressive: statements, negatives, and questions.**
(Charts 4-1 → 4-4)
Complete the sentences with the correct form of the verb **work**.

Part I: Statement Forms

1. I ___ *am working* ___ right now.

2. They _____ right now.

3. She _____ right now.

4. You _____ right now.

5. He _____ right now.

Part II: Negative Forms

6. I ___ *am not working* ___ right now.

7. They _____ right now.

8. She _____ right now.

9. You _____ right now.

10. He _____ right now.

11. _____Are_____ you _____working_____ right now?

12. _____ he _____ right now?

13. _____ they _____ right now?

14. _____ we _____ right now?

15. _____ she _____ right now?

▶ **Practice 11. The simple present: statements, negatives, and questions.**
   (Charts 4-1 → 4-4)
Complete the sentences with the correct form of the verb **work**.

Part I: Statement Forms

1. I _____work_____ every day.

2. They _____ every day.

3. She _____ every day.

4. You _____ every day.

5. He _____ every day.

Part II: Negative Forms

6. I _____do not work_____ every day.

7. They _____ every day.

8. She _____ every day.

9. You _____ every day.

10. He _____ every day.

Part III: Question Forms

11. _____Do_____ you _____work_____ every day?

12. _____ he _____ every day?

13. _____ they _____ every day?

14. _____ we _____ every day?

15. _____ she _____ every day?

Practice 12. Simple present vs. the present progressive. (Chart 4-5)
Choose the correct completion for each sentence.

1. I send text messages   now.   (every day.)
2. I am not sending a text message   (now.)   every day.
3. I receive text messages   now.   every day.
4. I look at magazines   now.   every day.
5. I'm reading a book   now.   every day.
6. It's raining   now.   every day.
7. My kids play outside   now.   every day.
8. My kids are playing outside   now.   every day.
9. My computer isn't working   now.   every day.
10. I work at my computer   now.   every day.

▶ **Practice 13. Simple present vs. the present progressive.** (Chart 4-5)
Check (✓) the sentences that describe activities happening right now.

1. _✓_ The phone is ringing.
2. ____ I'm talking to my sister.
3. ____ We talk two or three times a week.
4. ____ Ruth exercises in the mornings.
5. ____ She lifts weights.

6. ____ The baby is crying.
7. ____ She cries when she is hungry.
8. ____ Her mother is feeding her.
9. ____ We are listening to music.
10. ____ We listen to music in the car.

▶ **Practice 14. Simple present vs. the present progressive.** (Chart 4-5)
Complete each sentence with the correct form of the verb in parentheses.

Right now the sun (*shine*) _____*is shining*_____ . I (*look*)
_____*am looking*_____ out my window at the lake. A man and a young boy
(*fish*) _____*are fishing*_____ from a small boat. A mother with a baby (*sit*)
_____*is sitting*_____ on the grass. They (*play*) _____*are playing*_____ with
a ball. Two girls (*swim*) _____*are swimming*_____ near the shore. Some teenage boys
(*jump*) _____*are jumping*_____ off the dock.

I (*swim*) _____swim_____ in the lake every day in the summer for exercise.
8
In the winter, I usually (*walk*) _____walk_____ around the lake, or I (*go*)
9
a ____go____ to a gym.
10
Today I (*work*) ____am working____ at home. I usually
11
(*work*) ____work____ at home three days a week. I (*write*)
12
____write____ stories for children's books. Right now I (*write*)
13
am writing ____ a story about a young boy and girl and a magic hat.
14

▶ **Practice 15. Simple present vs. the present progressive.** (Chart 4-5)
Complete each sentence with *Do*, *Does*, *Is*, or *Are*.

1. ____Do____ you study every day?

2. ____Are you____ you working hard now?

3. ____Is____ your class working hard now?

4. ____Are____ you learning a lot of English?

5. ____Do____ you memorize vocabulary every day?

6. ____is____ your teacher helping you now?

7. ____Does____ your teacher help you after class?

8. ____Do____ you do your homework every day?

9. ____Does____ the homework take a long time?

10. ____Do____ you understand your classmates?

11. ____Does____ your teacher understand you?

12. ____Do____ you ask a lot of questions?

13. ____Do____ you studying with friends right now?

14. ____Do____ you often study with friends?

▶ **Practice 16. Non-action verbs.** (Chart 4-6)
Choose the correct verb form in each sentence.

1. (*Do you know* / *Are you knowing*) the names of all the students in your class?

2. Mmm. I (*smell* / *am smelling*) something good in the oven.

3. The baby (*cries* / *is crying*) right now. She (*is wanting* / *wants*) her mother.

4. This coffee (*is tasting / tastes*) wonderful. I (*like / am liking*) strong coffee.

5. The cat and dog (*are running / run*) outside right now. The dog (*likes / is liking*) the cat, but the cat (*is hating / hates*) the dog.

▶ **Practice 17. Non-action verbs.** (Chart 4-6)
Complete each sentence with the correct form of the verb in parentheses.

1. A: Mmm. This bread (*taste*) _____tastes_____ delicious.

   B: Thank you. I (*think*) _____think_____ it has honey in it.

2. A: What (*Jan, want*) __does Jan wants__ for her birthday?

   B: Well, she (*need*) ___needs_____ a winter coat, but she (*want*) ___wants_____ leather boots.

3. A: Shhh. (*you, hear*) __Do you_____ a siren?

   B: I (*hear*) ___hear_____ it, but I (*see, not*) __dont seem___ it.

4. A: Jackie (*love*) ___loves_____ Carl.

   B: What? I (*believe, not*) __dont believe___ you. Carl (*love*) ___loves_____ me!

▶ **Practice 18. *See, look at, watch, hear,* and *listen to*.** (Chart 4-7)
Choose the correct sentence in each pair.

1. a. I am hearing the neighbor's TV. It's very loud.
   (b.) I hear the neighbor's TV. It's very loud.

2. (a.) Look! I see a deer.
   b. Look! I am seeing a deer.

3. (a.) Annette isn't listening to me right now.
   b. Annette doesn't listen to me right now.

4. a. Shhh. I watch a movie.
   (b.) Shhh. I'm watching a movie.

a deer

5. a. I look at the clock. We are late.
   b. I'm looking at the clock. We are late. *(b circled)*

6. a. Mary, what are you looking at? *(a circled)*
   b. Mary, what do you look at?

7. a. Do you hear that noise? It sounds like an earthquake. *(a circled)*
   b. Are you hearing that noise? It sounds like an earthquake.

8. a. I am listening to the radio at night. It helps me fall asleep.
   b. I listen to the radio at night. It helps me fall asleep. *(b circled)*

9. a. I hear my cell phone. I need to answer it right now. *(a circled)*
   b. I am hearing my cell phone. I need to answer it right now.

▶ **Practice 19. See, look at, watch, hear, and listen to.** (Chart 4-7)
Complete each sentence with the correct form of the verb in parentheses.

Andy is sitting in his living room right now. He
(*watch*) __is watching__ a football game on TV. His
1
favorite team (*play*) __play__. He
2
(*listen, also*) __is also listening__ to the game
3
on the radio and (*look*) __is looking__
4
at sports information in the newspaper. He
(*wear*) __is wearing__
5
headphones. His wife (*talk*) __is talking__ to him. She (*tell*)
6
__is telling__ him her plans for the day. He (*listen, not*)
7
__isn't listening__ because he (*hear, not*) __doesn't hear__
8   9
her. Suddenly, she turns off the TV. Now Andy (*listen*) __is listening__
10
very carefully.

▶ **Practice 20. See, look at, watch, hear, and listen to.** (Chart 4-7)
Choose the correct verb in each sentence.

1. In the evenings, I like to sit in front of the TV and (*watch* / see) old movies. *(watch circled)*

2. The neighbors are having a party. I (*hear* / listen to) a lot of loud noise.

3. Shhh. I (*hear* / listen to) something. Is someone outside?

4. I love rock music. When I'm at home, I put on my headphones, sit down, and
   (*hear* / listen to) rock music.

5. A: Let's go shopping. I want to (*look at* / watch) clothes.
   B: Okay. You can (*look at* / see) clothes. I want to sit on a bench and (*see* / watch) the
      people at the mall.

6. A: Look out the window. (*Do you see / Do you watch*) the storm clouds?

    B: I (*see / look at*) several dark rain clouds.

▶ **Practice 21. Review.** (Charts 4-6 and 4-7)
Write true sentences using the given verbs.

Right now I. . .

1. (*look at*) I am looking at the clock .

2. (*see*) _____ .

3. (*hear*) I hear a Police siren .

4. (*listen to*) I am listening to the radio .

5. (*watch*) I am watching a Tv show. .

6. (*want*) I want to eat pizza. .

7. (*need*) I Need food. .

▶ **Practice 22. *Think about* and *think that*.** (Chart 4-8)
Choose the correct sentence in each pair.

1. a. You are very quiet. What do you think about?
   b. You are very quiet. What are you thinking about?

2. a. I am thinking about my plans for today.
   b. I think about my plans for today.

3. a. I am thinking that grammar is difficult.
   b. I think that grammar is difficult.

4. a. What are you thinking? Does this shirt look okay?
   b. What do you think? Does this shirt look okay?

5. a. Joe, do you think that sports stars get too much money?
   b. Joe, are you thinking that sports stars get too much money?

▶ **Practice 23. *Think about* and *think that*.** (Chart 4-8)
Complete each sentence with the correct form of ***think that*** or ***think about***.

1. A: What _____*are*_____ you _____*thinking about*_____
      right now?

    B: I _am thinking about_ my family. I miss them.

    A: You have a nice family. I _think that_ you are lucky.

2. A: Some people _____*think that*_____ English is an easy language.

   B: I (*not*) _____*don't think that*_____ it is easy to learn. I
   _____*an think that*_____ it is difficult.

3. A: I have a new game. I _____*am thinking about*_____ an animal. It
   is very long and sometimes dangerous. Do you know the animal? Can you guess?

   B: _____*Am thinking about*_____ you _____*are think about*_____ a snake?

   A: Yes!

   B: I _____*think that*_____ snakes make nice pets, but many people are
   afraid of them.

   A: I'm afraid of them. I _____*think that*_____ they are scary.

▶ **Practice 24. Verb review.** (Chapters 3 and 4)
   Complete each sentence with the correct form of the verb in parentheses.

1. Tony's family (*eat*) _____*eats*_____ dinner at the same time every day.
   During dinner, the phone sometimes (*ring*) _____*rings*_____.
   Tony's mother (*answer, not*) _____*doesn't answer*_____ it. She
   (*want, not*) _____*doesn't want*_____ her teenagers to talk on the phone
   during dinner. She (*believe*) _____*believes*_____ dinner is an important
   time for the family.

2. Olga Burns is a pilot for an airline company in Alaska. She (*fly*) _____*flies*_____
   almost every day. Today she (*fly*) _____*is flying*_____ from Juneau to
   Anchorage.

3. A: Excuse me. (*you, wait*) _____*Are you waiting*_____ for the downtown bus?

   B: Yes, I (*be*) _____*am*_____.

   A: What time (*the bus, stop*) _____*does the bus stop*_____ here?

   B: Ten thirty-five.

   A: (*be, usually, it*) _____*is it usually*_____ on time?

   B: Yes. It (*come, rarely*) _____*rarely come*_____ late.

4. A: What (*your teacher, do, usually*) _____*does your teacher usually do*_____
   at lunchtime every day?

   B: I (*think*) _____*think*_____ she (*correct*) _____*corrects*_____
   papers in the classroom and (*have*) _____*has*_____ lunch.

   A: What (*she, do*) _____*is she doing*_____ right now?

   B: She (*talk*) _____*is talking*_____ to a student.

5. A: (you, know) _Do you now_ the capital of Australia?

   B: I (believe) _believe_ it (be) _is_ Vienna.

   A: Not Austria. Australia!

   B: Oh. Wait a minute. Let me think. I (know) _Know_ . It's Canberra.

▶ **Practice 25. Verb review.** (Chapters 3 and 4)
Complete each sentence with the word or words in parentheses. Use the simple present or the present progressive. Use an infinitive where necessary.

   The Lind family is at home. It is evening. Jens (sit) _sits_ on the couch. He (look at) _is looking at_ a weather report on his computer. Brita (work) _works_ at her desk. She (study) _studies_ and (listen to) _listening to_ music. Jens (hear) _is hearing._ the music, but he (listen to, not) _doesn't listening_ it right now. He (think about) _is thinking about_ the weather report.

   Brita (memorize) _memorizes_ chemistry formulas. She (like) _likes_ chemistry. She (think) _thinks_ that chemistry is easy. She (understand) _understands_ it. Chemistry (be) _is_ her favorite course. She (like, not) _doesn't like_ history.

$$2H_2 + O_2 \rightarrow 2H_2O$$

a chemistry formula

Mr. Lind is in the kitchen. He (cook) _is cooking_ (15) dinner. He (cook) _cooks_ (16) three or four times a week. He (cut) _is cutting_ (17) vegetables for a salad. Steam (rise) _rising_ (18) from a pot on the stove.

Mrs. Lind (stand) _is standing_ (19) near the front door. She (take off) _is taking off_ (20) her jacket. She (wear) _is wearing_ (21) exercise clothes because she (exercise, usually) _usually exercises_ (22) after work. She (think about) _is thinking about_ (23) dinner. She (be) _is_ (24) very hungry, and the food (smell) _smells_ (25) good. After dinner, she (want) _wants_ (26) (watch) _watch_ (27) a TV show with her family. Their favorite show (be) _is_ (28) on tonight. She (need) _needs_ (29) (go) _to go to_ (30) to bed afterwards because she has a busy day at work tomorrow.

In the corner of the living room, a mouse (eat) _is eating_ (31) a piece of cheese. Their cat (be) _is_ (32) nearby, but she (sleep) _is sleeping_ (33). She (dream about) _is dreaming about_ (34) a mouse.

Nine-year-old Axel is in the middle of the living room. He (play) _is playing_ (35) with a toy train. He (see, not) _doesnt see_ (36) the mouse because he (look at) _is looking at_ (37) his train. Their bird (sing) _is singing_ (38). Axel (listen to, not) _isnt listening to_ (39) it. But Mrs. Lind (hear) _hears_ (40) the bird. She (like) _likes_ (41) (listen to) _to listen to_ (42) it sing.

Chapter 5

Talking About the Present

▶ **Practice 1. Using *it* with time and dates.** (Chart 5-1)
Read the email message. Make questions for the answers. Begin each question with **What**.

To:	Brooks, Jim
From:	Hernandez, Sue
Date:	Tue 3/5/2014 6:00 A.M.
Subject:	See you soon

Hi Jim,

It's 6:00 Tuesday morning in Tokyo. I'm sitting in my hotel room. I'm waiting for the airport bus. Great trip. Miss you—see you tomorrow!

Sue

1. _____*What day is it?*_____ It's Tuesday.
2. _____*What time is it?*_____ It's 6:00 A.M.
3. _____*What's the date today?*_____ It's March 5th.
4. _____*What year is it?*_____ It's 2014.
5. _____*What month is it?*_____ It's March.
6. _____*What time is it?*_____ It's six o'clock.
7. _____*What's date is it?*_____ It's the 5th of March.

▶ **Practice 2. Using *it* with time and dates.** (Chart 5-1)
Choose the correct response to each question.

1. What's the date today?
   (a.) It's April 1. b. It's Monday.

2. What day is it?
   a. It's February 2. (b.) It's Friday.

3. What month is it?
   a. It's January 2nd. (b.) It's December.

4. What time is it?
   (a.) It's 9:55.   b. It's 9:55 o'clock.

5. What's the date today?
   a. It's Monday.   (b.) It's the 2nd of May.

► **Practice 3. Prepositions of time.** (Chart 5-2)
Complete each sentence with the correct preposition.

1. I wake up . . .

   a. ____in____ the morning.

   b. ___at___ 7:00.

2. My husband goes to work . . .

   a. ___at___ 1:00 P.M.

   b. ___in___ the afternoon.

   c. ___on___ Mondays, Wednesdays, and Thursdays.

3. I work . . .

   a. ___in___ the evening.

   b. ___at___ night.

   c. ___from___ 5:00 ___to___ midnight.

   d. ___on___ Saturday.

   e. ___on___ Saturdays.

4. My husband was born . . .

   a. ___on___ December.

   b. ___on___ December 26.

   c. ___in___ the afternoon.

   d. ___at___ 1:00 ___in___ the afternoon.

   e. ___on___ December 26, 1989.

   f. ___in___ 1989.

► **Practice 4. Prepositions of time.** (Chart 5-2)
Complete each sentence with *in*, *on*, *at*, *from*, or *to*.

1. I have English class ___in___ the morning.

2. My first class begins ___at___ 9:00 A.M.

3. The class goes ___from___ 9:00 ___to___ 9:55.

4. I don't have class ___on___ Fridays.

5. My math class meets ___in___ the evenings.

6. I don't like to study ___at___ night.

7. I prefer to study ___in___ the afternoon.

8. There is no class ___on___ May 1st.

9. Summer vacation goes ___from___ June ___to___ September.

► **Practice 5. Talking about the weather.** (Chart 5-3)
Use the weather information in the box.

Moscow	0°C	32°F	partly cloudy, snow
Sydney	24°C	75°F	clear, dry
Seoul	5°C	41°F	heavy rain, strong winds
Cairo	38°C	100°F	clear, dry

Part I. Make questions for the given answers.

1. ___How's the weather / What's the weather like in Cairo?___ It's hot.

2. How's the weather / what's the weather like in Sydney? It's warm.

3. How's the weather / what's the weather like in Seoul It's stormy.

4. How's the weather / What's the weather like in Sydney It's beautiful.

5. How's the weather / what's the weather like in Moscow? It's freezing.

Part II. Circle *yes* or *no*.

6. It is chilly in Moscow.   (yes)   no

7. It is wet in Cairo.   yes   (no)

8. It is freezing in Seoul.   yes   (no)

9. It is humid in Sydney.   (yes)   no

10. It is nice in Sydney.   (yes)   no

11. It is clear in Seoul.   yes   (no)

▶ **Practice 6. Asking about the weather.** (Charts 5-1 and 5-3)
Complete the questions with words from the box.

how's	like	temperature	the weather

1. What's the weather __like__ in your hometown?

2. __how's__ the weather in your hometown?

3. What's the average __Temperature__ in the summer?

4. What's the average __Temperature__ in the winter?

5. How's __the weather__ in Singapore right now?

▶ **Practice 7. Questions: time and weather.** (Charts 5-1 and 5-3)
Choose the correct completion for each sentence.

1. What ____ the weather like today?
   a. is it   (b.) is

2. What month ____?
   (a.) is it   b. is

3. What ____ the date today?
   a. is it   b. (is)

4. What day ____?
   (a.) is it   b. is

5. What time ____?
   (a.) is it   b. is

6. How ____ the weather?
   a. is it   (b.) is

7. What year ____?
   (a.) is it   b. is

▶ **Practice 8. *There + be.*** (Chart 5-4)
Look around the room you are in. Choose the correct verb, and then circle *yes* or *no*.

1. There (is / are) one student in this room.   yes   no
2. There (is / are) two students in this room.   yes   (no)
3. There (is / are) a desk.   yes   no
4. There (is / are) one door.   yes   no
5. There (is / are) two doors.   yes   no
6. There (is / are) three windows.   yes   no
7. There (is / are) a computer.   yes   no

8. There (is / are) a TV.   yes   no
9. There (is / are) chairs.   yes   no

▶ **Practice 9. *There + be.*** (Chart 5-4)
Make sentences about the picture using the given words.

1. (*two chairs*) _____There are two chairs._____
2. (*one couch*) _____There is one couch_____
3. (*one table*) _____There is one table_____
4. (*four books*) _____There are four books_____
5. (*one lamp*) _____There is one lamp_____
6. (*two pillows*) _____There are two pillows_____

▶ **Practice 10. *There + be*: yes/no questions.** (Chart 5-5)
Think about your bedroom. Circle the correct form of *be*. Then write short answers.

1. (**Is** / Are)   there a bed in your bedroom?   _Yes, there is. / No, there isn't._
2. (**Is** / Are)   there a window in your bedroom?   Yes, there is / No, there isn't
3. (Is / **Are**)   there four windows in your bedroom? Yes, there are / no there aren't
4. (Is / Are)   there a pillow on your bed?   Yes, there is / no there isn't
5. (Is / Are)   there six pillows on your bed?   Yes, there is , No there aren't
6. (Is / Are)   there sheets on your bed?   _____
7. (Is / Are)   there a TV in your bedroom?   _____
8. (Is / Are)   there two closets in your bedroom? _____
9. (Is / Are)   there a mirror in your bedroom?   _____

► **Practice 11. *There + be*: yes/no questions.** (Chart 5-5)
You are new to a town. Make questions about the places in parentheses. Begin with ***Is there***
or ***Are there***.

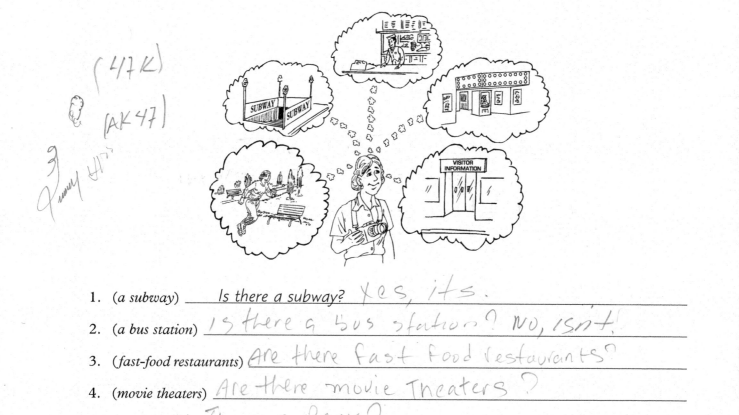

1. (*a subway*) _____ Is there a subway? Yes, its. _____

2. (*a bus station*) _____ Is there a bus station? No, isn't! _____

3. (*fast-food restaurants*) _____ Are there fast food restaurants? _____

4. (*movie theaters*) _____ Are there movie Theaters ? _____

5. (*a park*) _____ Is There a Park? _____

6. (*places to exercise*) _____ Are There Places to exercise ? _____

7. (*a visitor information office*) _____ Is there a visitor information Office? _____

► **Practice 12. *There + be*: questions with *how many*.** (Chart 5-6)
Choose the correct noun in each question.

1. How many (*boy* / *boys*) are there in the world?

2. How many (*girl* / *girls*) are there in the world?

3. How many (*car* / *cars*) are there in the world?

4. How many (*word* / *words*) are there in a dictionary?

5. How many (*minute* / *minutes*) are there in a day?

6. How many (*second* / *seconds*) are there in a day?

7. How many (*star* / *stars*) are there in the sky?

8. How many (*snowflake* / *snowflakes*) are there in a snowball?

a snowflake

► **Practice 13. *There + be*: questions with how many.** (Chart 5-6)
Complete each question with a word or phrase from the box. Begin with ***How many***.

— colors	— countries	- main languages
✓ continents	letters	- states

1. ___How many continents are there___ in the world? There are seven.
2. ___How many states are there___ in Australia? There are six.
3. ___How many colors are there___ on the Thai flag? There are three.
4. ___How many countries are there___ in North America? There are three.
5. ___How many letters are there___ in the English alphabet? There are twenty-six.
6. ___How many main languages are there___ in Canada? There are two: French and English.

► **Practice 14. *There + be*: questions with *how many*.** (Chart 5-6)
Make questions using the given words and ***How many***. Then give short answers.

1. sentence \ in this exercise

   ___How many sentences are there in this exercise?___ ___There are seven.___

2. exercise \ in this chapter

   ___How many exercises are there in this chapter?___
   ___there are #2's___

3. page \ in your dictionary

   ___How many pages are in your dictionary?___
   ___there are 1023___

4. student \ in your class

   ___How many students are there in your class?___

5. male \ in your class

   ___How many males are there in your class?___

6. female \ in your class

   ___How many females are there in your class?___

7. teacher \ at your school

   ___How many teachers are there at your school?___

► **Practice 15. Prepositions of place.** (Chart 5-7)
Complete each sentence with the correct preposition: *in, on,* or *at.*

1. Marco lives ____in____ Italy.

2. Tina lives ____in____ Vancouver, Canada.

3. Tina works ____on____ Robson Street.

4. Margaret lives ____at____ 6456 1st Street.

5. Margaret lives ____on____ 1st Street.

6. Jeffrey lives ____in____ Australia.

7. Jeffrey works ____on____ 2nd Street.

8. Jeffrey works ____at____ 5725 2nd Street.

► **Practice 16. *At* or *in*.** (Chart 5-7)
Complete the sentences with *at* or *in*.

1. Renata is sleeping. She is ___in___ bed ___in___ her bedroom.

2. Jack is very sick. He is a patient. He is ___in___ the hospital.

3. Mrs. Nelson is a university professor. Her students are ___in___ class. They are sitting ___in___ the classroom.

4. Everyone in class is listening to the teacher. They are ___at___ school right now.

5. Kellen is absent today. He is ___at___ home.

6. His wife is not ___at___ home. She is ___at___ work.

7. Your shoes are ___in___ the hall.

8. Extra chairs are ___in___ the kitchen.

9. Carlos is a thief. He is ___in___ jail.

10. His father is also a thief. He is ___in___ prison.

► **Practice 17. *At* or *in*.** (Chart 5-7)
Complete the sentences with *at* or *in*.

Last week, Ben was . . .

1. ____at____ home.

2. ____at____ school for a meeting.

3. ____at____ work.

4. ____in____ the bedroom.

5. __in__ bed.

6. __in__ the hospital visiting a friend.

7. __at__ the post office.

8. __in__ class.

9. __in__ his hometown of Mountain View.

10. on the phone with someone __in__ jail.

► **Practice 18. At or in.** (Chart 5-7)
Complete the sentences about the Johnson family. Use **at** or **in**.

It's 10:00 A.M. Where is everyone?

1. Mr. Johnson is ___in___ his office ___at___ work.

2. Mrs. Johnson is ___at___ the library with her first-grade class.

3. Joe is ___in___ class ___at___ school.

4. Beth is sick ___at___ home ___in___ bed.

5. Rita is on vacation ___in___ Hawaii.

6. Bob is ___at___ work. He is working ___at___ a bookstore.

7. Grandma Johnson is ___in___ the hospital. She is very sick.

► **Practice 19. Prepositions of place.** (Chart 5-8)
Complete each sentence with a preposition. There may be more than one possible completion.

1. The rabbit is _____ *in / inside* _____ the hat.

2. The rabbit is _____ in / front _____ the hat.

3. The rabbit is _____ behind / in back of _____ the hat.

4. The rabbit is _____ on top _____ the hat.

5. The rabbit is _____ Next to / beside / nex _____ the hat.

6. The rabbit is _____Above_____ the hat.

7. The rabbit is _____Under_____ the hat.

8. The rabbit is _____between_____ the hats.

▶ **Practice 20. Prepositions of place.** (Chart 5-8)
Answer the questions with prepositional expressions.

1. Where are your legs?

    _____Under my desk. / On the floor. / Etc._____

2. Where are your feet?

    _____On the floor_____

3. Where is your left hand?

    _____on my desk_____

4. Where is your right hand?

    _____

5. Where is your workbook?

    _____

6. Where is your pen or pencil?

    _____

▶ **Practice 21. *Would like*.** (Chart 5-9)
Complete each sentence with the correct form of **would like**.

1. I _____would like_____ to leave.

2. You _____would like_____ to leave.

3. He _____would like_____ to leave.

4. She _____would like_____ to leave.

5. The cat _____would like_____ to leave.

6. Mrs. Jones _____would like_____ to leave.

7. We _____would like_____ to leave.

8. They _____would like_____ to leave.

9. The students _____would like_____ to leave.

10. Their teacher _____would like_____ to leave.

11. My friend _____would like_____ to leave.

12. My parents _____would like_____ to leave.

▶ **Practice 22. *Would like* vs. *like*.** (Chart 5-10)
Decide the meaning of each sentence. Choose ***want*** or ***like***.

1. I would like a cup of coffee.   (want)   like

2. I enjoy coffee in the morning.   want   (like)

3. My husband enjoys tea.   wants   (likes)

4. He would like to try decaffeinated tea.   (wants)   likes

5. I don't enjoy decaffeinated coffee.   want   (like)

6. We would like some coffee now.   (want)   like

▶ **Practice 23. *Would like* vs. *like*.** (Chart 5-10)
Rewrite the sentences with ***would like*** where possible.

1. Mark wants to have a large family. _____*Mark would like to have a large family.*_____

2. He enjoys children. _____*(no change)*_____

3. Children enjoy Mark. _____

4. Mark wants to get married this year. h_____

5. He wants a pet this year too. he would like a pet this year too.

6. He enjoys cats, dogs, and birds. he would like enjoys, cats, dogs a

7. What does he want first? what would he like first?

► **Practice 24. Review.** (Chapters 4 and 5)

Part I. Answer the questions. Use vocabulary from the box.

sleep	a bed	a dream
(be) in love	a blanket	a head
dream	a clock	a pillow
dream about (someone/something)		

Is It a clook in the room?
Is there a blanket
Is there a clook in the room

Are Iuith and mary in love

1. What is Mary doing?
2. What is John doing?
3. What are Mary and John doing?
4. What do you see in the picture?
5. Is Mary in her bedroom?

6. Is John in class? Where is he?
7. Is John standing or lying down?
8. Is Mary dreaming?
9. Are Mary and John dreaming about each other?
10. Are John and Mary in love?

Part II. Complete the sentences.

11. John and Mary ____are____ sleeping. They are ____in____ bed.

12. John ____is____ dreaming ____about____ Mary. Mary ____is____ dreaming ____about____ John. They ____are____ dreaming ____about____ each other.

13. Mary's head is ____on____ a pillow.

14. John and Mary ____are____ in the living room.

15. They ____are____ asleep. They ____aren't____ awake.

16. John and Mary love each other. They are ____in____ love.

17. They would like ____to____ get married someday.

► **Practice 25. Review.** (Chapter 5)
Choose the correct completion for each sentence.

1. There _____ in our classroom.
   a. is twenty desks   (b.) are twenty desks   c. is twenty desk   d. are twenty desk

2. What _____ today?
   (a.) day is it   b. is day   c. day it   d. is it day

3. How many _____ there in your class?
   a. students are   b. student is   c. students   d. student

4. Dr. Smith is tired. She _____ to go home and sleep now.
   a. likes   b. would likes   c. would like   d. like

5. There _____ in a minute.
   a. is sixty second   b. are sixty second   c. is sixty seconds   d. are sixty seconds

6. The students _____ finish their work.
   a. needs to   b. need   c. needs   d. need to

7. What _____ the weather like in Bangkok?
   a. is   b. does   c. do   d. are

8. Philip lives _____ Dexter Avenue.
   a. in   b. at   c. on   d. next

9. Jason likes to sit _____ the room.
   a. in middle of   b. in the middle of   c. middle of   d. in middle

10. How _____ in Tokyo?
    a. the weather   b. is the weather   c. weather   d. is weather

11. Pam works _____ Tenth Avenue.
    a. next   b. at   c. in   d. on

12. I'm getting my hair cut _____ 2:45.
    a. in   b. on   c. from   d. at

13. The weather in my country is very hot _____ August.
    a. from   b. in   c. at   d. on

Chapter 6
Nouns and Pronouns

▶ **Practice 1. Identifying nouns.** (Chart 6-1)
Check (✓) the words that are nouns. Remember, nouns are *persons*, *places*, or *things*.

1. __✓__ father
2. _____ happy
3. _____ choose
4. _____ young
5. _____ snacks
6. _____ radio
7. _____ Beijing
8. _____ Mary
9. _____ hospital
10. _____ eat

Beijing
CHINA

▶ **Practice 2. Identifying nouns.** (Chart 6-1)
Read the message. Underline the nouns.

Mike,
I am shopping at the store. On my list I have eggs, bananas, rice, and tea. What else do you want? Call me on my cell.*

Judy

▶ **Practice 3. Identifying subjects.** (Chart 6-1)
Underline the subjects.

1. The weather is very cold today.
2. Snow is falling.
3. The sun isn't shining.

---

cell = cell phone.

4. The children and their parents are playing outside in the snow.

5. Some people are throwing snowballs.

6. Teenagers are building a huge snowman.

▶ **Practice 4. Identifying objects.** (Chart 6-1)
Read the sentences and answer the questions. Then write the object of each sentence. Remember:

1. Objects come after the verb.

2. Objects are **nouns**.

a worm

1. Birds eat worms. What do birds eat? _____Worms._____ OBJECT: _____Worms._____

2. Fish swim. What do fish do? _____They swim._____
   OBJECT: _____∅_____

3. Doctors help patients. Who do doctors help? _Patients_____
   OBJECT: _Patients_

4. Babies drink milk. What do babies drink? _Milk_____
   OBJECT: _Milk_

5. Babies drink several times a day. What do babies do? _Drink drink_____
   OBJECT: _____

6. Babies watch their mothers carefully.

   Who do babies watch? _their Mothers_____
   OBJECT: _Mothers_

▶ **Practice 5. Identifying objects.** (Chart 6-1)
Check (✓) the sentences that have objects of verbs. Underline the objects.

1. a. _✓_ I read the newspaper.

   b. _____ I read every morning.

   c. _✓_ I read the newspaper every morning.

2. a. _____ The children play every day.

   b. _____ The children play at the park.

   c. _____ The children play soccer.

3. a. _____ My father cooks several times a week.

   b. _____ My father cooks eggs.

   c. _____ My father cooks eggs several times a week.

4. a. _____ Dogs chew bones.

   b. _____ Dogs chew furniture.

   c. _____ Dogs chew with their sharp teeth.

5. a. _____ We are eating.

   b. _____ We are eating lunch.

6. a. _____ Jan teaches English.

   b. _____ Jan teaches at a private college.

   c. _____ Jan teaches three days a week.

   d. _____ Jan teaches English three days a week.

7. a. _____ Joe is staying with his cousins.

   b. _____ Joe is staying with his cousins for one week.

8. a. _____ Pedro helps with the housework.

   b. _____ Pedro helps Maria with the housework.

a bone

▶ **Practice 6. Prepositions.** (Chart 6-2)
Check (✓) the prepositional phrases. Then underline the noun that is the object of each preposition. Remember, prepositions are words like *in, on, at, from, to, with, by*, etc.

1. _____ every day
2. ✓ in the morning
3. _____ with her children
4. _____ on the table
5. _____ is paying money

6. _____ some trees and flowers
7. _____ across the street
8. _____ three times a week
9. _____ at work
10. _____ near my house

▶ **Practice 7. Identifying objects of prepositions.** (Chart 6-2)
Check (✓) the sentences that have objects of prepositions. Underline the objects.

1. a. ✓ Samira works at a bakery.

   b. _____ Samira works very hard.

2. a. _____ I have chocolate in my backpack.

   b. _____ I have chocolate a few times a week.

   c. _____ I have chocolate for a snack.

3. a. _____ Jake and Monica study together.

   b. _____ Jake and Monica study in the library.

   c. _____ Jake and Monica study every evening.

   d. _____ Jake and Monica study at night.

4. a. _____ The teacher is speaking with her students.

   b. _____ The teacher is speaking quickly.

   c. _____ The teacher is speaking in the classroom.

► **Practice 8. Identifying nouns and adjectives.** (Chart 6-3)
Write the words from the box in the correct column.

✓bright	easy	job	poor	tree
✓car	food	leg	quiet	wet
chair	fresh	nervous	rain	

nervous

Nouns	Adjectives
car	bright
Food	Fresh

► **Practice 9. Nouns and adjectives.** (Chart 6-3)
Write the adjective that has the opposite meaning.

1. happy _____ sad _____
2. new _____ old _____
3. soft _____ hard _____
4. beautiful _____ ugly _____
5. young _____ old _____
6. boring _____ interesting _____
7. fast _____ slow _____
8. tall _____ short _____
9. easy _____ hard - difficult _____
10. noisy _____ quiet _____

► **Practice 10. Identifying nouns and adjectives.** (Charts 6-1 and 6-3)
Write "N" over the nouns and "A" over the adjectives.

　　　　　　　　　N　　　　　　A　　N
1. My sister lives in a new apartment.

　　　　　　　　A
2. It is very bright.

　　　N　　　　　　　A　　　　　A　　N
3. The rooms are large and have tall ceilings.

　　　N　　　　　　　　　　A　　N
4. Her building is next to a Japanese restaurant.

　　　　N　　　　　　　N
5. I love food from other countries.

　A　　　N　　　A　　　　A
6. Mexican food is spicy and delicious.

　　　　　A　　N　　　　　　N
7. There is a wonderful café in my neighborhood.

　　　N　　　　　　　　　　　N
8. My neighbors like to meet there for coffee.

► **Practice 11. Using adjectives.** (Chart 6-3)
Choose two to four adjectives to describe the given nouns. Adjectives may be used more than once. Use Chart 6-3, p. 164, in the Student Book for ideas.

1. ___smart,_____ students

2. _____ tests

3. _____ neighbors

4. _____ fruit

► **Practice 12. Adjectives.** (Chart 6-3)
Some nationality adjectives are listed below. Write the country next to each adjective.

Nationality	Country
1. American	the United States (America)
2. Australian	Australia
3. Canadian	Canada
4. Chinese	China
5. Egyptian	Egypt
6. Indian	India
7. Indonesian	Indonesia
8. Italian	Italy
9. Japanese	Japan

10. Korean _Korea_

11. Malaysian _Malaysia_

12. Mexican _Mexico_

13. Russian _Russia_

14. Saudi Arabian _Saudi Arabia_

Write two more nationalities and countries.

_____ _____

_____ _____

▶ **Practice 13. Using adjectives.** (Chart 6-3)
Answer the questions. Use nationality adjectives in your answers.

1. What are your favorite ethnic foods? (Ethnic food is food from another country.)

_____

2. What kind of foreign films do you enjoy? (Foreign films are movies from other countries.)

_____

3. What cultures do you know something about?

_____

▶ **Practice 14. Subject and object pronouns.** (Chart 6-4)
Complete the sentences. Use pronouns (*I*, *me*, *he*, *him*, etc.).

1. Susan knows Thomas. _She_ knows _him_ well.

2. Thomas knows Susan. _he_ knows _her_ well.

3. Susan helps her co-workers. _she_ helps _Them_ a lot.

4. Thomas helps his co-workers. _he_ helps _Them_ a lot.

5. Susan and Thomas help their co-workers. _They_ help _them_ a lot.

6. Thomas and Susan rarely see Mr. Jones. _they_ don't know _him_ well.

7. Thomas and Susan rarely see Mrs. Jones. _they_ don't know _Ther_ well.

8. Susan and Thomas don't talk to their neighbors very much. _They_ don't know _Them_ well.

9. The neighbors don't talk to Susan and Thomas very much. _they_ don't know _Them_ well.

► **Practice 15. Subject and object pronouns.** (Chart 6-4)
Complete each sentence with the correct subject or object pronoun.

1. Grandpa John is in the picture. Do you see _____*him*_____?

2. Grandma Ella is in the picture. Do you see ___*her*_____?

3. My son and daughter are in the picture. Do you see ___*Them*_____?

4. Your brother is in the picture. Do you see ___*him*_____?

5. I am in the picture. Do you see ___*Me*_____?

6. Your brother and I are in the picture. Do you see ___*US*_____?

7. King, our dog, is in the picture. Do you see ___*him it*_____?

8. Queen, our cat, is in the picture. Do you see ___*her It*_____?

9. I don't see your sister. Where is ___*she*_____?

10. I don't see King. Where is ___*he*_____?

11. I don't see the dog and cat. Where are ___*they*_____?

12. I don't see my son. Where is ___*him*_____?

13. I don't see my brother and you. Where are ___*try*_____?

14. I don't see you. Where are ___*tw*_____?

► **Practice 16. Object pronouns.** (Chart 6-4)
Complete each sentence with the correct pronoun (*her*, *him*, *it*, *them*).

1. A: When do you take your children to school?

   B: I take _____*them*_____ at 8:30.

2. A: When do you have breakfast?

   B: I have _____*it*_____ at 9:00.

3. A: When do you call your friends?

   B: I call _____*Thym*_____ in the evening.

4. A: When do you call your husband?

   B: I call ___*him*___ during lunch.

5. A: When do you visit your parents?

   B: I visit ___*them*___ on weekends.

6. A: When do you check your email messages?

   B: I check ___*them*___ when I wake up.

7. A: When do you listen to the radio?

   B: I listen to ___*it*___ in the car.

8. A: When do you talk to your teacher, Mrs. Davis?

   B: I talk to ___*her*___ after class.

9. A: When do you see Mr. Gomez?

   B: I see ___*him*___ in class.

▶ **Practice 17. Object pronouns.** (Chart 6-4)
Choose the correct response for each question.

1. Where do you buy organic apples?
   a. I buy at the farmers' market.   (b.) I buy them at the farmers' market.

2. When do you see the manager, Mr. Owens?
   (a.) I see him on Mondays.   b. I see on Mondays.

3. When do you get your newspaper?
   a. I get in the morning.   (b.) I get it in the morning.

4. Where do you watch TV?
   a. I watch in the living room.   (b.) I watch it in the living room.

5. What time do you set your alarm clock for?
   (a.) I set it for 7:00 A.M.   b. I set for 7:00 A.M.

▶ **Practice 18. Subject and object pronouns.** (Chart 6-4)
Use pronouns to complete the sentences.

1. A: How are Mr. and Mrs. Carson?

   B: ___*They*___ are fine. ___*They*___ are taking care of their grandchildren right now. They enjoy taking care of ___*them*___.

2. A: Do you know Nathan and Vince?

   B: Yes, I do. _____ are in my chemistry class. I sit behind
      _____. _____ help me with my homework. The class is
      really hard, and I don't always understand _____.

3. A: That's Ms. Williams. Do you know _____?

   B: Yes, I do. _____ is the kindergarten teacher. The kids love
      _____.

4. A: Would you like to join Paul and me for dinner this evening?

   B: Yes, _____ would. Thank you. Can I bring something? Do you want
      _____ to bring a salad?

   A: No, thanks. Paul is cooking, and _____ has everything he needs.

▶ **Practice 19. Review: subject and object pronouns and possessive adjectives.**
  (Charts 2-5 and 6-4)
Review the information. Complete the sentences.

SUBJECT PRONOUNS	POSSESSIVE ADJECTIVES	OBJECT PRONOUNS
I	my	me
you	your	you
she	her	her
he	his	him
it	its	it
we	our	us
they	their	them

1. I have a book. ____My____ book is red. Please give it to ____me____.

2. You have a book. ____Your____ book is red. I'm giving it to ____you____.

3. She has a book. __her__ book is red. Please give it to __her__.

4. He has a book. __he__ book is red. Please give it to __him__.

5. We have books. __Our__ books are red. Please give them to __us__.

6. They have books. __their__ books are red. Please give them to __then__.

7. I have a female cat. __hisit__ fur is black. I like to play with __her it__.

8. I have a male cat. __his it__ fur is brown. I like to play with __her it__.

9. My new car is blue. __its__ seats are red. I love driving __it__.

► **Practice 20. Review: subject and object pronouns and possessive adjectives.**
(Charts 2-5 and 6-4)

Complete each sentence with the correct word.

1. Hi. (*I / My / Me*) _____My_____ name is Kathy. How are you?

2. This isn't my textbook. It doesn't belong to (*I / my / me*) _____.

3. Where is Jon? I don't see (*he / his / him*) _____. I don't see
   (*he / his / him*) _____ bike.

4. Your dress is beautiful. Is (*it / your / she*) _____ new?

5. Do (*you / your / you're*) _____ have a map? We are lost.

6. We have two young children. (*We / Our / Us*) _____ son is three, and
   (*we / our / us*) _____ daughter is five.

7. Dogs like to hide (*it / their / them*) _____ bones.

► **Practice 21. Review: subject and object pronouns and possessive adjectives.**
(Charts 2-5 and 6-4)

Complete each sentence with the correct word.

1. Frederick is an artist. (*He / His / Him*) _____He_____
   draws cartoons. (*He / His / Him*) _____
   cartoons are very funny. I like to watch (*he / his / him*)
   _____ when he draws.

2. The kids are doing (*they / them / their*) _____
   homework. (*They / Them / Their*) _____ are working hard.
   Sometimes I help (*they / them / their*) _____ with (*they / them / their*)
   _____ homework.

3. Mary is a surgeon. (*She / Her*) _____ works long hours. (*She / Her*)
   _____ family doesn't see (*she / her*) _____ very
   much.

4. Mr. and Mrs. Cook are on vacation. I am taking care of (*they / them / their*)
   _____ dog and cat. (*They / Them / Their*) _____ dog
   likes to play, but (*they / them / their*) _____ cat likes to sleep.

5. My husband and (*I / me / my*) _____ own a restaurant together.
   We enjoy (*we / our / us*) _____ work. Sometimes (*we / our / us*)
   _____ friends and family help (*we / our / us*) _____
   at the restaurant.

► **Practice 22. Singular and plural nouns.** (Chart 6-5)
Complete the lists with the correct forms of the given nouns.

	Singular	**Plural**
1.	box	boxes
2.	tomato	tomatos
3.	zoo	
4.	Pen	pens
5.	baby	babies
6.	key	Keys
7.	City	cities
8.	wife	wives
9.	dish	dishes
10.	thief	thieves

► **Practice 23. Singular and plural nouns.** (Chart 6-5)
Write the plural form of the noun in the correct column.

baby	city	girl	lady	life	potato	tax	tray
bush	✓ coin	glass	✓ leaf	party	shoe	thief	wife

-s	**-ies**	**-ves**	**-es**
coins	babies	leaves	Taxes
shoes	Cities	lives	glasses
girls	ladies	thieves	bushes
Trays	parties	wives	potatoes

► **Practice 24. Spelling of nouns.** (Chart 6-5)
Complete each sentence with the plural form of the noun in parentheses.

1. (*Potato*) Potatoes are my favorite vegetable.

2. Where are the car (*key*) Keys ?

3. The English (*class*) classes meet in the afternoon.

4. The police want to catch the car (*thief*) thives soon.

5. The students are studying for their (*test*) tests .

6. (*Baby*) Babies don't like loud noises.

7. I need two (box) _boxes_ for these gifts.

8. Why does Richard have three (radio) _radios_ in his kitchen?

9. During the holidays, we go to many (party) _parties_.

10. Miriam has ten (cat) _cats_ in her apartment.

11. The (match) _matches_ are wet. They don't work.

12. How many (textbook) _textbooks_ do you need for your English class?

13. I like (dictionary) _dictionaries_ with easy definitions.

14. Do you think cats have nine (life) _lives_?

15. Before you cook carrots, you need to cut off the (top)
    tops.

16. The wind is blowing the (leaf)
    leaves off the trees.

carrots

17. They make good (sandwich) _sandwiches_ at that restaurant.

▶ **Practice 25. Irregular plural nouns.** (Chart 6-6)
Complete each sentence with the plural form of the appropriate noun.

child	foot	mouse	✓ tooth
fish	man	sheep	woman

1. A dentist fixes _teeth_.

2. Cats like to catch _mouses_.

3. Are men and _women_ very different?

4. There are many different kinds of _fish_ in the sea.

5. We put shoes on our _foot_.

6. In your culture, do _men_ and women have the same freedoms?

7. Some movies are very violent. They are not good for _children_.

8. Baby lambs become _sheep_.

a lamb

► **Practice 26. Complete/incomplete sentences.** (Charts 6-1 → 6-6)
Check (✓) the incorrect sentences and correct them. Remember: A *complete sentence* is a group of words that has a subject and a verb. An *incomplete sentence* is a group of words that does not have a subject and a verb.

work
1. ✓ I ^ in my home office in the morning.
2. _____ My parents work at a university.
3. _is_ My father in the library.
4. _he_ Is a teacher.
5. _____ My mother _is_ a professor.
6. _she_ Is an excellent professor.
7. _____ I study at the university.
8. _____ The university _has_ many interesting and useful classes.
9. _____ Education is important for my family.

► **Practice 27. Review.** (Charts 6-1 → 6-6)
Choose the correct completion for each sentence.

1. Where do _____ live?
   a. she   b. he   (c.) you   d. them

2. Dr. Ruiz is my dentist and neighbor. _____ is very helpful.
   a. We   (b.) She   c. They   d. You

3. This is our apartment. _____ is very comfortable.
   (a.) It   b. We   c. She   d. He

4. These are our seats. Do you want to sit next to _____?
   a. we   b. our   c. it   (d.) us

5. The students are going to the movies. Their teacher is taking _____.
   a. we   b. us   c. they   (d.) them

6. Many _____ in the neighborhood work from their homes.
   a. womens   b. woman   (c.) women   d. womans

7. You and _____ like to read the same books and listen to the same music.
   a. me   (b.) I   c. him   d. her

8. Paul is an active child. Children like to play with _____.
   a. her   b. he   (c.) him   d. she

9. _____ bird has a vocabulary of fifteen words.
   (a.) Our   b. We   c. I   d. Us

10. I love _____.
    a. China food   b. food Chinese   c. food China   (d.) Chinese food

► **Practice 28. Possessive pronouns and possessive adjectives.** (Chart 6-7)
Complete each sentence with the correct possessive pronoun (*mine*, *yours*, etc.) or possessive adjective (*my*, *your*, etc.).

1. It's his car. It's _____ *his* _____.

2. It's her car. It's ___ her _____.

3. They're our cars. They're ___ ours _____.

4. It's my car. It's ___ mine _____.

5. It's your car. It's ___ your _____.

6. It's their car. It's ___ their _____.

7. The car belongs to her. It's _____ *her* _____ car.

8. The car belongs to me. It's ____ MY _____ car.

9. The car belongs to him. It's ____ him _____ car.

10. The car belongs to them. It's ____ then _____ car.

11. The car belongs to you. It's ____ your _____ car.

12. The car belongs to us. It's ____ our _____ car.

► **Practice 29. Possessive nouns.** (Chart 6-8)
Choose the meaning of each noun in **bold**: "one" or "more than one."

		How Many?
1. My **friends'** parents are very friendly.	one	(more than one)
2. The **dog's** toys are all over the yard.	(one)	more than one

3. Where is your **parents'** house?	one	more than one
4. The **doctors'** offices are near the hospital.	one	more than one
5. The **doctor's** offices are near the hospital.	(one)	more than one
6. Our **co-worker's** schedule changes every week.	(one)	more than one
7. Your **daughters'** bedroom is very large.	one	more than one

► **Practice 30. Possessive nouns.** (Chart 6-8)
Complete each sentence with the correct nouns.

1. Jim's dog is active.

   The _____*dog*_____ belongs to _____*Jim*_____.

2. Bill's car is new.

   The ___*Car*___ belongs to ___*Bill*___ _job of preposition_.

3. The teacher's desk is next to mine.

   The ___*desk*___ belongs to ___*The teacher*___.

4. The students' schedules are ready.

   The ___*schedules*___ belong to ___*The students'*___.

5. I'm going to buy my parents' truck.

   The ___*truck*___ belongs to ___*My parents*___.

6. Where are the professors' offices?

   The ___*offices*___ belong to ___*The professors*___.

► **Practice 31. Possessive nouns** (Chart 6-8)
Add an apostrophe (') where necessary.

1. Where is Ben's calculator?
2. Dan's daughter is a university professor.
3. Who has the teacher's pen?
4. My sister's baby doesn't sleep very much.
5. Dr. Smith's nurse is very helpful.
6. My pets' names are Ping and Pong.
7. All our neighbors' yards have flower and vegetable gardens.
8. What is your mother's maiden* name?

APPLICATION FORM

Name:	*Sanchez,*	*Rosa*	*T*
	(last)	(first)	(middle initial)

Address:	*720 Lake Street, Green Hills, Texas*

Phone number:	*253 — 555 — 7063*

Mother's maiden name:	*Santos*

Maiden name is a married woman's last name (family name) before she got married.

▶ **Practice 32. Possessive nouns.** (Chart 6-8)
Add **'s** where necessary or **Ø** (nothing).

1. Tom _'s_____ job is very interesting.

2. Tom ___Ø___ works for a large airline.

3. Tom ___Ø___ buys airplanes.

4. Tom ___'s___ wife, Olga, works at home.

5. Olga ___Ø___ designs web pages.

6. Olga ___Ø___ is artistic.

7. Olga ___'s___ websites are very creative.

▶ **Practice 33. Possessive nouns.** (Chart 6-8)
Read the story. Then complete each sentence with the correct possessive name.

John   Jane

Mike   Marie   Belle   Ruff

Jane and John are married. They have one son and one daughter. Their son is Mike and their daughter is Marie. They also have two dogs: Belle and her puppy, Ruff.

1. Jane is _____John's_____ wife.

2. John is ___Jane's___ husband.

3. Marie is ___Mike's___ sister.

4. Belle is ___Ruff's___ mother.

5. Mike is ___Marie's___ brother.

6. Ruff is ___Belle's___ son.

7. Mike is Jane and ___John's___ son.

8. Marie is John and ___Jane's___ daughter.

► **Practice 34. Possessive noun or *is*.** (Chart 6-8)
Circle the meaning of **'s**: possessive or *is*.

1. Bob's happy.	possessive	(is)
2. Bob's bird sounds happy.	possessive	is
3. My teacher's not at school today.	possessive	is
4. The substitute teacher's nice.	possessive	is
5. Bill's manager went on vacation.	possessive	is
6. Bill's managing the office.	possessive	is
7. Bill's a good manager.	possessive	is
8. Bill's co-workers like him.	possessive	is

► **Practice 35. *Whose* and *who's*.** (Chart 6-9)
Choose the correct response for each sentence.

1. Whose are these?
   (a.) Pat's.   b. Pat.

2. Who's on the phone?
   (a.) Mr. Smith.   b. Mr. Smith's.

3. Who's coming?
   (a.) Some teachers.   b. Some teachers'.

4. Whose sweater is on the chair?
   a. Pam.   (b.) Pam's.

5. Who's going to help you with your homework?
   (a.) Andy.   b. Andy's.

6. Whose schedule do you have?
   a. Mark.   (b.) Mark's.

7. Whose is this?
   a. My.   (b.) Mine.

► **Practice 36. *Whose*.** (Chart 6-9)
Make questions with **Whose**.

1. book \ this _____ *Whose book is this?* _____

2. glasses \ these _____

3. toy \ this _____

4. keys \ these _____

5. shoes \ these _____

6. shirt \ this _____

7. cell phone \ this _____

8. pens \ these _____

▶ **Practice 37. *Whose* and *who's*.** (Chart 6-9)
Complete the sentences with ***Whose*** or ***Who's***.

1. _____*Who's*_____ that?

2. _____ is that?

3. _____ coming?

4. _____ ready?

5. _____ glasses are these?

6. _____ lunch is this?

7. _____ car is in the driveway?

8. _____ working tomorrow?

9. _____ outside?

10. _____ work is this?

▶ **Practice 38. *Whose*.** (Chart 6-9)
Make questions with the given words.

1. is \ project \ that \ whose

    _____*Whose project is that?*_____

2. whose \ are \ children \ those

    _____

3. who \ next \ is

    _____

4. are \ whose \ shoes \ in the middle of the floor

    _____

5. today \ absent \ is \ who

    _____

6. package \ whose \ this \ is

    _____

▶ **Practice 39. Regular and irregular possessives.** (Charts 6-8 and 6-10)
Circle the meaning of each noun in **bold**: "one" or "more than one."

How many?

1.	The **dogs'** food is in the kitchen.	one	(more than one)
2.	The **cat's** dishes are in the garage.	one	more than one
3.	The **teachers'** office is near the classrooms.	one	more than one
4.	That **woman's** grandkids are noisy.	one	more than one
5.	Where is the **women's** clothing department?	one	more than one
6.	Is there a **men's** restroom nearby?	one	more than one
7.	The **man's** children are waiting outside.	one	more than one
8.	The **child's** toys are on the floor.	one	more than one
9.	The **children's** toys aren't in the closet.	one	more than one

▶ **Practice 40. Regular and irregular possessives.** (Charts 6-8 and 6-10)
Make possessive phrases with the given words.

1.	(one)	*boy \ truck*	the	*boy's truck*
2.	(five)	*boys \ trucks*	the	*boys' trucks*
3.	(three)	*girls \ bikes*	the	_____
4.	(one)	*girl \ bike*	the	_____
5.	(four)	*children \ toys*	the	_____
6.	(six)	*students \ passwords*	the	_____
7.	(one)	*woman \ wages*	the	_____
8.	(five)	*women \ wages*	the	_____
9.	(two)	*people \ ideas*	some	_____
10.	(one)	*person \ ideas*	a	_____
11.	(two)	*men \ coats*	the	_____

► **Practice 41. Regular and irregular possessives.** (Charts 6-8 and 6-10)
Check (✓) the incorrect sentences and correct them.

children's
1. ✓ The ~~childrens'~~ school is down the street.

2. ____ Several student's parents help at school.

3. ____ I have one brother. I like my brother's friends'.

4. ____ My brother's friend is very funny.

5. ____ I offered to fix my neighbor's computer.

6. ____ I like hearing other peoples' opinions.

7. ____ Womans' opinions are frequently different from men's opinions.

8. ____ Do you and your husband's agree very often?

► **Practice 42. Review.** (Charts 6-7 → 6-10)
Choose the correct completions.

1. This newspaper is yours. That newspaper is ____.
   a. our   (b.) ours   c. our's   d. ours'

2. My ____ name is Ernesto.
   a. father   b. fathers   c. fathers'   d. father's

3. ____ books are these?
   a. Who's   b. Whose   c. Who   d. Who are

4. ____ coming to the party?
   a. Who's   b. Whose   c. Who   d. Who are

5. I found two ____ backpacks in the park.
   a. girls   b. girl's   c. girls'   d. girl

6. My ____ are older than me.
   a. brother   b. brother's   c. brothers   d. brothers'

7. My ____ teacher is very patient.
   a. children's   b. childrens'   c. childs'   d. children

8. This is our hotel room and that room is ____.
   a. theirs'   b. their's   c. their   d. theirs

Chapter 7
Count and Noncount Nouns

▶ **Practice 1. Singular and plural.** (Chart 7-1)
Write "S" for singular or "P" for plural in front of each noun.

1. ___S___ boy
2. ___P___ boys
3. ___S___ car
4. ___S___ job

5. ___P___ passengers
6. ___S___ house
7. ___P___ apartments
8. ___S___ computer

▶ **Practice 2. Singular and plural.** (Chart 7-1)
Circle all the words that can come in front of each noun.

1. a   an   one   (five)   (a lot of)   cell phones
2. (a)   (an)   (one)   five   a lot of   cell phone
3. a   an   one   (five)   (a lot of)   buses
4. a   an   one   (five)   (a lot of)   oranges
5. (a)   an   (one)   five   a lot of   mistake
6. a   an   one   (five)   (a lot of)   rules
7. a   (an)   (one)   five   a lot of   envelope

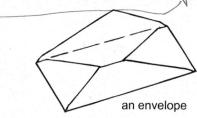

an envelope

▶ **Practice 3. Count and noncount nouns.** (Chart 7-1)
Write "C" for count or "NC" for noncount in front of each noun.

1. ___C___ girls
2. ___C___ girl
3. ___NC___ homework
4. ___NC___ traffic

5. ___C___ infants
6. ___NC___ rice
7. ___NC___ money
8. ___C___ coin

► **Practice 4. Count and noncount nouns.** (Chart 7-1)
Write all the correct words from the box in front of each noun.

a	a lot of	ten
an	one	twenty

1. _____*a, one*_____ coin _C_
2. _____*a lot 10,120r*_____ coins _C_
3. _____*a lot of*_____ water _NC_
4. _____*a lot of*_____ jewelry _NC_

5. _____*a lo oR ten, twenty*_____ eggs _C_
6. _____*a one*_____ ring _C_
7. _____*a lot ten, twenty*_____ rings _C_
8. _____*a lot OF*_____ advice _NC_

articles/pieces

► **Practice 5. Count and noncount nouns.** (Chart 7-1)
Complete each word with **-s** or **Ø** (nothing).

1. a book ___Ø___, one book ___Ø___, two book ___S___, fifty book ___S___

2. a job ___Ø___, one job ___Ø___, five job ___S___, a lot of job ___S___

3. information ___Ø___, some information ___Ø___, a lot of information ___Ø___

4. a fact ___Ø___, one fact ___Ø___, three fact ___S___, a lot of fact ___S___

► **Practice 6. Count and noncount nouns.** (Chart 7-1)
Circle all the words that can come before each noun.

1. a   an   one   (a lot of)   homework _NC_
2. (a)   an   (one)   a lot of   letter _C_
3. a   an   one   (a lot of)   letters _C_
4. (a)   an   (one)   a lot of   textbook _C_
5. a   (an   one)   a lot of   apple _C_
6. a   an   one   (a lot of)   music _NC_
7. a   an   one   (a lot of)   vocabulary _NC_
8. (a)   an   (one)   a lot of   word _C_
9. a   an   one   (a lot of)   words _C_
10. a   an   one   (a lot of)   ideas _C_

► **Practice 7. Count and noncount nouns.** (Chart 7-1)
Write a noncount noun that is close in meaning to the count noun.

Count	Noncount
1. a job	*work*
2. an assignment (for school)	*homework*
3. a song	*Music*

4. a word   *Count*

5. a fact   *vocabulary*

6. a suggestion   *information*

7. a chair, a desk, a table   *advice*

8. a banana, an apple   *furniture*

9. a coin   *Fruit*

10. a ring, a bracelet   *Money*

Jewelry

a bracelet

▶ **Practice 8. Noun review.** (Charts 6-4, 6-5, and 7-1)
Complete each sentence with a word from the box. Make the word plural when necessary. Use each word only one time.

advice	fruit ✓	✓ money	weather
child ✓	furniture ✓	monkey ✓	work
city ✓	help ✓	potato	
country ✓	horse ✓	tool	
foot ✓	man	traffic ✓	

1. I have a lot of _____ *money* _____ in my wallet. I'm rich.

2. Cowboys ride *horses* .

3. I would like to visit many *cities* in Canada. I'd like to visit Vancouver, Victoria, Quebec City, Toronto, and some others.

4. There are three *Contries* *C* in North America: Canada, the United States, and Mexico.

5. Birds and *Monkeys* *C* live in trees.

6. Barbara has four suitcases. She can't carry all of them. She needs some *help* *NC* .

7. There is a lot of *Traffic* *NC* on the street during rush hour.

8. Susie and Bobby are seven years old. They aren't adults. They're *children* *C* .

9. We need a new bed, a new couch, and some new chairs. We need some new *furniture* *NC* .

10. People wear shoes on their *feet* *C* .

11. I like pears, oranges, and bananas. I eat a lot of *fruit* *NC* .

a pear

12. Sometimes I have a steak, a salad, and French-fried _potatoes C_ for dinner.

13. When the temperature is around 35°C (77°F), I'm comfortable. But I don't like very hot _weather NC_.

14. I'm not busy today. I don't have much _work_ to do. NC

a hammer

TOOLS

15. I have a problem. I need your help. I need some _advice_ from you. NC

a saw

16. Some _men_ have mustaches. C

17. Where is my hammer? Do you have a saw? I need some _tools_ . C

a screwdriver

▶ **Practice 9.** *A* vs. *an* (Chart 7-2)
Write *a* or *an*.

1. _an_ idea
2. _an_ office
3. _an_ elephant
4. _an_ university
5. _an_ uncle

6. _an_ interesting idea
7. _an_ hour
8. _a_ house
9. _an_ hungry animal
10. _an_ upset child

▶ **Practice 10.** *A* vs. *an* (Chart 7-2)
Write *a*, *an*, or *Ø*.

1. _Ø_ happy
2. _a_ happy man
3. _Ø_ exciting
4. _an_ exciting day
5. _an_ hot oven

6. _an_ easy test
7. _an_ honest man
8. _Ø_ honest
9. _Ø_ my father
10. _Ø_ his job

an oven

► **Practice 11. *A* vs. *an*** (Chart 7-2)
Write *a*, *an*, or Ø.

1. I need to see _____a_____ doctor.

2. I have _____a_____ headache. C

3. It is _____Ø_____ painful.

vowel sound

4. Mary is reading _____an_____ article in the newspaper.

5. The article is _____Ø_____ interesting.

age

6. _____A_____ healthy person gets regular exercise.

7. The Browns own _____a_____ house. C

8. Gary and Joel are having _____an_____ argument in the cafeteria. It is _____an_____
   uncomfortable situation. C

9. I feel _____Ø_____ uncomfortable.

10. Are you _____a_____ hard worker? C

11. Was the test _____Ø_____ hard? *abjective*

12. Janet is _____an_____ honest person.

13. The store manager is talking to _____an_____ angry woman. *vowel singular*

14. Bill is _____an_____ uncle. He has _____a_____ niece and two nephews.
    C   P

Bill

uncle

niece   nephew   nephew

► **Practice 12. A/an and some.** (Chart 7-3)
Write each word from the box in the correct column.

advice	earache	elevator	furniture	letter	packages	umbrella
✓ dog	eggs	flower	gardens	mail	suggestion	umbrellas

a	*an*	*some*
_____dog_____	_____	_____
_____	_____	_____
_____	_____	_____
_____		_____
		_____
		_____
		_____

ELEVATOR

► **Practice 13. A/an and some.** (Chart 7-3)
Use **a/an** or **some**. Are the nouns singular or plural?

1. Bob has _____a_____ book on his desk.   singular   plural

2. Bob has _____some_____ books on his desk.   singular   plural

3. I see _____ desk in this room.   singular   plural

4. I see _____ desks in this room.   singular   plural

5. I would like _____ apple.   singular   plural

6. The kids want _____ apples too.   singular   plural

7. Is there _____ mail for me?   singular   plural

8. I need to move _____ furniture downstairs. singular   plural

9. Did you pay _____ tax?   singular   plural

10. Did you pay _____ taxes?   singular   plural

▶ **Practice 14.** *A/an* and *some*. (Chart 7-3)
Complete each sentence with *a/an* or *some*.

1. Here is _____*a*_____ letter for you.

2. There is ____*some*____ mail on the kitchen table.

3. *Some* _____ teachers give a lot of homework.

4. I have ____*a*____ long assignment.

5. The teacher has ____*an*____ interesting idea for today's discussion.

6. ____*Some*____ ideas take several days to discuss.

7. Dr. Roberts is ____*a*____ very special teacher.

8. He gives *some* ____ interesting lectures.

9. Are ____*some*____ students working on their projects?

10. Is ____*an*____ assistant teacher helping them?

▶ **Practice 15. Review.** (Charts 7-1 → 7-4)
Choose all the correct sentences.

1. (a.) We are learning a lot of vocabulary.
   (b.) We are learning some vocabulary.
   c. We are learning some vocabularies.

2. a. Our teacher gives a lot of homeworks.
   (b.) Our teacher gives a lot of homework.
   c. Our teachers gives a lot of assignment.

3. (a.) Let's listen to music.
   (b.) Let's listen to some music.
   c. Let's listen to a music.

4. (a.) Do you have some advice for me?
   b. Do you have an advice for me?
   (c.) Do you have a suggestion for me?

5. a. I have job.
   (b.) I have a job.
   c. I have some job.

6. a. I would like interesting job.
   (b.) I would like an interesting job.
   c. I would like some interesting job.

▶ **Practice 16. Units of measure.** (Chart 7-4)
Write the name of the item for each picture. Use the expressions in the box.

1   2   3   4

5   6   7   8   9

✓a bag of	a box of	a carton of
a bar of	a bunch of	a jar of
a bottle of	a can of	a tube of

1. ___*a bag of rice*___

2. _____

3. _____

4. _____

5. _____

6. _____

7. _____

8. _____

9. _____

▶ **Practice 17. Units of measure.** (Chart 7-4)
What can you find at a store or restaurant? Complete each phrase with nouns from the box.
You may use some nouns more than once.

bananas	✓ cereal	ice cream	mayonnaise	✓ rice
bread	cheese	lettuce	paper	water

1. a box of ___*cereal, rice, paper*___

2. a sheet of _____

3. a head of _____

4. a piece of _____

5. a loaf of _____

6. a bunch of _____

7. a bowl of _____

8. a bottle of _____

9. a jar of _____

▶ **Practice 18. Review: *A/an/some* and units of measure.** (Charts 7-3 and 7-4)
Complete the sentences with *a*, *an*, or *some*.

1. I'm hungry. I'd like . . .

   a. _____*a*_____ piece of chicken.

   b. _____Some_____ fruit

   c. _____Some_____ food

   d. _____a_____ bowl of ice cream

   e. _____an_____ apple

   f. _____a_____ can of soup

   g. _____Some_____ rice

   h. _____Some_____ strawberries

   strawberries

2. I'm thirsty. I'd like . . .

   a. _____*some*_____ water

   b. _____ bottle of water

   c. _____ juice

   d. _____ glass of milk

   e. _____ cup of coffee

   f. _____ strong coffee

   g. _____ tea

   h. _____ milk

► **Practice 19. Much/many.** (Chart 7-5)
Complete the sentences with **much** or **many**.

I need to go to the store. I don't have . . .

1. _____much_____ coffee
2. _____Many_____ bananas
3. _____Much_____ fruit
4. _____Much_____ lamb
5. _____Much_____ rice

6. _____Much_____ sugar
7. _____Much_____ bread
8. _____Much_____ food
9. _____Many_____ peaches
10. _____Many_____ cans of soup

peaches

► **Practice 20. A few/a little.** (Chart 7-5)
Complete the sentences with **a few** or **a little**.

I need to go shopping. I need . . .

1. _____a little_____ salt
2. _____a few_____ strawberries
3. _____a few_____ pens
4. _____a little_____ cheese
5. _____a little_____ tea
6. _____a few_____ teabags

7. _____a few_____ bottles of water
8. _____a few_____ sandwiches
9. _____a little_____ flour
10. _____a few_____ rolls of toilet paper

a teabag

► **Practice 21. Much/many/a few/a little.** (Chart 7-5)
Choose the correct words. Add **-s** or **Ø** (nothing) to the nouns where necessary.

1. The teacher needs (a few / (a little)) information ___Ø___ about her students.

2. Do the students have (much / (many)) question _s___?

3. Here are ((a few / a little) new pen _s___ for you.

4. Do you have ((a few / a little) minute _s___ to talk?

5. Andy doesn't drink (*much* / *many*) coffee _____. He drinks (*a few* / *a little*) tea _____.

6. There are (*much* / *many*) beautiful flowers _S_ in your garden.

7. I have (*a few* / *a little*) flower _S_ in my garden and (*much* / *many*) vegetable _S_.

▶ **Practice 22. *How much/how many*.** (Chart 7-5)
Rick is going shopping. His roommate gives him a list. He needs to know the amount to buy.
Write questions with *How much/How many . . . do we need?*

✓ carrots	eggs	fruit
cheese	flour	olive oil

1. ___How many carrots do we need?___

2. ___How much cheese do we need?___

3. ___How many eggs do we need?___

4. ___How much Flour do we need___

5. _____

6. _____

▶ **Practice 23. First mention vs. second mention.** (Chart 7-6)
Complete each sentence with *the* or *a*.

1. These pants and shirts don't fit. __The__ pants are too big, and __the__ shirts are too tight.

2. Here's some chicken. Be careful! __the__ chicken is very spicy.

3. Andrew drives __a__ company truck. __the__ truck is big and uses a lot of gas. His company pays for __the__ gas.

4. Rudy wants to give his wife __a__ ring for their anniversary. __the__ ring has three diamonds, and __the__ diamonds are very large.

5. Rachel is looking at __a__ picture of __a__ dog and __a__ baby. __the__ baby is sleeping, and __the__ dog is watching her.

6. Tommy is getting __a__ new bike for his birthday. __the__ bike is very fast, and he is excited to ride it.

7. Dr. Olsson is speaking with __a__ new patient. __the__ patient is scared because she needs emergency surgery.

8. Do you have __a__ minute? I have __a__ problem and would like your advice.

► **Practice 24. General vs. specific.** (Chart 7-7)
Decide if the word in *italics* has a general or specific meaning.

1. *Clothes* are expensive. — (general) specific
2. The *clothes* in Jan's closet are expensive. — general (specific)
3. *Lemons* are sour. — (general) specific
4. I love *vegetables*. — (general) specific
5. The *vegetables* on the counter are from my garden. — (general) specific
6. How are the *carrots* in your salad? Are they sweet? — general (specific)
7. *Rabbits* like carrots. — (general) specific
8. What are you doing about the *rabbits* in your garden? — general (specific)

► **Practice 25. General vs. specific.** (Chart 7-7)
Complete the sentences with **a/an**, **the**, or **Ø** (nothing).

1. I need ___Ø___ sugar for my coffee.
2. ___the___ sugar is in the cupboard.
3. Dentists say ___Ø___ sugar is not good for our teeth.
4. I'd like ___a___ glass of water.
5. Ann would like ___an___ orange for a snack.
6. ___Ø___ oranges grow on trees.
7. Ken has ___an___ egg every day for lunch.
8. Are ___Ø___ eggs healthy?
9. I'm going shopping. I need ___Ø___ bread and ___Ø___ cheese.
10. Jack is having ___Ø___ rice, ___Ø___ fish, and ___a___ bowl of soup for dinner.
11. Johnny, please feed ___the___ cat. He's hungry.
12. Do you like ___Ø___ cats? Would you like ___a___ cat?

brothers'
Kevin's

► **Practice 26. Article review.** (Charts 7-3, 7-6, and 7-7)
Choose the sentence that is closest in meaning to the given situation.

1. Mark is at a toy store. There are five fire trucks. He buys one for his son.
   a. He buys a fire truck.   b. He buys the fire truck.

2. Pat is at a pet store. There is one turtle. She buys it.
   a. She buys a turtle.   b. She buys the turtle.

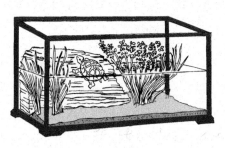

3. Martha is leaving her apartment. There are three bags near the door. She takes one.
   a. She takes the bag.   b. She takes a bag.

4. Jane is sitting outside in her garden. It is midnight. She is looking up at the sky.
   a. She sees the moon.   b. She sees a moon.

5. I love ice cream. Vanilla ice cream is my favorite.
   a. I love the vanilla ice cream. b. I love vanilla ice cream.

6. Alice is picking apples from an apple tree. It has only five apples. She picks all five.
   a. She takes the apples home.   b. She takes apples home.

7. Paul drives a small car. He wants to save gas.
   a. He doesn't like to drive big cars.   b. He doesn't like to drive the big cars.

► **Practice 27. Some/any.** (Chart 7-8)
Choose the correct word. In some cases, both words are correct.

1. Let's go outside. I need (some / any) fresh air.

2. There aren't (some / any) clouds in the sky.

3. There is (some / any) wind.

4. I don't feel (some / any) wind.

5. Do you have (some / any) time?

6. Sorry, I don't have (some / any) time right now.

7. I have (some / any) time tomorrow.

8. I need (some / any) money for the store.

9. Do you have (some / any) money?

10. (Some / Any) people carry a lot of money in their wallets.

► **Practice 28. Some/any.** (Charts 7-3 and 7-8)

Think about shopping. Write sentences about what you need and don't need. Use **some/any** and the words from the list. Add **-s/-es** where necessary. You can also use your own words.

avocado	egg	fruit	potato	soup
banana	fish	grape	rice	toothpaste
coffee	flour	meat	soap	vegetable

1. I need _____, _____, _____,

   _____, and _____ .

2. I don't need _____, _____,

   _____, _____, or _____ .

an avocado

grapes

► **Practice 29. A/an or any.** (Chart 7-8)

Circle **a**, **an**, or **any**. Remember, use **any** with noncount nouns and plural count nouns. Use **a** with singular count nouns.

I don't want . . .

1.	(a)	an	any	low grade on my test.
2.	a	an	any	low grades this year.
3.	a	an	any	pets.
4.	a	an	any	pet.
5.	a	an	any	ice cream for dessert.
6.	a	an	any	bowl of ice cream for dessert.
7.	a	an	any	cup of coffee.
8.	a	an	any	help.
9.	a	an	any	homework.
10.	a	an	any	assignment.
11.	a	an	any	assignments.

► **Practice 30. A/any.** (Chart 7-8)
Use *any* or *a*. Use *any* with noncount nouns and plural count nouns. Use *a* with singular count nouns.

1. I don't have _____*any*_____ money.

2. I don't have _____*a*_____ job.

3. I don't have _____*any*_____ brothers or sisters.

4. We don't need to buy _____ new furniture.

5. Mr. and Mrs. Kelly don't have _____ children.

6. There isn't _____ coffee in the house.

7. Ann doesn't want _____ cup of coffee.

8. I don't like this room because there aren't _____ windows.

9. Amanda is very unhappy because she doesn't have _____ friends.

10. I don't need _____ help. I can finish my homework by myself.

11. I don't have _____ comfortable chair in my dorm room.

12. I'm getting along fine. I don't have _____ problems.

13. Joe doesn't have _____ car, so he takes the bus to school.

14. I don't have _____ homework to do tonight.

15. I don't need _____ new clothes.

16. I don't need _____ new suit.

► **Practice 31. Review.** (Chapter 7)
Draw a line through the expressions that <u>cannot</u> complete the sentences.

1. I need to buy ____ white sugar.
   a. ~~a~~
   b. an
   c. some
   d. any
   e. two
   f. a lot of
   g. a bag of
   h. Ø

2. I don't need ____ brown sugar.
   a. some
   b. much
   c. a
   d. a lot of
   e. any
   f. two
   g. three bags of
   h. Ø

3. Do you need ____ flour?

   a. an

   b. any

   c. a

   d. a bag of

   e. some

   f. two bags of

   g. a lot of

   h. Ø

▶ **Practice 32. Review.** (Chapter 7)
Correct the mistakes.

                countries
1. Korea and Japan are ~~country~~ in Asia.
2. Is there many traffics at 5:00 P.M.?
3. Are you a hungry? Do you want some food?
4. My children come home every day with a lot of homeworks.
5. The digital cameras take wonderful pictures.
6. My eggs and coffee don't taste very good. Eggs are very salty, and coffee is weak.
7. What do you like better for a snack: orange or the orange juice?
8. I wear dresses for work and the jeans at home.
9. I'm going to bank. I need money.
10. We need to get any furniture. Do you know good furniture store?

Chapter 8
Expressing Past Time, Part 1

▶ **Practice 1. Simple past forms of *be*.** (Chart 8-1)
Complete the sentences with the correct form of *be*.

Now	**An hour ago**
1. I am tired.	I _____ *was* _____ tired.
2. We are tired.	We _____ tired.
3. She is tired.	She _____ tired.
4. They are tired.	They _____ tired.
5. He is tired.	He _____ tired.
6. The cat is tired.	The cat _____ tired.
7. My kids are tired.	My kids _____ tired.
8. Al and Todd are tired.	Al and Todd _____ tired.
9. Our teacher is tired.	Our teacher _____ tired.
10. You are tired.	You _____ tired.

▶ **Practice 2. Past forms of *be*.** (Chart 8-1)
Choose the correct form of the verb in each sentence.

1. My parents (*was* / (*were*)) at home last night.
2. Our next-door neighbors (*was* / *were*) at work.
3. I (*was* / *were*) at the library.
4. My roommate (*was* / *were*) there too.
5. She (*was* / *were*) across the table from me.
6. Our teacher (*was* / *were*) at the table next to us.
7. He (*was* / *were*) half-asleep.
8. We (*was* / *were*) at the library until closing time.
9. The library (*was* / *were*) open until 9:00 P.M.
10. My roommate and I (*was* / *were*) the last people to leave.

► **Practice 3. Past forms of *be*: negative.** (Chart 8-2)
Complete the sentences with the correct negative form: ***wasn't*** or ***weren't***.

1. I _____ *wasn't* _____ at school yesterday.

2. You _____ at school yesterday.

3. Some students _____ at school yesterday.

4. They _____ at school yesterday.

5. Toshi _____ at school yesterday.

6. He _____ at school yesterday.

7. My teacher _____ at school yesterday.

8. Beth and Mark _____ at school yesterday.

9. Sarah _____ at school yesterday.

10. She and I _____ at school yesterday.

11. We _____ at school yesterday.

► **Practice 4. Simple past tense of *be*: negative.** (Chart 8-2)
Complete the sentences with the correct negative form: ***wasn't*** or ***weren't***.

A bad hotel

1. The hotel _____ *wasn't* _____ nice.

2. My room _____ clean.

3. The beds _____ comfortable.

4. The pillows _____ soft.

5. The shower water _____ warm.

6. The elevators _____ fast.

7. The restaurant _____ good.

8. The food _____ fresh.

9. The hotel clerks _____ polite.

▶ **Practice 5. Simple past tense of *be*: negative.** (Chart 8-2)
Write sentences about the people in the chart.

	Mike	**Lori**	**Ricardo**	**Eva**
at work	x			
at school				
on vacation			x	
out of town		x		x

Where were they yesterday?

1. Mike ____*wasn't out of town yesterday. He was at work.*____

2. Ricardo _____

3. Lori _____

4. Lori and Eva _____

▶ **Practice 6. Simple past tense of *be*: negative.** (Chart 8-2)
Think about your elementary school years. Write sentences about yourself. Use *was* or *wasn't*.

1. (*shy*) ____*I was / wasn't shy.*____   4. (*active*) _____

2. (*happy*) _____   5. (*serious*) _____

3. (*quiet*) _____   6. (*noisy*) _____

▶ **Practice 7. Simple past tense of *be*: questions.** (Chart 8-3)
Complete the questions with *Was* or *Were*.

1. ____*Were*____ you home yesterday evening?

2. _____ your husband home yesterday evening?

3. _____ he home yesterday evening?

4. _____ your parents home last weekend?

5. _____ they home last weekend?

6. _____ I home last weekend?

7. _____ the teacher home last night?

8. _____ your teacher home last night?

9. _____ Jan and I home yesterday evening?

10. _____ we home last weekend?

▶ **Practice 8. Simple past tense of *be*: questions.** (Chart 8-3)
Make two questions for each situation. The first question is a yes/no question, and the second is a ***where*** question. Give the answers for both questions. Use the places from the box.

at the grocery store	at the library	at the train station
at home	at the mall	at the zoo

1. Jake and Kevin \ at a swimming pool

   A: _____Were Jake and Kevin at a swimming pool?_____

   B: _____No, they weren't._____

   A: _____Where were they?_____

   B: _____They were at the grocery store._____

2. Ellen \ at the library

   A: _____

   B: _____

   A: _____

   B: _____

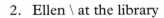

3. you \ at a party

   A: _____

   B: _____

   A: _____

   B: _____

4. Thomas \ at the airport

   A: _____

   B: _____

   A: _____

   B: _____

5. your kids \ at school

   A: _____

   B: _____

   A: _____

   B: _____

6. Liz and you \ at the park

A: _____

B: _____

A: _____

B: _____

▶ **Practice 9. Simple past tense of *be*: questions.** (Chart 8-3)
Your friend was at a movie last night. Ask questions about the movie. Use **was** or **were**.

1. _____*Was*_____ it scary?

2. _____ you afraid?

3. _____ the characters interesting?

4. _____ the movie funny?

5. _____ the main actor good?

6. _____ she or he a good actor?

7. _____ the actors good?

8. _____ they good?

▶ **Practice 10. Simple past tense -*ed*.** (Chart 8-4)
Complete the sentences with the simple past tense form of the verbs.

Every day	**Yesterday**
1. I study English.	I ____*studied*____ English.
2. He studies English.	He __studied__ English.
3. We walk in the park.	We __walked__ in the park.
4. You work hard.	You __worked__ hard.
5. They smile.	They __smiled__ .
6. The baby smiles.	The baby __smiled__
7. Sonja talks on the phone.	Sonja __Talked__ on the phone.
8. Tim helps his parents.	Tim __helped__ his parents.
9. I help my parents.	I __helped__ my parents.
10. She listens carefully.	She __listened__ carefully.
11. They listen carefully.	They __listened__ carefully.

► **Practice 11. Simple past tense -ed.** (Chart 8-4)
Look at the activities and write sentences about the people.

Yesterday	Ruth	Deb	Bill	Stuart
cook breakfast	x		x	
watch TV		x	x	
talk to friends on the phone	x			
exercise at a gym				x

1. Deb _____ *watched TV.* _____

2. Stuart _____

3. Ruth and Bill _____

4. Ruth also _____

5. Bill also _____

► **Practice 12. Simple past tense -ed.** (Chart 8-4)
Complete each sentence with the simple past tense form of a verb from the box.

Group A:

asked	erased	kissed	touched	✓ watched
cooked	finished	laughed	walked	worked
coughed	helped	stopped	washed	

1. I _____ *watched* _____ TV last night.

2. Anna _____ walked _____ to class yesterday instead of taking the bus.

3. I _____ washed _____ the dirty dishes after dinner last night.

4. Jim _____ erased _____ the board with an eraser.

5. Robert loves his daughter. He __kissed__ her on the forehead.

6. The joke was funny. We __laughed__ at the funny story.

7. The train suddenly __stopped__. There was a cow on the tracks.

8. I cleaned for three hours last night. I __finished__ my housework at about nine o'clock.

9. Steve __touched__ my shoulder with his hand to get my attention.

10. Mr. Wilson __worked__ in his garden yesterday morning.

11. Judy __coughed__ a lot. She had a bad cold.

12. Dan is a good cook. He __cooked__ some delicious food last night.

13. Linda __asked__ a question in class yesterday.

14. I had a problem with my homework. The teacher __helped__ me before class.

Group B:

— arrived	—killed	—remembered	smiled
—closed	⌣ played	—shaved	sneezed
enjoyed	rained	signed	✓ snowed

15. It's winter. The ground is white because it _____snowed_____ yesterday.

16. Anita __arrived__ at the airport on September 3.

17. The girls and boys __played__ baseball after school yesterday.

18. When Ali got a new credit card, he __signed__ his name in ink on the back of the card.

19. Rick had a beard yesterday, but now he doesn't. He __shaved__ it this morning.

20. The students' test papers were very good. The teacher, Mr. Jackson, was very pleased. He __smiled__ when he returned the test papers.

21. I __enjoyed__ the party last night. It was fun. I had a good time.

22. The window was open. Mr. Chan __closed__ it because it was cold outside.

23. The streets were wet this morning because it _____rained_____ last night.

24. "Achoo!" When Judy _____sneezed_____, Ken said, "Bless you." Oscar said, "Gesundheit!"

25. I have my books with me. I didn't forget them today. I _____remembered_____ to bring them to class.

26. Mrs. Lane was upset because there was a fly in the room. The fly was buzzing all around the room. Finally, she _____killed_____ it with a rolled-up newspaper.

Group C:

— added	folded	— needed	— waited
counted	— invited	visited	✓ wanted

27. The children _____wanted_____ some candy after dinner.

28. Mr. Miller _____need_____ to stay in the hospital for several days after his operation.

29. I _____added_____ the number of students in the room. There were twenty.

30. Mr. and Mrs. Johnson _____invited_____ us to come to their house last Sunday.

31. Last Sunday we _____visited_____ the Johnsons. We had dinner with them.

32. I _____folded_____ the letter before I put it in the envelope.

33. Kim _____waited_____ for the bus at the corner of Fifth Avenue and Main Street.

34. The boy _____counted_____ the numbers on the board in math class yesterday.

8-A Summary of Spelling Rules for *-ed* Verbs		
	END OF VERB- → *-ED* FORM	
Rule 1:	CONSONANT + *-e* → ADD *-d*.	
	smi*le* → smi*led*	
	era*se* → era*sed*	
Rule 2:	ONE VOWEL + ONE CONSONANT → DOUBLE THE CONSONANT.* ADD *-ed*.	
	st*op*	st*opped*
	r*ub*	r*ubbed*
Rule 3:	TWO VOWELS + ONE CONSONANT → ADD *-ed*. DO NOT DOUBLE THE CONSONANT.	
	r*ain*	r*ained*
	n*eed*	n*eeded*
Rule 4:	TWO CONSONANTS → ADD *-ed*. DO NOT DOUBLE THE CONSONANT.	
	cou*nt*	cou*nted*
	he*lp*	he*lped*
Rule 5:	CONSONANT + *-y* → CHANGE *-y* TO *-i*. ADD *-ed*.	
	stu*dy*	stu*died*
	car*ry*	car*ried*
Rule 6:	VOWEL + *-y* → ADD *-ed*. DO NOT CHANGE *-y* TO *-i*.	
	pl*ay*	pl*ayed*
	enj*oy*	enj*oyed*

*EXCEPTIONS: Do not double *x* (*fix* + *-ed* = *fixed*). Do not double *w* (*snow* + *-ed* = *snowed*).

▶ **Practice 13. Spelling rules: *-ed* verbs.** (Chart 8-A)
Study each rule and the examples. Then write the simple past tense of the given verbs.

Rule 1. END OF VERB: CONSONANT + *-e* → ADD *-d*.

1. like → _____

2. close → _____

3. shave → _____

4. love → _____

5. hate → _____

6. exercise → _____

Rule 2. END OF VERB: ONE VOWEL + ONE CONSONANT → DOUBLE THE CONSONANT. ADD *-ed*.

7. plan → planned

8. drop → dropped

9. clap → clapped

Rule 3. END OF VERB: TWO VOWELS + ONE CONSONANT → ADD **-ed**. DO NOT DOUBLE
    THE CONSONANT.

10. join *ed* → _____

11. shout *ed* → _____

12. wait *ed* → _____

Rule 4. END OF VERB: TWO CONSONANTS → ADD **-ed**. DO NOT DOUBLE THE CONSONANT.

13. point   → _____

14. touch *ed* → _____

15. melt   → _____

Rule 5. END OF VERB: CONSONANT + **-y** → CHANGE **-y** TO **-i**. ADD **-ed**.

16. marry   → *Married* _____

17. try   → _____

18. hurry   → _____

19. reply   → _____

20. dry   → _____

Rule 6. END OF VERB: VOWEL + **-y** → ADD **-ed**. DO NOT CHANGE **-y** TO **-i**.

21. stay   → _____

22. delay *ed* → *NO chem* ✓y *consonant*

▶ **Practice 14. Spelling practice: -ed.** (Chart 8-4)
Write the **-ed** forms of these verbs.

                        -ed

1. count   _____ *counted* _____

2. rain   _____

3. help   _____

4. plan   _____

5. dream   _____

6. erase   _____

NOTE: Spelling rules for the two-syllable verbs *visit, answer, happen, occur, listen, open,* and *enter* are in Appendix 5 at the back of
this Workbook.

7. close   _____

8. yawn   _____

9. study   _____

10. worry   _____

11. drop   _____

▶ **Practice 15. Spelling review: -ed.** (Chart 8-4)
Use the correct form of a verb in the box to complete each sentence.

carry	fail	rub	stop
clap	✓ finish	smile	taste
cry	learn	stay	wait

1. I _____finished_____ my homework at nine o'clock last night.

2. We _____ some new vocabulary yesterday.

3. I _____ the soup before dinner last night. It was delicious.

4. Linda _____ for the bus at the corner yesterday.

5. The bus _____ at the corner. It was on time.

6. Ann _____ her suitcases to the bus station yesterday. They weren't heavy.

7. The baby _____ her eyes because she was sleepy.

8. I _____ home and watched a sad show on TV last night. I _____ at the end of the show.

9. Mike _____ his examination last week. He got most answers wrong.

10. Jane _____ at her kids. She was happy to see them.

11. The audience loved the movie. They _____ loudly at the end.

▶ **Practice 16. Yesterday, last, and ago.** (Chart 8-5)
Complete each sentence with **yesterday**, **last**, or **ago**.

My soccer team played . . .

1. _____ *last* _____ night.   7. _____ evening.

2. _____ afternoon.   8. three months _____.

3. _____ Wednesday.   9. two weeks _____.

4. _____ week.   10. one year _____.

5. _____ summer.   11. _____ morning.

6. _____ month.   12. _____ weekend.

▶ **Practice 17. Yesterday, last, and ago.** (Chart 8-5)
Rewrite each *italicized* sentence using a time expression with **yesterday**, **last**, or **ago**.

1. It's 7:00. *At 6:55, Tim brushed his teeth.*

   _____ *Tim brushed his teeth five minutes ago.* _____

2. It's 3:00 P.M. *The day before at 3:00, Bonnie walked to the park.*

   _____

3. This week Tom is working. *The week before, he was at home on vacation.*

   _____

4. It's 2014. *In 2010, Sam graduated from high school.*

   _____

5. It's Saturday. *The Thursday before, Jan worked 12 hours.*

   _____

6. It's March. *The January before, Thomas stayed with his parents.*

   _____

7. It's 10:00 P.M. *The night before at 10:00, we watched a DVD.*

   _____

▶ **Practice 18. Irregular verbs: Group 1.** (Chart 8-6)
Complete each sentence with the simple past tense form of the verb.

Every day   **Yesterday**

1. I eat vegetables.   I _____*ate*_____ vegetables.

2. You eat vegetables.   You ___ate___ vegetables.

3. He eats vegetables.   He ___ate___ vegetables.

4. She eats vegetables.   She ___ate___ vegetables.

5. We eat vegetables.   We ___ate___ vegetables.

6. They eat vegetables.   They ___ate___ vegetables.

7. Sam and I eat vegetables. Sam and I ___ate___ vegetables.

8. I do my homework.   I ___did___ my homework.

9. You do your homework.   You ___did___ your homework.

10. He does his homework.   He ___did___ his homework.

11. We do our homework.   We ___did___ our homework.

12. I sleep eight hours.   I ___slept___ eight hours.

13. They sleep eight hours.   They ___slept___ eight hours.

14. We sleep eight hours.   We ___slept___ eight hours.

15. She sleeps eight hours.   She ___slept___ eight hours.

▶ **Practice 19. Irregular verbs: Group 1.** (Chart 8-6)
Which sentences are true for you? Write the present form for each verb in italics.

                                              Present Form

1. _____ I *got* a package in the mail yesterday.   _____*get*_____

2. _____ I *came* home early yesterday.   _____

3. _____ I *went* out to dinner last night.   _____

4. _____ I *had* a headache yesterday.   _____

5. _____ I *put* on sunglasses yesterday.   _____

6. _____ I *slept* for nine hours last night.   _____

7. _____ I *saw* my parents yesterday.   _____

8. _____ I *did* homework last night.   _____

9. _____ I *ate* fish for dinner.   _____

10. _____ I *wrote* an email last night.   _____

11. _____ I *sat* in the sun yesterday.   _____

12. _____ I *stood* outside in the rain yesterday.   _____

▶ **Practice 20. Irregular verbs: Group 1.** (Chart 8-6)
Complete each sentence with the simple past tense form of a verb from the box. In some sentences, more than one verb fits. The number in parentheses tells you how many verbs you can use.

come	eat	go	put	sit	stand
✓ do	get	have	see	sleep	write

1. Last week, I _____*did*_____ something really fun. (1)

2. I _____ to the mountains for a camping trip. (1)

3. At night, I _____ under the stars. (3)

4. I _____ millions of stars in the sky. (1)

5. I _____ three fish from the river with my fishing pole. (1)

6. I cooked them over a fire and _____ them for dinner. (2)

7. One day I walked in the woods for several hours. I _____ deer and foxes with my binoculars. (1)

8 I _____ home late Monday night. (3)

9. I _____ an email to my parents. (1)

10. I _____ some photos in the email. (2)

▶ **Practice 21. Simple past: negative.** (Charts 1-5 and 8-7)
Choose the true completion for each sentence.

When my parents were teenagers, they . . .

1.	had	didn't have	computers.
2.	walked	didn't walk	to school.
3.	did	didn't do	chores on weekends.
4.	drank	didn't drink	sodas.
5.	used	didn't use	microwave ovens.
6.	watched	didn't watch	videos.
7.	talked	didn't talk	on cell phones.

▶ **Practice 22. Simple past: negative.** (Charts 1-5 and 8-7)
Complete each sentence with the negative form of the verb.

1. I came home late.   I _____*didn't come*_____ home late.

2. You came home late.   You ___didn't come___ home late.

3. He came home late.   He ___didn't come___ home late.

4. She came home late.   She ___didn't come___ home late.

5. We came home late.   We ___weren't___ home late.

6. They came home late.   They ___weren't___ home late.

7. He played soccer.   He ___didn't play___ soccer.

8. They played soccer.   They ___didn't play___ soccer.

9. She answered the phone.   She ___didn't answer___ the phone.

10. I saw a UFO.*   I ___didn't see___ a UFO.

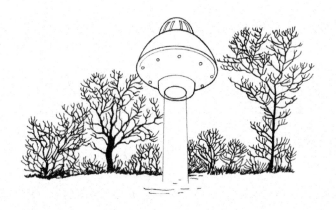

*UFO = unidentified flying object.

11. You slept late.   You _didn't sleep_ late.

12. I did my homework.   I _didn't do_ my homework.

13. I was late.   I _wasn't_ late.

14. They were late.   They _weren't_ late.

▶ **Practice 23. Simple past: negative.** (Chart 8-7)
Write sentences that are true for you.

1. eat \ a big dinner \ last night

    _____ *I ate a big dinner last night.* OR *I didn't eat a big dinner last night.* _____

2. sleep \ on the floor \ last night

    _____

3. write \ a long email \ earlier today

    _____

4. walk \ to school \ last month

    _____

5. get \ some money from the bank \ yesterday

    _____

6. go \ to my cousins' house\ last week

    _____

7. do \ some housework \ yesterday

    _____

8. work \ outside \ yesterday

    _____

9. put on \ my shoes \ yesterday

    _____

10. stop \ at a café \ earlier today

    _____

► **Practice 24. Simple past: negative.** (Chart 8-7)
Part I. Read the story.

A Bad Day

Derek had a lot of trouble yesterday. He woke up with a sore throat and headache. Then he dropped his breakfast of eggs on the floor. The plate broke on his foot. He cleaned up the eggs and the broken plate. Then he decided to have coffee. He found a little cream in his fridge, but when he drank the coffee, he realized the cream was sour. He decided to have breakfast at school.

Derek waited for the bus for half an hour, but it didn't come. He got his bike and went to school. During a class break, someone stole his money. Derek left school early, but his bike had a flat tire, so he took a taxi. When he got to his apartment, he remembered he didn't have any money to pay the driver. Fortunately, his neighbor paid the fare for him.

Part II. Make true sentences. Write one negative and one affirmative statement.

1. Derek woke up feeling good. *He didn't wake up feeling good. He woke up sick / with a sore throat, etc.*

2. He broke a glass on the floor. _____

3. He ate a delicious breakfast. _____

4. He took the bus to school. _____

5. He left school late. _____

6. He took the bus home. _____

7. He paid the driver. _____

▶ **Practice 25. Review of yes/no questions: past and present.** (Charts 3-9 and 8-8)
Make yes/no questions.

1. ___Do they play___ tennis?   Yes, they do. They play tennis.

2. ___Did they play___ tennis?   Yes, they did. They played tennis.

3. _____ tennis?   Yes, she does. She plays tennis.

4. _____ tennis?   Yes, she did. She played tennis.

5. _____ to work?   Yes, he does. He walks to work.

6. _____ to work?   Yes, he did. He walked to work.

7. _____ at home?   Yes, she does. She works at home.

8. _____ at home?   Yes, she did. She worked at home.

9. _____ your new job?   Yes, I do. I like my new job.

10. _____ your old job?   Yes, I did. I liked my old job.

▶ **Practice 26. Yes/no questions.** (Charts 8-3 and 8-8)
Complete each sentence with **did**, **was**, or **were**.

Tell me about your trip.

1. _____Did_____ you have a good time?

2. _____ it fun?

3. _____ you see a lot of interesting sights?

4. _____ you meet many people?

5. _____ the people friendly?

6. _____ you learn a lot?

7. _____ the trip long enough?

8. _____ you want to come home?

9. _____ you ready to come home?

▶ **Practice 27. Review: questions and negatives.** (Charts 8-7 and 8-8)
Make questions and negative sentences from the given sentences.

	Question	**Negative**
1. a. They play.	_Do they play?_	_They don't play._
b. They played.	_Did they play?_	_They didn't play._

		Question	Negative

2. a. They help. _____ _____

   b. They helped. _____ _____

3. a. She listens. _____ _____

   b. She listened. _____ _____

4. a. He works. _____ _____

   b. He worked. _____ _____

5. a. The baby cries. _____ _____

   b. The baby cried. _____ _____

6. a. We are sick. _____ _____

   b. We were sick. _____ _____

► **Practice 28. Review: Yes/no questions.** (Charts 8-2, 8-3, 8-7, and 8-8)
Make yes/no questions. Give short answers.

1. A: _Were you at home last night?_

   B: _No, I wasn't._ (I wasn't at home last night.)

   A: _Did you go to a lake last weekend?_

   B: _Yes, I did._ (I went to a lake last weekend.)

2. A: _Is it cold today?_

   B: _No, it isn't_ (It isn't cold today.)

3. A: _Do you come to class every day?_

   B: _Yes, I do_ (I come to class every day.)

4. A: _Was Robert absent yesterday?_

   B: _Yes, he was_ (Roberto was absent yesterday.)

5. A: _Did Robert stay home yesterday?_

   B: _Yes, he did_ (Roberto stayed home yesterday.)

6. A: _Does Phillip change his passwords very often?_

   B: _No, he doesn't_ (Phillip doesn't change his passwords very often.)

7. A: _Is Mohammed in class today?_

   B: _No, he isn't_ (Mohammed isn't in class today.)

8. A: ___Was he here yesterday___

   B: ___Yes, he was___ (He was here yesterday.)

9. A: ___Did he come to the day before yesterday___

   B: ___Yes, he did___ (He came to class the day before yesterday.)

10. A: ___Does he usually come to class every day?___

    B: ___Yes, he does___ (He usually comes to class every day.)

▶ **Practice 29. Irregular verbs: Group 2.** (Chart 8-9)
Check (✓) the sentences that are true for you. Write the present form for each verb in italics.

Present Form

1. _____ I *bought* some snack food yesterday.   ___*buy*___

2. _____ I *read* a newspaper last week.   _____

3. _____ I *rode* a horse last year.   _____

4. _____ I *ran* up some stairs yesterday.   _____

5. _____ I *drank* tea yesterday.   _____

6. _____ I *caught* a taxi last week.   _____

7. _____ I *drove* a car yesterday.   _____

8. _____ I *thought* about English yesterday evening.   _____

9. _____ I *brought* this book to school last week.   _____

10. _____ My teacher *taught* me new vocabulary last week.   _____

▶ **Practice 30. Irregular verbs: Group 2.** (Chart 8-9)
Complete each sentence with the simple past tense form of a verb from the box. The number in parentheses tells you how many verbs you can use.

bring	catch	drive	✓ ride	teach
buy	drink	read	run	think

Jane is a teacher.

1. She didn't drive to work yesterday. She _____*rode*_____ her bike to school. (1)

2. In the morning, she _____ math and science to her students. (1)

3. At lunch time, she went home and got her car. She _____ her car to the mall. (1)

4. She _____ a sweater for her husband at a clothing store. (1)

5. She stopped at a café and _____ some coffee. (2)

6. Then she went home and _____ her students' science projects. (1)

7. Before dinner, she put on her running clothes and shoes. She walked outside and _____ down the street to the store. (1)

8. During her run, she _____ about her favorite foods: potato chips, ice cream, and chocolate. (1)

9. But she _____ home healthy foods: chicken, rice, and vegetables. (1)

10. Her husband _____ a cold last week, and she wants to stay healthy. (1)

▶ **Practice 31. Irregular verbs: Group 3.** (Chart 8-10)
Check (✓) the sentences that are true for you. Write the present form for each verb in italics.

                                                                    Present Form

1. _____ I *flew* in a small airplane last year.   _____fly_____

2. _____ I *spoke* a little English two years ago.   _____

3. _____ I *took* the bus to school last week.   _____

4. _____ I *paid* bills last month.   _____

5. _____ I *woke up* early this morning.   _____

6. _____ I *broke* my arm when I was a child.   _____

7. _____ I *sent* an email to a friend last week.   _____

8. _____ I *sang* a song this morning.   _____

9. _____ I *left* my home today.   _____

10. _____ I *met* a famous person at a party.   _____

11. _____ A cell phone *rang* in my English class last week.   _____

12. _____ I *heard* a funny story yesterday.   _____

► **Practice 32. Irregular verbs: Group 3.** (Chart 8-10)
Complete each sentence with the simple past tense form of a verb from the box. There is only one correct verb for each sentence.

break	hear	meet	ring	sing	take
✓ fly	leave	pay	send	speak	wake

1. It was 7:00 A.M. Jerry was asleep. A bird _____*flew*_____ into his open bedroom window.

2. Jerry _____ a noise.

3. The noise _____ him up. He saw the bird.

4. The bird looked hurt. Jerry _____ the bird to the veterinarian.*

5. A nurse _____ Jerry in the parking lot and helped him with the bird.

6. Jerry _____ the bird at the vet's office and went to work.

7. An hour later, Jerry's office phone _____. It was the vet.

8. The vet _____ to Jerry. He said, "The bird _____ its wing, but it's okay."

9. Jerry took the bird home. After a week, its wing got better. Jerry put the bird outside. The bird _____ a few songs and flew away. Jerry watched his little friend, feeling both happy and sad.

10. The vet _____ Jerry a bill for a small amount.

11. Jerry happily _____ the bill.

► **Practice 33. Irregular verbs: Group 4.** (Chart 8-11)
Check (✓) the sentences that are true for you. Write the present form for each verb in *italics*.

Present Form

1. _____ I *wore* a hat yesterday.   _____*wear*_____

2. _____ I *said* "Good morning" to my teacher yesterday.   _____

3. _____ I *found* money on the street last week.   _____

---

*veterinarian (vet) = an animal doctor.

4. _____ I *lost* something expensive in the past.   _____

5. _____ Someone *stole* something expensive from me once.   _____

6. _____ I *hung* up my clothes before I went to bed last night.   _____

7. _____ I *told* a funny joke last week.   _____

8. _____ My classes *began* on time last week.   _____

9. _____ I *sold* something on the Internet.   _____

10. _____ The last time I paid bills, I *tore* up a check.   _____

▶ **Practice 34. Irregular verbs: Group 4.** (Chart 8-11)
Complete each sentence with the simple past tense form of a verb from the box. There is only one correct verb for each sentence. Note the use of **tell** and **say**: **tell** + person but **say** + **to** + person.

✓begin	hang	say	steal	tell
find	lose	sell	tear	wear

1. Martha's school day _____*began*_____ with bad news.

2. Her husband said, "The dog _____ your students' work into small pieces. Now he's looking at your leather jacket."

3. Martha _____ her leather jacket to school every day. It was her favorite jacket.

4. She picked up her jacket and the homework, and _____ the dog, "No."

5. She went to school. She took off her jacket and _____ it up on a hanger in the closet.

6. At the end of the day, there was no jacket. A student _____ to her, "Maybe a thief _____ it."

7. Someone else said to her, "Maybe you left it somewhere else and don't remember. Maybe you _____ it."

8. Martha wondered, "Did someone steal it? Maybe someone _____ it for money."

9. An hour later, another student _____ Martha's jacket in the closet. It was on a hanger under another teacher's jacket!

► **Practice 35. Review: -ed spelling.**
Write the correct spelling of the **-ed** form.

	-ed form			**-ed form**
1. wait	*waited*	9. point		
2. spell	*spelled*	10. pat		
3. kiss	*kissed*	11. shout		
4. plan		12. reply		
5. join		13. play		
6. hope		14. touch		
7. drop		15. end		
8. add		16. dance		

► **Practice 36. Verb review: simple past tense.** (Chapter 8)
Complete the sentences. Use the verbs in parentheses.

1. Mari and I (*go*) _____*went*_____ to the pharmacy yesterday. I (*buy*) _____ some aspirin and (*pick up*) _____ a prescription.

2. I had to go downtown yesterday. I (*catch*) _____ the bus in front of my apartment and (*ride*) _____ to Grand Avenue. Then I (*get off*) _____ the bus and transferred to another one. It (*be*) _____ a long trip.

3. Sue (*eat*) _____ popcorn and (*drink*) _____ a soft drink at the movie theater last night. I (*eat, not*) _____ anything. Movie theater prices are too high.

4. Maria (*ask*) _____ the teacher a question in class yesterday. The teacher (*think*) _____ about the question for a few minutes and then said, "I don't know."

5. I (*want*) _____ to go to the basketball game last night, but I (*stay*) _____ home because I had to study.

6. Last night I (*read*) _____ an interesting article online. It (*be*) _____ about the superstorm.

7. Rita (*pass, not*) _____ the test yesterday. She (*fail*) _____ it.

8. Last summer we (*drive*) _____ to Colorado for our vacation. We (*visit*) _____ a national park, where we (*camp*) _____ out in a tent for a week. We (*go*) _____ fishing one morning. I (*catch*) _____ a big fish, but my husband (*catch, not*) _____ anything. We (*enjoy*) _____ cooking and eating the fish for dinner. It (*be*) _____ delicious. I like fresh fish.

▶ **Practice 37. Verb review: past and present.** (Chapters 1–4 and 8)
Complete the sentences with the words in parentheses. Use the simple present, present progressive, or simple past. The sentence may require an affirmative statement, a negative statement, or a question form.

1. Tom (*walk*) _____ *walks* _____ to work almost every day.

2. I can see Tom from my window. He's on the street below. He (*walk*) _____ to work right now.

3. (*Tom, walk*) _____ to work every day?

4. (*you, walk*) _____ to work every day?

5. I usually take the bus to work, but yesterday I (*walk*) _____ to my office.

6. On my way to work yesterday, I (*see*) _____ an accident.

7. Alex (*see, not*) _____ the accident.

8. (*you, see*) _____ the accident yesterday?

9. Tom (*walk, not*) _____ to work last week. The weather was too cold. He (*take*) _____ the bus.

10. I (*walk, not*) _____ to work last week either.

► **Practice 38. Verb review: past and present.** (Chapters 1–4 and 8)
Complete the sentences. Use the words in parentheses. Use any appropriate verb form.

1. I (*finish, not*) _____*didn't finish*_____ my chores last night. I (*go*)
_____ to bed early.

2. Jasmin (*stand, not*) _____ up right now. She (*sit*)
_____ down.

3. The weather (*be, not*) _____ cold today, but it (*be*)
_____ cold yesterday.

4. It (*rain, not*) _____ right now. The rain (*stop*)
_____ a few minutes ago.

5. Tina and I (*go, not*) _____ shopping yesterday. We (*go*)
_____ shopping last Monday.

6. I (*go*) _____ to a party last night, but I (*enjoy, not*)
_____ it. It (*be, not*) _____ a lot of fun.

7. I (*write*) _____ a paragraph for my history class last night, but I
(*spend, not*) _____ much time on it.

8. My husband (*come, not*) _____ home for dinner last night.

9. The twins (*go*) _____ to bed a half an hour ago. They (*sleep*)
_____ now.

10. We (*be*) _____ late for a meeting at our son's school last
night. The meeting (*start*) _____ at 7:00, but we (*arrive, not*)
_____ until 7:15.

11. Olga (*ask*) _____ Hamid a question a few minutes ago, but he
(*answer, not*) _____ her.

12. When Ben and I (*go*) _____ to the mall yesterday,
I (*buy*) _____ some new shoes. Ben (*buy, not*)
_____ anything.

13. A: What did you do yesterday?

    B: Well, I (*wake up*) _____ around 9:00 and (*go*)
    _____ shopping. While I was downtown, someone (*steal*)
    _____ my purse. I (*take*) _____
    a taxi home. When I (*get*) _____ out of the taxi, I (*tear*)
    _____ my blouse. I (*borrow*) _____
    some money from my roommate to pay the taxi driver.

A: Did anything good happen to you yesterday?

B: Let me think. Yeah. I (*lose*) _____ my grammar book, but I (*find*) _____ it later.

14. A: May I use your laptop?

B: Sure.

A: Thanks. I (*want*) _____ to look for apartment rentals. I (*need*) _____ to find a new apartment.

15. A: I (*see, not*) _____ you yesterday. (*be*) _____ you sick?

B: No, but my daughter (*feel, not*) _____ well, so I (*be*) _____ home with her. She's fine now. She (*be*) _____ at school.

A: That's good to hear.

16. A: Wait! Where (*go, you*) _____?

B: My dentist's office just (*call*) _____. Someone (*pick*) _____ up my wallet in the parking lot. I (*need*) _____ to go get it.

A: Wow! You're lucky.

B: I (*know*) _____.

Chapter 9
Expressing Past Time, Part 2

▶ **Practice 1.** *Where, when, what time, why.* (Chart 9-1)
Make simple past questions and answers. Use **Where . . . go?**, **When/What time . . . leave?**, **Why . . . go there?** and the given information.

> Oscar's travel plans
>
> To Mexico City
> Leave on March 22
> To visit family

> Serena's travel plans
>
> the Canary Islands
> Leave at 6 AM
> For vacation

Oscar's plans

1. A: _____ *Where did Oscar go?* _____

   B: _____ *He went to Mexico City.* _____

2. A: _____

   B: _____

3. A: _____

   B: _____

Serena's plans

4. A: _____

   B: _____

5. A: _____

   B: _____

6. A: _____

   B: _____

► **Practice 2. *Where, when, what time, why.*** (Chart 9-1)
Write the letter of the correct response next to the question.

1. Who did you invite to your party? __*b*__   a. A new TV.

2. When did your plane arrive? _____   ✓ b. My best friends.

3. Why did you eat two breakfasts? _____   c. In 2003.

4. When did you travel to Peru? _____   d. In Toronto.

5. Where did you live during high school? _____   e. Because I was very hungry.

6. What did you buy? _____   f. A few minutes ago.

► **Practice 3. *Where, when, what time, why.*** (Chart 9-1)
Make questions for the given answers.

1. A: _____*Where did you study last night?*_____

   B: At the library. (I studied at the library last night.)

2. A: When did you leave the library?

   B: At 10:00. (I left the library at 10:00.)   — base vers

3. A: Why did you (leave) the library?

   B: Because it closed at 10:00. (I left because the library closed at 10:00.)

4. A: Where did you (go) yesterday afternoon

   B: To the park. (My friends and I went to the park yesterday afternoon.)

5. A: _____

   B: Two days ago. (Sandra got back from Brazil two days ago.)

6. A: Why was Bobby in bed?

   B: Because he was sick. (Bobby was in bed because he was sick.)

7. A: Why was Bobby SICK?

   B: Because he didn't get enough sleep. (Bobby was sick because he didn't get enough sleep.)

8. A: Where did you buy your sandals?

   B: Online. (I bought my sandals online.)

sandals

▶ **Practice 4. Why didn't.** (Chart 9-1)
Make questions. Begin with **Why didn't**.

1. A: I looked for you at the meeting, but you didn't come. ___Why didn't you come?___
   B: Because I had to work overtime.

2. A: You needed help, but you didn't ask the teacher. _____
   B: Because no one else had questions, and I felt stupid.

3. A: The homework is due today, and you didn't bring it. _____
   B: Because I fell asleep while I was studying last night.

4. A: You told a lie. You didn't tell me the truth. _____
   B: Because I was afraid of your reaction.

5. A: Sharon looked sad. You didn't go to her party. _____
   B: Because I forgot it was her birthday.

6. A: Look at this mess! You didn't clean your bedroom. _____
   B: Because I was too tired.

▶ **Practice 5. What + verb review.** (Chart 9-2)
Make questions. Pay attention to verb tenses.

1. A: ___What did you buy?_____
   B: A digital camera. (We bought a digital camera.)

2. A: ___Did you buy a digital camera?_____
   B: Yes, we did. (We bought a digital camera.)

3. A: _____
   B: Math. (I studied math.)

4. A: _____
   B: Yes, I did. (I studied math.)

5. A: _____
   B: A map. (They're looking at a map.)

6. A: _____
   B: Yes, they are. (They're looking at a map.)

7. A: _____
   B: English grammar. (I dreamed about English grammar last night.)

8. A: _____
   B: Yes, she is. (She's a new employee.)

9. A: _____

    B: Algebra. (She tutors algebra.)

10. A: _____

    B: His country. (David talked about his country.)

11. A: _____

    B: Yes, he did. (David talked about his country.)

12. A: _____

    B: Nothing in particular. (I'm thinking about nothing in particular.)

13. A: _____

    B: Nothing special. (*Nothing in particular* means "nothing special.")

14. A: _____

    B: Spiders. (I am afraid of spiders.)

a spider

▶ **Practice 6. Understanding questions with *who*.** (Chart 9-3)
Write questions and short answers for the given sentences.

1. Julie called the police.

    a. Who called _____ *the police?* _____ Julie.

    b. Who did _____ *Julie call?* _____ The police.

2. The nurse checked Lea.

    a. Who checked _____ The nurse.

    b. Who did _____ Lea.

3. Felix helped the new assistant.

    a. Who did _____ The new assistant.

    b. Who helped _____ _____

4. Professor Jones taught the advanced students.

    a. Who taught _____ Professor Jones.

    b. Who did _____ _____

5. The police caught the thief.

    a. Who did _____ _____

    b. Who caught _____ _____

6. Tommy dreamed about a monster.

    a. Who dreamed about _____ _____

    b. Who did _____ _____

▶ **Practice 7. Using *who*.** (Chart 9-3)
Make questions with *who*.

1. Ron helped Judy.

    a. _____*Who helped Judy?*_____ Ron.

    b. _____*Who did Ron help?*_____ Judy.

2. The doctor examined the patient.

    a. _____ The patient.

    b. _____ The doctor.

3. Miriam called the supervisor.

    a. _____ Miriam.

    b. _____ The supervisor.

4. The students surprised the teacher.

    a. _____ The students.

    b. _____ The teacher.

5. Andrew and Catherine waited for Mrs. Allen.

    a. _____ Mrs. Allen.

    b. _____ Andrew and Catherine.

▶ **Practice 8. Using *who*.** (Chart 9-3)

There were some parties last week. Write questions and answers using the words from the box.

Questions: Who had a ＿＿＿＿ party?

Who did ＿＿＿＿ invite?

Host*	Party	Guests
Mrs. Adams	birthday party for her son	her son's friends
Dr. Martin	New Year's party	her employees
Professor Brown	graduation party	his students

1. ＿＿＿*Who had a birthday party?*＿＿＿＿   Mrs. Adams.

2. ＿＿＿*Who did Mrs. Adams invite?*＿＿＿   Her son's friends.

3. ＿＿＿＿＿＿＿＿＿＿＿＿＿＿＿＿＿   Professor Brown.

4. ＿＿＿＿＿＿＿＿＿＿＿＿＿＿＿＿＿   His students.

5. ＿＿＿＿＿＿＿＿＿＿＿＿＿＿＿＿＿   Dr. Martin.

6. ＿＿＿＿＿＿＿＿＿＿＿＿＿＿＿＿＿   Her employees.

▶ **Practice 9. Using *who*.** (Chart 9-3)

Make questions with *who*.

1. A: ＿＿＿*Who did you see?*＿＿＿＿＿＿＿＿＿＿＿＿＿

   B: Ken. (I saw Ken.)

2. A: ＿＿＿＿＿＿＿＿＿＿＿＿＿＿＿＿＿＿＿＿＿＿＿＿＿

   B: Ken. (I talked to Ken.)

3. A: ＿＿＿＿＿＿＿＿＿＿＿＿＿＿＿＿＿＿＿＿＿＿＿＿＿

   B: Nancy. (I visited Nancy.)

4. A: ＿＿＿＿＿＿＿＿＿＿＿＿＿＿＿＿＿＿＿＿＿＿＿＿＿

   B: Ahmed. (Ahmed answered the question.)

5. A: ＿＿＿＿＿＿＿＿＿＿＿＿＿＿＿＿＿＿＿＿＿＿＿＿＿

   B: Mr. Lee. (Mr. Lee taught the English class.)

＊host = the person who gives a party.

6. A: _____

   B: Carlos. (Carlos helped me.)

7. A: _____

   B. Gina. (I helped Gina.)

8. A: _____

   B: My brother. (My brother carried the suitcases.)

9. A: _____

   B: Yuko. (Yuko called.)

▶ **Practice 10. Irregular verbs: Group 5.** (Chart 9-4)
Check (✓) the sentences that are true for you. Write the present form for each verb in *italics*.

		Present Form
1. _____	I *forgot* to do my homework last week.	*forget*
2. _____	My teacher *gave* me extra work last week.	
3. _____	I *understood* my teacher on the first day of class.	
4. _____	I *hurt* my back last year.	
5. _____	I *spent* money on snack food yesterday.	
6. _____	I *shut* a window last night.	
7. _____	I *lent* some money to a friend last year.	
8. _____	I *cut* something with a sharp knife yesterday.	
9. _____	I once *hit* my finger with a hammer.	
10. _____	I *made* only one mistake on my last grammar test.	
11. _____	Ice-cream cones *cost* a lot when I was a child.	

an ice-cream cone

▶ **Practice 11. Irregular verbs: Group 5.** (Chart 9-4)
Complete each sentence on the next page with the simple past form of a verb from the box.
In some sentences, more than one verb is correct. The number in parentheses tells you how
many verbs you can use.

cost	forget	hit	lend	✓ shut	understand
cut	give	hurt	make	spend	

Jonathan had a bad day yesterday.

1. He woke up early because a dog was barking outside. He _____*shut*_____ his
   bedroom window too hard and cracked the glass. (1)

2. He _____ to bring his homework to class. His teacher wasn't
   happy. (1)

3. He _____ a lot of mistakes on his math quiz. (1)

4. His teacher _____ him a low grade on his research paper. (1)

5. He thought he _____ the research assignment, but his teacher said he
   did it wrong. (1)

6. He broke a glass container in chemistry class. When
   he picked up the glass, he _____ his
   hand. (2)

7. He left his lunch at home, so he bought food in the
   cafeteria. It _____ a lot. He had
   no money left. (1)

8. Because he _____ all his money, he had no money for the bus. (1)

9. A friend _____ him some bus money, but he lost it. (2)

10. During lunch, he played soccer with his friends. Someone kicked the ball, and it
    _____ him in the face. (2)

11. He couldn't open his eye, and his face _____ the rest of the day. (1)

▶ **Practice 12. Irregular verbs: Group 6.** (Chart 9-5)
   Check (✓) the sentences that are true for you. Write the present form for each verb in *italics*.

   Present Form

1. _____ I *knew* all the answers in the last exercise.   _____*know*_____

2. _____ I *felt* happy all day yesterday.   _____

3. _____ When I was a child, I *kept* animals for pets.   _____

4. _____ I *swam* in a pool last month.   _____

5. _____ I *threw* away some homework yesterday.   _____

6. _____ I *drew* pictures in my grammar book yesterday.   _____

7. _____ I *grew* vegetables last summer.   _____

8. _____ I often *fell* down when I was a child.   _____

9. _____ I *won* a prize when I was a child.   _____

10. _____ I *blew* bubbles with bubblegum yesterday.   _____

bubblegum

▶ **Practice 13. Irregular verbs: Group 6.** (Chart 9-5)
Complete each sentence with the simple past form of a verb from the box. There is only one correct verb for each sentence.

✓ blow	fall	grow	know	throw
draw	feel	keep	swim	won

A crazy day in the classroom

1. Every time the teacher spoke, she _____*blew*_____ a whistle.

2. Some students _____ funny pictures on the ceiling.

3. It was a hot, sunny day. Snow _____ outside the classroom.

4. The students _____ happy when they heard there was a test. They cheered.

5. The teacher didn't want her lesson plans. She _____ them in the garbage can.

6. Flowers _____ on the teacher's desk. They smelled wonderful.

7. One student _____ a pet mouse in a box on her desk.

8. A goldfish _____ upside down in the fish bowl.

9. The class played a game. The teacher asked questions, but no one _____ the answers.

10. Both teams _____ a prize.

▶ **Practice 14. Irregular verbs: Group 7.** (Chart 9-6)
Check (✓) the sentences that are true for you. Write the present form for each verb in *italics*.

Present Form

1. _____ I once *held* a big spider in my hand. _____*hold*_____

2. _____ I once *bent* an iron bar. _____

3. _____ I *shook* the hand of a famous person once. _____

4. _____ I *became* friends with a famous person. _____

5. _____ I *fed* a pet (dog, cat, fish, etc.) last week. _____

6. _____ When I was a baby, I *bit* people. _____

7. _____ I once *hid* some keys and later couldn't find them. _____

8. _____ I sometimes *fought* with my friends when I was young. _____

9. _____ When I was a child, I *built* sand castles at the beach. _____

a sand castle

▶ **Practice 15. Irregular verbs: Group 7.** (Chart 9-6)
Complete each sentence with the simple past form of a verb from the box. In some sentences, more than one verb fits. The number in parentheses tells you how many verbs you can use.

become	bite	feed	hide	shake
bend	✓ build	fight	held	

Puppy trouble

Thomas got a new puppy. He's having trouble with her. Here's what happened last week.

1. He _____*built*_____ a dog house for her, but she didn't want to sleep outdoors. She wanted to be inside. (1)

2. She likes to play in the rain. Yesterday, she got all wet. Then she came inside and _____ her tail. She got Thomas all wet. (1)

3. Thomas _____ her dog food, but she didn't eat it. She only wanted meat. (1)

4. He gave her dog toys, but she _____ the toys. He can't find them. (1)

5. The puppy likes to play with people. On Monday, she got excited and _____ the mail carrier's pant leg. Fortunately, her teeth didn't touch the skin. (3)

6. The mail carrier didn't understand and _____ upset. (1)

7. Thomas's big cat, Snow, doesn't like the puppy. Snow jumps at her and tries to scratch her. All last week, they _____. (1)

8. Thomas didn't want the puppy to get hurt. He _____ her in his arms a lot. (1)

9. The puppy likes to chew. She chewed Thomas's glasses. She _____ the frames, and now they are crooked. (2)

▶ **Practice 16. Complete and incomplete sentences.**
(Chart 9-7)
Write the phrases or sentences in the correct column on the next page. Add capitalization and punctuation where necessary.

✓ we slept	before school starts
✓ at the store	before school starts, I help the teacher
they left	we ate at a restaurant
after they left	after we finish dinner
after several minutes	we were at home

Incomplete sentence	Complete sentence
at the store	*We slept.*

▶ **Practice 17. After.** (Chart 9-7)

Look at the pairs of sentences. Decide which action happened first and which action happened second. Then write sentences with **after**. Pay special attention to the punctuation.

1. __1__ My computer crashed.

   __2__ I lost my information.

   ⌐ *After my computer crashed, I lost my information.* _____ OR

   _____ *I lost my information after my computer crashed.* _____

2. __2__ I closed the freezer door.

   __1__ I looked in the freezer.

   After I looked freezer, I closed OR

   I close the freezer afte i

3. _____ I stood on the scale.

   _____ The nurse wrote down my weight.

   _____ OR

   _____

4. _____ I exercised.

   _____ I put on my exercise clothes.

   _____ OR

   _____

5. _____ The alarm rang at the fire station.

   _____ The firefighters got in their truck.

   _____ OR

   _____

▶ **Practice 18. _Before_ and _after_.** (Chart 9-7)
Look at the pairs of sentences. Decide which action happened first and which action happened
second. Then choose the two sentences that have the same meaning.

1. __1__ Joan washed the dishes.

   __2__ Joan dried the dishes.

   (a.) After Joan washed the dishes, she dried them.

   b. Before Joan washed the dishes, she dried them.

   c. After Joan dried the dishes, she washed them.

   (d.) Before Joan dried the dishes, she washed them.

2. __2__ It rained.

   __1__ The rain clouds came.

   a. After it rained, the rain clouds came.

   (b.) Before it rained, the rain clouds came.

   (c.) After the rain clouds came, it rained.

   d. Before the rain clouds came, it rained.

3. __2__ Luis drove away.

   __1__ Luis started the car.

   a. Before Luis drove away, he started the car.

   b. Before Luis started the car, he drove away.

   c. After Luis drove away, he started the car.

   d. After Luis started the car, he drove away.

4. _____ I opened my eyes.

    _____ I looked around the room.

    a. Before I opened my eyes, I looked around the room.

    b. After I opened my eyes, I looked around the room.

    c. Before I looked around the room, I opened my eyes.

    d. After I looked around the room, I opened my eyes.

▶ **Practice 19. *When* in questions and time clauses.** (Chart 9-8)
In each of the following pairs, one is a question and one is a time clause. Add the necessary punctuation: question mark or a comma.

1. a. When you called**,**
   b. When did you call**?**

2. a. When did the movie start
   b. When the movie started

3. a. When you were in high school
   b. When were you in high school

4. a. When it snowed
   b. When did it snow

5. a. When was Dave sick
   b. When Dave was sick

▶ **Practice 20. *When* in questions and time clauses.** (Chart 9-8)
Add punctuation: a question mark or a comma. Then make each time clause a complete sentence by adding another clause from the box.

> we felt sad.
> everyone clapped.
> ✓ I met them at the airport.
> we were happy to see you.
> the class had a test.

1. When was the Smiths' party**?**

2. When the Browns came**,** *I met them at the airport.*

3. When did you hear the good news

4. When Mr. King died

5. When were you here

6. When did we meet

7. When you arrived

8. When Kevin was absent

9. When the TV show ended

10. When was Mrs. Allen a teacher

▶ **Practice 21. *When* in questions and time clauses.** (Chart 9-8)
Use the given words to make (a) a simple past question and (b) a simple past clause. Then use your own words to complete the sentence in (b).

1. when \ rain \ it

   a. _____ *When did it rain?* _____

   b. _____ *When it rained, I went inside.* _____

2. when \ get sick \ you

   a. When did tou Get Sick _____

   b. When you got sick, tou stayed in bed?

3. when \ begin \ the problem

   a. _____

   b. _____

4. when \ visit \ they

   a. _____

   b. _____

▶ **Practice 22. Forms of the past progressive.** (Chart 9-9)
Create your own chart by completing the sentences with ***study*** and the correct form of the past progressive.

1. I _____ *was studying.* _____

2. You _____

3. He _____

4. She _____

5. Ray and I _____

6. Several students _____

7. We (not) _____

8. My children (not) _____

9. Dr. Roberts (not) _____

10. My friends and I (not) _____

11. Your friends (not) _____

12. I (not) _____

► **Practice 23. Forms of the present and past progressive.** (Chart 9-9)
Complete the sentences. Use a form of **be + sit**.

1. I _____ *am sitting* _____ in class right now.

2. I _____ *was sitting* _____ in class yesterday too.

3. You _____ in class right now.

4. You _____ in class yesterday too.

5. Tony _____ in class right now.

6. He _____ in class yesterday too.

7. We _____ in class today.

8. We _____ in class yesterday too.

9. Rita _____ in class now.

10. She _____ in class yesterday too.

11. Rita and Tony _____ in class today.

12. They _____ in class yesterday too.

► **Practice 24. *While* + past progressive.** (Chart 9-10)
Combine the sentences in each pair and add the correct punctuation. Use **while**.

1. We felt an earthquake.
   We were sitting in our living room last night.

   a. _____ *We felt an earthquake while we were sitting in our living room last night.* _____

   b. _____ *While we were sitting in our living room last night, we felt an earthquake.* _____

2. I was talking to the teacher yesterday.
   Another student interrupted me.

   a. While I was Talking to the teacher Yesterday
      another student interrupted me.

   b. _____ another student interrupted while I was
      Talking to the teacher

3. A police officer stopped another driver for speeding.
   We were driving to work.

   a. _____

   b. _____

4. I was walking in the forest.
   A dead tree fell over.

   a. _____

   b. _____

5. I was planting flowers in the garden.
   My dog began to bark at a squirrel.

   a. _____

   b. _____

a squirrel

▶ **Practice 25. *While* + past progressive.** (Chart 9-10)
Complete each sentence with the correct form of the verb.

While Tom (*drive*) _____*was driving*_____ down the road yesterday, his cell phone
                              1

(*ring*) _____. He (*answer, not*) _____ it because he
              2   3

(*want*) _____ to be careful. He (*notice*) _____ many drivers with
              4   5

cell phones. While he (*slow*) _____ down to make a turn, the driver
                                          6

in front of him suddenly (*drive*) _____ off the road into a ditch. Tom (*see*)
                                              7

_____ a cell phone in her hand.
        8

► **Practice 26. *While* + past progressive.** (Chart 9-10)
Complete each sentence with the correct form of the verb in parentheses.

A: My husband and I (*be*) _____were_____ at my cousin's last night. While we (*sit*)
    1

_____ outside in the garden after dinner, her cat (*come*)
                    2

_____ up to us with a snake in its mouth. I (*scream*) _____.
        3   4

B: What (*your cousin, do*) _____?
                                                        5

A: She (*yell*) _____.
                        6

B: (*your husband, do*) _____ something?
                                                    7

A: He (*run*) _____ to the house. While he (*run*) _____,
                    8   9

the cat (*run*) _____ after him. It was so funny. My cousin and I
                            10

(*begin*) _____ to laugh until tears ran down our faces.
                    11

► **Practice 27. Simple past vs. past progressive.** (Chart 9-11)
Complete each sentence with the correct form of the verb in parentheses.

1. My roommate came home late last night. I (*sleep*) _____*was sleeping*_____ when
   she (*get*) _____ home.

2. When Gina (*call*) _____ last night, I (*take*) _____ a
   bubble bath.

3. I (*eat*) _____ lunch with my brother when I suddenly (*remember*)
   _____ my promise to pick my cousin up at school.

4. When the president (*begin*) _____ to speak, everyone (*become*)
   _____ quiet.

5. While I (*drive*) _____ to the airport, I (*see*) _____ an
   accident.

6. While Joan (*exercise*) _____, a salesperson (*come*)
   _____ to the door.

7. Pete (*send*) _____ a text message while his teacher (*talk*)
   _____. She (*tell*) _____ him to put his phone away.

8. When Albert (*hear*) _____ the police siren, he (*stop*)
   _____ on the side of the road.

▶ **Practice 28. Using *while* and *when*.** (Chart 9-11)
Read the story. Complete the sentences with information from the story.

A Nonstop Talker

    While I was riding the train, a man sat down
next to me. I was reading a book, and he asked
me about it. I didn't want to talk. I just wanted to
read my book, so I tried to answer quickly. While
I was trying to finish, he interrupted me. He told
me about his job, his boss, and his family. When I
looked away, he continued to talk. When I looked
at my watch, he continued to talk. Finally, I told
him I wasn't feeling well. He began to tell me about
his health. While he was giving me details about
his doctor visits, I stood up. I excused myself and
walked to the back of the train. When I looked ten
minutes later, he was talking to another passenger.
I'm sure he is talking to someone right now!

1. While the woman was reading a book, _____

2. When she answered the man's question, _____

3. When she looked away, _____

4. When she told him she wasn't feeling well, _____

5. While he was talking about doctors, _____

6. When she looked at him later, _____

▶ **Practice 29. Question review.** (Chapter 9)
Make questions. Use any appropriate question word: ***where, when, what time, why, who,***
or ***what***.

1. A: _____*Where did Simone go?*_____
   B: To a conference. (Simone went to a conference.)

2. A: _____
   B: Last month. (Simone went to a conference last month.)

3. A: _____
   B: Simone. (Simone went to a conference last month.)

4. A: _____
   B: Ali. (I saw Ali.)

5. A: _____
   B: At the train station. (I saw Ali at the train station.)

6. A: _____
   B: At 10:00. (I saw Ali at the train station at 10:00.)

7. A: _____

   B: Grammar. (The teacher is talking about grammar.)

8. A: _____

   B: Because the weather was hot. (The kids played in the pool because the weather was hot.)

9. A: _____

   B: The doctor's office. (The doctor's office called.)

10. A: _____

    B: Yesterday afternoon. (They called yesterday afternoon.)

11. A: _____

    B: The nurse. (I talked to the nurse.)

12. A: _____

    B: At home. (I was at home last night.)

13. A: _____

    B: "Very old." (*Ancient* means "very old.")

14. A: _____

    B: In an apartment. (I live in an apartment.)

15. A: _____

    B: A frog. (Annie has a frog in her pocket.)

▶ **Practice 30. Question review.** (Chapter 9)
Make questions for the given answers.

1. A: *When did you get up this morning? / What time do we need to leave? / Etc.*
   B: At 7:00.

2. A: _____
   B: In an apartment.

3. A: _____
   B: Yesterday.

4. A: _____
   B: It means "very, very good."

5. A: _____
   B: At 7:30.

6. A: _____
   B: A shirt.

7. A: _____
   B: My professor.

8. A: _____
   B: No, I didn't.

9. A: _____
   B: Because I wanted to.

10. A: _____
    B: Chemistry.

11. A: _____
    B: Yes, I did.

12. A: _____
    B: Nothing.

13. A: _____
    B: In the dormitory.

14. A: _____
    B: Because I was tired.

15. A: _____
    B: Last night.

▶ **Practice 31. Review: irregular verbs.** (Chapters 8 and 9)
Choose a sentence from the box that best completes each idea.

It sold in three days.	He ate too much for lunch.
Someone stole his wallet.	I caught a taxi.
She hung up after midnight.	She caught a cold yesterday.
✓ He said they were too noisy.	Sam bent over and picked it up for her.
It tore when she played outside.	I grew up there.
Several students came to class without their homework.	She found it on the teacher's desk.

1. The teacher told the students to work more quietly. ___*He said they were too noisy.*___

2. Laurie doesn't feel good. _____

3. Beth lost her grammar book. _____

4. Jack had no money. _____

5. Peter didn't want dinner. _____

6. Susan didn't want to sell her car, but she needed money. _____

   _____

7. Maria wore her best dress to school. _____

   _____

8. Shelley's phone conversation began at 9:00 P.M. _____

   _____

9. Kathy dropped her pen on the floor. _____

   _____

10. I missed the bus for the airport yesterday. _____

11. The teacher was unhappy. _____

12. My hometown is Ames, Iowa. _____

▶ **Practice 32. Review: irregular verbs.** (Chapters 8 and 9)
   Complete the sentences. Use the simple past form of the verbs from the box.

break	fall	lose	meet	steal	✓ throw
cost	know	make	spend	tell	wear

1. The baseball player _____ *threw* _____ the ball to the catcher.

2. Rick _____ his arm when he fell on the ice.

3. Maggie didn't tell a lie. She _____ the truth.

4. We _____ a lot of money at the restaurant last night. The food was
   good but expensive.

5. I wrote a check yesterday. I _____ a mistake on the check, so I tore it
   up and wrote another one.

6. I _____ my winter jacket yesterday because the weather was cold.

7. Tom bought a new tie. It _____ a lot because it was a hand-painted
   silk tie.

8. Leo read the story easily. The words in the story weren't new for him. He
   _____ the vocabulary in the story.

9. I know Amanda Clark. I _____ her at a party a couple of weeks ago.

10. I dropped my book. It _____ to the floor.

11. Jack couldn't get into his apartment because he _____ his keys.

12. Someone _____ my bicycle, so I called the police.

▶ **Practice 33. Review: irregular verbs.** (Chapters 8 and 9)
Complete the sentences. Use the simple past form of the verbs from the box.

✓ begin	feed	fly	put	sing
build	fight	leave	shake	win

1. We were late for the graduation ceremony. It _____*began*_____ at 7:00, but we didn't get there until 7:15.

2. We _____ songs at the party last night and had a good time.

3. I _____ to Chicago last week. The plane was only five minutes late.

4. My plane _____ at 6:03 and arrived at 8:45.

5. We played a soccer game yesterday. The other team _____. We lost.

6. When I asked Dennis a question, he _____ his head no.

7. My daughter _____ a table in her woodworking class in high school.

8. Mike stole a spoon from the restaurant. He _____ it in his pocket before he walked out of the restaurant.

9. The two children wanted the same toy. They _____ for a few minutes. Then they decided to share it.

10. The baby was crying, so I _____ her some milk.

► **Practice 34. Verb review.** (Chapters 8 and 9)
Complete the sentences with the words in parentheses.

Part I.

Yesterday Fish (be) _____ *in the river. He*
1
(see) _____ *Bear on the bank of the river. Here is*
2
their conversation.

BEAR: Good morning, Fish.

FISH: Good morning, Bear. How (*you, be*) _____ today?
3

BEAR: I (*do*) _____ fine, thank you. And you?
4

FISH: Fine, thanks.

BEAR: (*you, would like*) _____ to get out of the river and
5

(*sit*) _____ with me? I (*need*) _____ someone to talk to.
6   7

FISH: I (*need, not*) _____ to get out of the river for us to talk. We
8

can talk just the way we are now.

BEAR: Hmm.

FISH: Wait! What (*you, do*)

_____?
9

BEAR: I (*get*) _____ in the river to join you.
10

FISH: Stop! This (*be*) _____ my river! I (*trust, not*) _____ you.
11   12

What (*you, want*) _____?
13

BEAR: Nothing. Just a little conversation. I (*want*) _____ to tell you about my
14

problems. I (*have*) _____ a bad day yesterday.
15

FISH: Oh? What happened?

Part II.

BEAR: While I was walking through the woods,

I (*see*) _____ a beehive. I (*love*)
16

_____ honey. So I (*stop*)
17

_____. When I (*reach*)
18

_____ inside the beehive
19

to get some honey, a great big bee

(come) _____ up behind me and stung* my ear. The sting (be)
            20
_____ very painful.
        21

FISH: I (believe, not) _____ you. Bees can't hurt bears. I
                            22
(believe, not) _____ your story about a great big bee. All bees (be)
                    23
_____ the same size, and they (be, not) _____ big.
        24   25

BEAR: But it is true! Here. Come a little closer and look at my ear. I'll show you where the

big bee stung it.

FISH: Okay. Where (it, be) _____? Where (the bee, sting)
                                26
_____ you?
            27

BEAR: Right here. See?

FISH: Stop! What (you, do) _____? Let go of me! Why (you, hold)
                                    28
_____ me?
            29

BEAR: I (hold) _____ you because I'm going to eat you for dinner.
                    30

FISH: Oh, no! You (trick) _____ me! Your story about the great big bee
                                31
never (happen) _____!
                    32

Part III.

BEAR: That's right. I (get) _____ in the river because I (want)
                                33
_____ (catch) _____ you for dinner. And I did! I
        34   35
(catch) _____ you for dinner.
            36

FISH: Watch out! Behind you! Oh, no! Oh, no! It's a very, very big bee. It's huge! It

(look) _____ really angry!
            37

BEAR: I (believe, not) _____ you!
                            38

FISH: But it (be) _____ true! A great big bee (come) _____
                    39   40
toward you. It's going to attack you and sting you!

---

*Stung is the past form of the verb *sting*, which means "to cause sharp pain."

BEAR: What? Where? I (*see, not*) _____ a bee! Oh, no,
41

Fish, you are getting away from me. Oh,

no! I (*drop*) _____ you!
42

Come back! Come back!

FISH: Ha! I (*fool*) _____ you too
43

Bear. Now you must find your dinner in another place.

BEAR: Yes, you (*trick*) _____ me too. We (*teach*)
44

_____ each other a good lesson today: Don't believe everything
45

you hear.

FISH: Thank you for teaching me that lesson. Now I will live a long and happy life.

BEAR: Yes, we (*learn*) _____ a valuable lesson today, and that's good.
46

But I (*be*) _____ still hungry. Hmm. I (*have*) _____
47   48

a gold tooth in my mouth. (*you, would like*) _____
49

to come closer and look at it?

Chapter 10

Expressing Future Time, Part 1

▶ **Practice 1. Forms of *be going to*.** (Chart 10-1)
Create your own chart by completing each sentence with the correct form of ***be going to***.

Tomorrow

1. I _____*am going to be*_____ absent.

2. We _____ absent.

3. She _____ absent.

4. You _____ absent.

5. They _____ absent.

6. Tim and I _____ absent.

7. Mr. Han _____ absent.

8. Mr. Han and you _____ absent.

9. He _____ absent.

10. Rick and Sam _____ absent.

▶ **Practice 2. *Be going to*.** (Chart 10-1)
Complete each sentence with the correct form of ***be going to***.

1. A: (*you, be*) _____*Are you going to be*_____ at home tomorrow morning around ten?

   B: No. I (*be*) _____ out.

2. A: (*Albert, fix*) _____ the bathroom faucet soon? It's still dripping.

   B: He already tried. I (*call*) _____ a plumber in the morning.

3. A: (*you, apply*) _____ for the security job at the mall?

   B: Yes. I (*complete*) _____ the online application tomorrow.

4. A: (*Ed and Nancy, join*) _____ us at the restaurant for dinner?

    B: Yes, they (*meet*) _____ us there at 7:00.

▶ **Practice 3. Be going to.** (Chart 10-1)
Read the story. Rewrite the second paragraph using **be going to**.

Mondays are always very busy for Antonia. She is the project manager for a construction company, and she has a long day. Here is her schedule.

She wakes up at 5:00. She has a quick breakfast of toast and coffee. She catches the 5:45 train to work. At 6:30, she has a weekly meeting with her employees. For the rest of the morning, she is at her desk. She answers phone calls and emails, and she works on project details. She answers a lot of questions. She has a big lunch at 11:00. In the afternoon, she visits job sites. She meets with builders and architects. She finishes by 7:00 and is home by 8:00.

Today is Monday. What is Antonia going to do?

_____*She is going to wake up at 5:00. She*_____

_____

_____

_____

_____

_____

_____

_____

▶ **Practice 4. Be going to.** (Chart 10-1)
Complete the sentences. Use **be going to** and the given expressions.

call the neighbors	eat a big lunch	take it back to the store
check the lost-and-found	✓ go back to bed	take some medicine
do a search on the Internet	look for a bigger place	

1. It's 8:00 A.M. and I'm very tired.

    I _____*am going to go back to bed.*_____

2. I'm hungry. I didn't have breakfast.

    I _____

3. I have a stomachache.

    I _____

4. The dog next door is barking loudly.

   I _____

5. Richard needs to get some information about earthquakes for a school project.

   He _____

6. The Smiths have a new baby. Their apartment is too small.

   They _____

7. Diane left her purse in the classroom.

   She _____

8. The zipper broke on my new dress.

   I _____

zipper

▶ **Practice 5. *Be going to.*** (Chart 10-1)
Write answers to the question ***What are you going to do?*** Use ***be going to*** in your answers.

1. You're thirsty. _____*I am going to get a drink of water.*_____

2. You have a sore throat. _____

3. You broke a tooth. _____

4. Your alarm didn't go off. You are in bed, and class starts in fifteen minutes. _____

   _____

5. It's midnight. You are wide awake, and you want to go to sleep. _____

   _____

6. You are at school. You locked your bike in a bike rack, and now it's not there. _____

   _____

► **Practice 6. Be going to: negative and question forms.** (Chart 10-1)
Create your own chart by rewriting the given sentences as negatives and questions.

	Negative	**Question**
1. I am going to eat.	_I am not going to eat._	_Am I going to eat?_
2. You are going to eat.	_____	_____
3. He is going to eat.	_____	_____
4. She is going to eat.	_____	_____
5. We are going to eat.	_____	_____
6. They are going to eat.	_____	_____
7. My friend is going to eat.	_____	_____
8. The students are going to eat.	_____	_____

► **Practice 7. Be going to: negative and question forms.** (Chart 10-1)
Complete each sentence with the correct form of the verb in parentheses. Use **be going to**.

1. A: What (*you, do*) _____are you going to do_____ next weekend?

   B: We (*go*) _are going to go_ (fishing) at a lake in the mountains.

   A: (*you, stay*) _Are you going to stay_ overnight?

   B: No. We (*come*) _Are going to come_ back the same day.

2. A: Where (*Sally, work*) _is sally going to work_ this summer?

   B: She (*work, not*) _isn't going to work_. She (*take*) _Is going to take_ summer school classes.

3. A: (*the students, have*) _Are the students going to have_ an end-of-the-year party?

   B: Yes, they are. They (*have*) _Are Going to have_ a picnic at the park near the beach.

4. A: (*Joan and Bob, move*) _Are they going to move_ next month?

   B: Yes. Joan (*start*) _Is going to start_ a new job in the city.

   A: (*they, look for*) _Are they going to look for_ a house?

   B: No, they (*look for, not*) _Aren't going to look for_ a house. They (*rent*) _Are going to rent_ an apartment.

▶ **Practice 8. Using the present progressive for future time.** (Chart 10-2)
Rewrite the sentences using the present progressive for the future verbs.

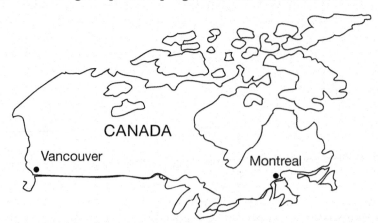

1. The Johnsons are going to take a camping trip across Canada this summer.

   The Johnsons are taking a camping trip across Canada this summer.

2. They are going to take their teenage grandchildren with them.

   _____

3. They are going to stay in parks and campgrounds.

   _____

4. They are going to leave from Vancouver in June.

   _____

5. They are going to arrive in Montreal in August.

   _____

6. Mr. and Mrs. Johnson are going to drive back home alone.

   _____

7. Their grandchildren are going to fly home because they don't want to miss the beginning of school.

   _____

   _____

8. Their parents are going to meet them at the airport.

   _____

▶ **Practice 9. Using the present progressive for future time.** (Chart 10-2)
Write "P" if the sentence has a present meaning. Write "F" if the sentence has a future meaning.

1. __P__ Wait! I'm coming.

2. _____ I'm coming at 8:00 tonight.

3. _____ Wait—what are you doing?

4. _____ Ron is taking us to the airport soon.

5. _____ I'm returning this library book. I'm sorry it's late.

6. _____ We're flying to Rome in a few weeks.

7. _____ A: Joe, are you leaving?

   _____ B: No, I'm not going. I'm staying.

8. _____ Claude and Marie are spending their next vacation hiking in the mountains.

▶ **Practice 10. Using *yesterday, last, tomorrow, next, in*, or *ago*.** (Chart 10-3)
Complete the phrases with the appropriate time word.

1. I left for my trip . . .

   a. ___yesterday___ afternoon.

   b. _____ fall.

   c. _____ week.

   d. _____ weekend.

   e. _____ morning.

   f. two hours _____.

   g. _____ month.

   h. three months _____.

   i. _____ night.

   j. _____ evening.

2. Sam is going to leave for his trip . . .

   a. ___tomorrow___ afternoon.

   b. _____ fall.

   c. _____ week.

   d. _____ weekend.

   e. _____ morning.

   f. _____ two hours.

   g. _____ month.

   h. _____ three months.

   i. _____ night.

   j. _____ evening.

► **Practice 11. Using *yesterday, last, tomorrow, next, in,* or *ago.*** (Chart 10-3)
Complete the sentences. Use *yesterday*, *last*, *tomorrow*, *next*, *in*, or *ago*.

1. I went to Hawaii _____*last*_____ year.

2. I went to Hawaii a year _____.

3. My sister went to Singapore a week _____.

4. My sister went to Singapore _____ week.

5. Our neighbors are going to Iceland _____ Friday.

6. We're going to Morocco _____ two weeks.

7. My parents went to Costa Rica _____ afternoon.

8. Their friends are going to Costa Rica _____ morning.

9. My cousins are going to Kenya _____ three weeks.

10. Were you home _____ afternoon around 4:00?

11. Were you home _____ night around 9:00?

12. Are you going to be in the office _____ afternoon around 3:00?

13. I wasn't at work two days _____.

14. I'm not going to be at work _____ Thursday.

► **Practice 12. Using *a couple of* with past and future.** (Chart 10-4)
Check (✓) the expressions that can mean *a couple of*. Rewrite the expressions using
a couple of.

1. ___✓___ two hours   _____*a couple of hours*_____

2. _____ seven minutes   _____

3. _____ five days   _____

4. _____ six years   _____

5. _____ three months   _____

6. _____ two years   _____

7. _____ four hours   _____

8. _____ one minute   _____

9. _____ two weeks   _____

▶ **Practice 13. Using *a few* with past and future.** (Chart 10-4)
Check (✓) the expressions that can mean *a few*. Rewrite the expressions using *a few*.

1. __✓__ five minutes   __a few minutes_____

2. _____ seven months   _____

3. _____ four hours   _____

4. _____ three days   _____

5. _____ ten weeks   _____

6. _____ five years   _____

7. _____ one day   _____

▶ **Practice 14. Using *a couple of* or *a few* with past and future.** (Chart 10-4)
Make sentences using the given words.

1. I \ leave

   a. (*in a few days*)

   _____ *I am going to leave in a few days.*_____

   b. (*a few days ago*)

   _____ *I left a few days ago.*_____

2. Susie \ marry Paul

   a. (*a couple of months ago*)

   _____

   b. (*in a couple of months*)

   _____

3. Dr. Nelson \ retire

   a. (*a few years ago*)

   _____

   b. (*in a few years*)

   _____

4. Jack \ begin a new job

    a. (*a couple of days ago*)

    _____

    b. (*in a couple of days*)

    _____

▶ **Practice 15. Using *this* with time words and *today* or *tonight*.** (Chart 10-5)
Circle the meaning of each sentence: past, present, or future time.

1. Tom is going to finish school this June.	past	present	(future)
2. We took my parents to the airport this morning.	past	present	future
3. Nancy is at her grandmother's. She is cleaning her house this morning.	past	present	future
4. Mrs. Andrew had lunch with friends today.	past	present	future
5. Our secretary is going to retire this month.	past	present	future
6. The children are studying dinosaurs this month.	past	present	future
7. I am doing a lot of work today.	past	present	future
8. We heard about an interesting movie this morning.	past	present	future
9. You are going to have a good time tonight.	past	present	future
10. I had fun this evening.	past	present	future
11. Are you going to be home this afternoon?	past	present	future

▶ **Practice 16. Using time words.** (Chart 10-5)
Read the description of Sophia's morning. Then choose all the correct completions.

It's 6:00 A.M. Sophia is late and needs to hurry. She is taking a shower. Then she is going to get dressed, have breakfast, and go to school.

1. Sophia woke up early	(this morning,)	(today.)	right now.
2. She is late	this morning.	today.	right now.
3. She is going to go to school	this morning.	today.	right now.
4. She is going to have breakfast	this morning.	today.	right now.
5. She is in a hurry	this morning.	today.	right now.
6. She got up before 6:00	this morning.	today.	right now.

▶ **Practice 17. Using *this* with time words.** (Chart 10-5)
Read the story about Sara. Then answer the questions.

   Right now, I'm sitting in my kitchen. I'm thinking about going to school. This morning I woke up late. I overslept and missed my math class. I have an important chemistry test this afternoon. I have a problem. I don't want to miss it, but my chemistry teacher is also my math teacher. I'm not sure what to do. How do I explain my absence from my math class? I'm going to sit at the kitchen table and think about a solution.

1. What are two things Sara did this morning?

   a. _____*She woke up late.*_____

   b. _____

2. What are two things Sara is going to do this morning?

   a. _____

   b. _____

3. What is one thing Sara is doing this morning?

   _____

▶ **Practice 18. Forms of *will*.** (Chart 10-6)
Create your own chart by completing the sentences with the correct forms of *will*.

1. We aren't late.	We	_____*will be*_____ there soon.
2. You aren't late.	You	_____ there soon.
3. They aren't late.	They	_____ there soon.
4. She isn't late.	She	_____ there soon.
5. I'm not late.	I	_____ there soon.
6. The students aren't late.	The students	_____ there soon.
7. My mother isn't late.	My mother	_____ there soon.
8. He isn't late.	He	_____ there soon.
9. Jill and I aren't late.	Jill and I	_____ there soon.
10. Eva and her son aren't late.	Eva and her son	_____ there soon.

► **Practice 19. Using *will*.** (Chart 10-6)
Imagine you are a tourist in San Francisco. What are you going to do? Complete the sentences with ***will*** or ***won't***.

1. I _____ take a tour of the city.

2. I _____ ride a cable car.

3. I _____ walk across the Golden Gate Bridge.

4. I _____ practice my English.

5. I _____ speak my own language.

6. I _____ visit the Walt Disney Family Museum.

7. I _____ see the famous flower gardens at Golden Gate Park.

8. I _____ walk to the top of Telegraph Hill for beautiful views of the city.

9. I _____ eat fresh seafood at Fisherman's Wharf.

10. I _____ take the ferry to Alcatraz Island.

a cable car

the Golden Gate Bridge

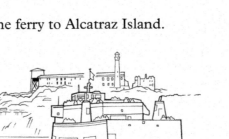

a ferry to Alcatraz Island

► **Practice 20. Using *will*.** (Chart 10-6)
What will happen fifty years from now? Complete each sentence with ***will*** or ***won't*** and the verb in parentheses.

Fifty years from now . . .

1. most people (*live*) _____ to be 100.

2. people (*travel*) _____ to other planets.

3. students (*study*) _____ at home with computers, not at school.

4. students (*study*) _____ in the classroom.

5. some people (*live*) _____ in underwater homes.

6. scientists (*discover*) _____ cures for serious diseases like cancer and AIDS.

7. there (*be*) _____ wars.

8. the world (*be*) _____ peaceful.

▶ **Practice 21. *Will.*** (Chart 10-6)
Change the sentences by using *will* to express future time.

1. Class is ~~going to finish~~ a few minutes early today.

   _____*Class will finish a few minutes early today.*_____

2. You are ~~going to need~~ extra chairs for the party.

   ~~*You* Will need extra chairs for the party~~

3. Hurry or we aren't ~~going~~ to be on time for the movie.

   Hurry will not be on time for the movie

4. Your brother and sister ~~are going~~ to help you with your science project.

   Will help you with your science

5. The bus isn't ~~going to~~ be on time today.

   Won't be on time today

6. Watch out! You're ~~going to~~ cut yourself with that sharp knife.

   will cut

7. Carlos and Olivia ~~are going~~ to graduate from nursing school with high grades.

   C Will graduate from nursing school with high grades.

▶ **Practice 22. Questions with *will.*** (Chart 10-7)
Make questions using the given words.

In the future

How did she do the Homework

1. you \ live to be 100 years old?

   _____*Will you live to be 100 years old?*_____

2. your friends \ live to be 100 years old?

   Will your friends live to be 100 years old

3. your children \ live to be 100 years old?

will your children live to 100 years old _____

4. we \ live on another planet?

will we live on another planet? _____

5. my friends \ live on another planet?

_____

6. some people \ live underwater?

_____

7. I \ live underwater?

_____

8. countries \ find a solution for poverty?

_____

▶ **Practice 23. Forms of *be going to* and *will*.** (Chart 10-8)
Complete each sentence with the correct form of the verb.

be going to + *go*	*will* + *go*

Statement

1. I _____ *am going to go* _____ .   I _____ *will go* _____ .

2. You _____ .   You _____ .

3. The students _____ .   The students _____ .

4. Ms. Jenkins _____ .   Ms. Jenkins _____ .

5. Our friends _____ .   Our friends _____ .

Negative

6. Mr. Davis (*not*) _____ .   Mr. Davis (*not*) _____ .

7. I (*not*) _____ .   I (*not*) _____ .

8. We (*not*) _____ .   We (*not*) _____ .

Question

9. (*she, go*) _____ ?   (*she, go*) _____ ?

10. (*they, go*) _____ ?   (*they, go*) _____ ?

11. (*you, go*) _____ ?   (*you, go*) _____ ?

► **Practice 24. Verb review: present, past, and future.** (Chart 10-8)
Make questions with the given words. Use **will** for future tense.

1. you \ need \ help \ now?

   Do you need help now?

2. you \ need \ help \ tomorrow?

   _____

3. you \ need \ help \ yesterday?

   _____

4. Eva \ need \ help \ yesterday?

   _____

5. Eva \ need \ help \ tomorrow?

   _____

6. Eva \ need \ help \ now?

   _____

7. the students \ need \ help \ now?

   _____

8. the students \ need \ help \ tomorrow?

   _____

9. the students \ need \ help \ yesterday?

   _____

► **Practice 25. Verb review: present, past, and future.** (Chart 10-8)
Complete each sentence with the correct form of the verb in parentheses.

1. Right now, Noor (*eat*) _____ _is eating_ _____ fish for lunch.

2. She (*eat*) _____ fish for lunch once or twice a week.

3. She also (*eat*) _____ chicken often.

4. She usually (*have*) _____ chicken for dinner.

5. Last night Noor (*cook*) _____ a spicy chicken and rice dish for her
   friends.

6. It (*be*) _____ delicious, and they (*love*) _____ it.

7. While she was cooking dinner, she (*drop*)

_____ a pan of hot oil on the floor, but

fortunately she (*be*) _____ okay.

It (*burn, not*) _____ her.

8. Tomorrow Noor (*invite*) _____ her

parents over for lunch.

9. (*she, cook*) _____ fish?

10. (*she, make*) _____ chicken?

11. Maybe she (*prepare, not*) _____ chicken

or fish.

12. Maybe she (*surprise*) _____ her parents

with a completely new dish.

▶ **Practice 26. Verb review: *be*** (Chart 10-9)
Make sentences with the given words.

1. you \ be \ sick \ now?

_____*Are you sick now?*_____

2. you \ be \ sick \ tomorrow?

_____

3. you \ be \ sick \ yesterday?

_____

4. Steve \ be \ sick \ yesterday?

_____

5. Steve \ be \ sick \ tomorrow?

_____

6. Steve \ be \ sick \ now?

_____

7. your kids \ be \ sick \ now?

_____

8. your kids \ be \ sick \ tomorrow?

_____

9. your kids \ be \ sick \ yesterday?

_____

▶ **Practice 27. Verb review: _be_.** (Chart 10-9)
Complete each sentence with the correct form of the verb in parentheses.

1. I (_be_) _____ _am_ _____ very busy today. Right now, I (_be_) _____ in Quebec. Tomorrow I (_be_) _____ in New York. Yesterday I (_be_) _____ in Paris. I (_be_) _____ home next week.

2. A: Where (_you, be_) _____ last night? (_you, be_) _____ _____ at home?

   B: No, I (_be, not_) _____. I (_be_) _____ at the library with my friends.

   A: I (_be_) _____ there too. Where (_you, be_) _____?

   B: We (_be_) _____ in the study area.

   A: Oh. I (_be_) _____ in the reference section.

3. A: (_the post office, be_) _____ open now?

   B: No, it (_be, not_) _____. Today (_be_) _____ a national holiday.

   A: What about banks? (_they, be_) _____ open?

   B: No, they (_be, not_) _____. All the banks (_be_) _____ closed.

▶ **Practice 28. Simple present questions.** (Charts 10-8 and 10-9)
Complete the sentences with _are_ or _do_.

Isabella is starting a new job this morning. Her mother is asking her questions on the phone.

1. _____ _Do_ _____ you need to get there early?

2. _____ you nervous or excited?

3. _____ you feel nervous or excited?

4. _____ you know your co-workers' names?

5. _____ you ready to begin?

6. _____ you need ID?

7. _____ you have your cell phone?

8. _____ you taking the bus or subway?

9. _____ you want me to call you later?

▶ **Practice 29. Simple past questions.** (Charts 10-8 and 10-9)
Complete the sentences with **were** or **did**.

Dan had an important math test this morning. A friend is asking him about it.

1. _____*Did*_____ you study for the test last night?

2. _____ you get enough sleep?

3. _____ you nervous this morning?

4. _____ you ready for the test?

5. _____ you do well?

6. _____ you make any mistakes?

7. _____ you get 100%?

8. _____ you happy when you finished?

Math test
$3(a+15)=60$
$3a+45=60$
100% $a=5$

▶ **Practice 30. Verb review: present, past, and future.** (Charts 10-8 and 10-9)
Complete the chart with the correct forms of the verbs.

Every Day / Now	Yesterday	Tomorrow
1. I **drink** tea every day. I _____*am drinking*_____ tea now.	I _____*drank*_____ tea yesterday.	I _____*am going to drink*_____ tea tomorrow. I _____*will drink*_____ tea tomorrow.
2. We **work** every day. We _____ now.	We _____ yesterday.	We _____ tomorrow. We _____ tomorrow.
3. She **is** late every day. She _____ late now.	She _____ late yesterday.	She _____ late tomorrow. She _____ late tomorrow.
4. You _____ me every day. You _____ me now.	You **helped** me yesterday.	You _____ me tomorrow. You _____ me tomorrow.

Every Day / Now	Yesterday	Tomorrow
5. She **doesn't come** every day. She _____ now.	She _____ yesterday.	She _____ tomorrow. She _____ tomorrow.
6. She _____ the dishes every day. She **isn't doing** the dishes now.	She _____ the dishes yesterday.	She _____ the dishes tomorrow. She _____ the dishes tomorrow.
7. _____ every day? **Are they exercising** now?	_____ yesterday?	_____ tomorrow? _____ tomorrow?
8. _____ on time every day? _____ on time now?	**Was he** on time yesterday?	_____ on time tomorrow? _____ on time tomorrow?
9. She **isn't** on time every day. She _____ on time now.	She _____ on time yesterday.	She _____ on time tomorrow. She _____ on time tomorrow.

▶ **Practice 31. Verb review: past, present, and future.** (Charts 10-8 and 10-9)
Complete the sentences. Use the words in parentheses. Use any appropriate verb form.

1. A: I (lose) _____ *lost* _____ my sunglasses yesterday.

   B: Where?

   A: I probably (leave) _____ them on a table at the restaurant.

2. A: What (you, wear) _____ to the party next weekend?

   B: I (wear) _____ my jeans. It (be) _____
   _____ a casual party.

3. A: Sometimes children tell little lies. You talked to Annie. (she, tell)
   _____ the truth, or (she, tell) _____ a lie?

   B: She (tell) _____ the truth. She's honest.

4. A: How are you getting along?

   B: Fine. (I, make) _____ a lot of friends, and my English (get)
   _____ better.

5. A: What are you going to do tonight? (*you, study*) _____
   _____?

   B: No. I (*have, not*) _____ any homework.

   A: Really?

   B: Our teacher (*give*) _____ us a lot of work last week. She (*give*)
   _____ us a break this week.

6. A: Mark's wedding is next weekend. (*you, be*) _____
   there?

   B: No. I have to take my dad home from the hospital on Saturday. He (*have*)
   _____ surgery in a few days.

   A: Really? That's too bad.

   B: He (*break*) _____ his leg last year, and it (*heal, not*)
   _____ properly.

7. A: Good morning.

   B: Excuse me?

   A: I (*say*) _____, "Good morning."

   B: Oh! Good morning! I'm sorry. I (*understand, not*)
   _____ at first.

8. A: Where (*Cathy, be*) _____? I need to talk to her.

   B: She (*meet*) _____ with some students right now.

9. I almost (*have*) _____ an accident yesterday. A dog (*run*)
   _____ into the street in front of my car. I (*slam*) _____
   on my brakes and just (*miss*) _____ the dog.

10. A: (*you, call*) _____ George tomorrow? It's his birthday.

    B: Thank you for the reminder! I always (*forget*) _____ his birthday.

▶ **Practice 32. Verb review: past, present, and future.** (Charts 10-8 and 10-9)
Choose the correct verbs.

Jack and the Beanstalk

A long time ago, a boy named Jack (*is living / lived*) with his mother. They (*are / were*) very
₁ poor. They (*didn't have / don't have*) money for food. His mother (*decided / was deciding*) to sell
₃ their cow.

So, Jack (*is taking / took*) the cow to town. He (*met / was meeting*) a man. The man said,
₅ "I (*buy / will buy*)" your cow. I (*will give / give*) you magic beans. Jack (*took / was taking*) the
₇ beans to his mother. She (*was / did*) very angry. She said, "You (*be / are*) a stupid boy. Now
₁₀ we (*don't have / not have*) anything."
₁₂

Before he went to bed, Jack (*threw / is throwing*) the beans out the window. The next
₁₃ morning, he (*was seeing / saw*) a big beanstalk outside his window. He (*climbed / is climbing*) it
₁₄ and (*found / was finding*) a castle. A giant's wife told him, "You need to hide. My husband
₁₆ (*eats / will eat*) you for breakfast." She hid Jack in the oven.
₁₇

The giant smelled Jack. He asked his wife, "(*Are you going to give / Do you give*) me a boy
₁₈ for breakfast? She answered, "No, that smell (*is / will be*) the boy from last week."
₁₉

After the giant (*fell / is going to fall*) asleep, Jack took some of the giant's money
₂₀ and escaped.

His mother (*did / was*) very happy. She (*didn't want / no want*)
₂₁   ₂₂
Jack to go back to the castle. But Jack (*was going / went*)
₂₃ back to the castle two more times. He got a hen, golden eggs,
and a harp.

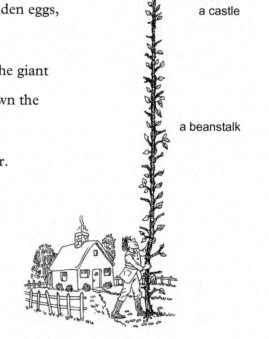

a castle

The giant (*never caught / is never catching*) Jack. The giant
₂₄ (*is going to run / ran*) after Jack, but Jack chopped down the
₂₅ beanstalk and the giant (*died / was dying*).
₂₆

a beanstalk

Jack and his mother (*lives / lived*) happily ever after.
₂₇

Chapter 11

Expressing Future Time, Part 2

▶ **Practice 1. May, might, or will.** (Chart 11-1)
Circle the meaning of each sentence: sure or unsure.

1. It may be stormy tomorrow.   sure   (unsure)
2. I will be absent next week.   sure   unsure
3. Joe and Jeff won't be at work tomorrow.   sure   unsure
4. We might take a trip next week.   sure   unsure
5. Sandra may take a vacation soon.   sure   unsure
6. We won't go camping next week.   sure   unsure
7. Our English class may get together for dinner soon.   sure   unsure
8. Some of our teachers might be there.   sure   unsure
9. Some of our teachers won't be there.   sure   unsure

▶ **Practice 2. May, might, or will.** (Chart 11-1)
Complete the sentences with **may**, **might**, **will**, or **won't** and the verb in parentheses. Give your own opinion.

One hundred years from now, . . .

1. the earth (*be*) _____ very hot.

2. cars (*fly*) _____ .

3. people (*travel*) _____ easily to space.

4. all school courses (*be*) _____ online.

5. there (*be*) _____ enough food and water for everyone in the world.

6. 100% of our energy for electricity (*come*) _____ from the sun.

7. everyone (*speak*) _____ the same language.

8. everyone (*live*) _____ in peace.

▶ **Practice 3. *Maybe* vs. *may be.*** (Chart 11-2)
Make sentences using the given words.

1. It \ be \ sunny tomorrow

   a. *(may)* _____ It may be sunny tomorrow. _____

   b. *(maybe)* Maybe it will be sunny tomorrow. _____

2. You \ need to see \ a doctor soon

   a. *(might)* _____

   b. *(maybe)* _____

3. We \ play \ basketball after school

   a. *(may)* _____

   b. *(might)* _____

4. Our class \ go \ to a movie together

   a. *(maybe)* _____

   b. *(may)* _____

▶ **Practice 4. *Maybe* vs. *may be.*** (Chart 11-2)
Circle the letters of the correct sentences. In some cases, both sentences may be correct.

1. ⓐ I may need your advice.
   ⓑ Maybe I will need your advice.

2. a. The teacher may give a surprise quiz tomorrow.
   b. The teacher maybe will give a surprise quiz tomorrow.

3. a. Maybe all the students do well.
   b. Maybe all the students will do well.

4. a. Maybe traffic will be heavy later.
   b. Maybe traffic is heavy later.

5. a. You may will need more time.
   b. Maybe you will need more time.

6. a. We may delay our trip for a few days.
   b. Maybe we will delay our trip for a few days.

7. a. Maybe they are come.
   b. Maybe they will come.

▶ **Practice 5. *May, might,* and *maybe.*** (Charts 11-1 and 11-2)
Rewrite the given sentences.

Tomorrow	*May*	*Might*
1. Maybe I will come.	I may come.	I might come.
2. Maybe they will come.		

	Might	*May*
3. Maybe she won't study.		
4. Maybe we won't need help.		
5. Maybe I won't need help.		

	May	*Maybe*
6. He might understand.		
7. You might understand.		
8. They might understand.		

▶ **Practice 6. Review: *Maybe, may, might,* and *will.*** (Chart 11-2)
Make sentences with the given words and the ideas in parentheses. Use *maybe*, *may*, *might*, or *will*.

1. It \ snow \ tomorrow (*you are sure*)

   _____It will snow tomorrow._____

2. It \ snow \ next week (*you are unsure*)

   _____

3. We \ go ice-skating on the lake (*you are unsure*)

   _____

4. The kids \ play in the snow (*you are sure*)

   _____

5. The snow \ melt, not \ for several days (*you are sure*)

   _____

▶ **Practice 7. Review:** *Maybe, may, might,* **and** *will.* (Chart 11-2)
Choose all the grammatically correct sentences.

1. (a.) Maybe I am going to skip class tomorrow.

   b. Maybe I skip class tomorrow.

  (c.) I might skip class tomorrow.

  (d.) Maybe I will skip class tomorrow.

2. a. It will snow in the mountains next week.

   b. It might snow in the mountains next week.

   c. Maybe it snows in the mountains next week.

   d. Maybe it will snow in the mountains next week.

3. a. We may not have a warm summer this year.

   b. We won't have a warm summer this year.

   c. Maybe we won't have a warm summer this year.

   d. Maybe we don't have a warm summer this year.

4. a. Maybe you are need extra time for the test tomorrow.

   b. You might need extra time for the test tomorrow.

   c. You may be need extra time for the test tomorrow.

   d. Maybe you will need extra time for the test tomorrow.

▶ **Practice 8.** *Before* **and** *after.* (Chart 11-3)
Look at the pairs of sentences. Decide which action happens first and which happens second. Then write two sentences: one with *before* and one with *after*. Use a form of *be going to* in the main clause.

1.   __1__ I boil the water.

   __2__ I put in the rice.

  a. ___*Before I put in the rice, I am going to boil the water.*___

  b. ___*After I boil the water, I am going to put in the rice.*___

2.   _____ I turn in my homework.

   _____ I check my answers.

  a. _____

  b. _____

3. _____ I wash the dishes.

    _____ I clear off the table.

    a. _____

    b. _____

4. _____ I get my umbrella.

    _____ I go out in the rain.

    a. _____

    b. _____

5. _____ I board the airplane.

    _____ I go to the departure gate.

    a. _____

    b. _____

▶ **Practice 9. _Before_, _after_, and _when_.** (Chart 11-3)
Write logical sentences with the given words.

Carlos is a student. What is he going to do tomorrow?

1. make breakfast \ get up

    After _____ _he gets up, he is going to make breakfast._ _____

2. eat breakfast \ go to school

    Before _____

3. go to his classroom \ get to school

    After _____

4. have lunch in the cafeteria \ talk to his friends

    When _____

5. cook dinner for his roommates \ pick up food at the grocery store

   Before _____

6. do his homework \ go to bed

   Before _____

7. fall asleep \ have good dreams

   After _____

▶ **Practice 10. *Before, after,* and *when.*** (Chart 11-3)
Complete each sentence with the verb in parentheses. Use ***be going to*** for future.

1. Before I (*fix*)_____*fix*_____ dinner tonight, I (*get*) _____*am going to get*_____
   fresh vegetables from my garden.

2. After I (*have*) _____ dinner, I (*go*) _____ out with
   friends for dessert.

3. When I (*see*) _____ my friends, we (*make*) _____
   plans for a camping trip this summer.

4. Before Susan (*take*) _____ the driving test next week, she (*practice*)
   _____ with her parents.

5. When Susan (*take*) _____ the test next week, she (*feel*)
   _____ nervous.

6. After Susan (*get*) _____ her license, she (*be*) _____ a
   careful driver.

▶ **Practice 11. Clauses with *if.*** (Chart 11-4)
Complete each sentence with the correct verb in parentheses.

1. If Ellen (*wins, will win*) _____*wins*_____ a scholarship, she
   (*attends, will attend*) _____*will attend*_____ a four-year college or university.

2. If she (*goes, will go*) _____ to a college or university, she
   (*is going to study, studies*) _____ chemistry.

3. If she (*enjoys, will enjoy*) _____ chemistry, she (*takes, will take*)
   _____ pre-med★ courses.

4. She (*applies, will apply*) _____ to medical school if she
   (*is going to do, does*) _____ well in her pre-med courses.

★*pre-med* = classes that prepare a student for medical school.

5. If she (*attends, will attend*) _____ medical school, she
(*studies, is going to study*) _____ family medicine.

6. If she (*completes, is going to complete*) _____ her training, she
(*works, is going to work*) _____ around the world helping people.

▶ **Practice 12. Clauses with *if*.** (Chart 11-4)
Complete each sentence with the verb in parentheses.

1. If it (*be*) _____*is*_____ sunny tomorrow, Jake (*spend*) ___*is going to spend*___ OR
_____*will spend*_____ the day at the beach.

2. If it (*rain*) _____ tomorrow, I (*spend, not*)
_____ the day at the beach.

3. If Beth (*get*) _____ a high score on her college entrance exams, her
parents (*be*) _____ proud of her.

4. Her parents (*get*) _____ her extra help if she (*do, not*) _____
well.

5. If Mark (*get*) _____ a job as a tour guide this summer, he (*earn*)
_____ enough money for school next year.

6. If Mark (*get, not*) _____ a good job, he (*delay*) _____
_____ school for a year.

7. If Lesley (*feel*) _____ sick tomorrow, she (*come, not*) _____
_____ to school.

8. She (*call*) _____ you for the homework assignments if she (*miss*)
_____ class.

9. If Brian (*need*) _____ help this weekend, we (*help*) _____ him.

10. We (*make*) _____ other plans if he (*need, not*) _____
help next week.

▶ **Practice 13. *Before, after*, and *if*.** (Charts 11-3 and 11-4)
Complete the sentences with the words in parentheses.

On Ana's birthday, Alex is going to ask Ana to marry him.

He (*ask*) _*is going to ask / will ask*_ her after they
                              1

(*celebrate*) _____*celebrate*_____ her birthday at a
                         2

restaurant. Before Alex (*talk*) _____ to Ana,
                                                3

he (*meet*) _____ with her parents.
                        4

If they (*agree*) _____ , Alex (*buy*) _____
₅   ₆

an engagement ring for Ana. If Ana (*say*) _____ "yes,"
₇

Alex (*surprise*) _____ her with the ring. If Ana (*say, not*)
₈

_____ "yes," Alex (*save*) _____ the ring and try
₉   ₁₀

again later.

▶ **Practice 14. Time clauses and questions.** (Charts 11-3 and 11-4)
Read the story about Frank. Write questions with ***will***. Then give short answers using ***will*** or
won't.

Frank has a good job as an IT* employee. He is the owner's son, but he is lazy. His co-
workers don't like to work with him. His father is going to fire him if he doesn't change his
work habits. Beginning Monday, Frank is going to get to work on time. He isn't going to stay
up late the night before work. He isn't going to fall asleep at his desk. He is going to read all
his emails before he deletes them. He is going to answer his phone and check his voice mails.
He is going to help his co-workers when they ask. He isn't going to tell them he is too busy.
His father and co-workers are going to be happy with Frank's work.

1. change his behavior

   _____ *Will he change his behavior? Yes, he will.* _____

2. get to work on time

   _____

   _____

*IT = information technology.

3. stay awake at work

_____

4. delete emails before he reads them

_____

5. answer his phone

_____

6. help his co-workers when they ask

_____

7. tell his co-workers he is too busy

_____

8. his father and co-workers be happy

_____

▶ **Practice 15. Habitual present.** (Chart 11-5)
Make sentences using the habitual present.

Part I. Match each word or phrase in Column A with a phrase in Column B. Write the letter in the blank.

Column A

1. __*f*__ drink too much coffee

2. _____ cry

3. _____ not pay my electric bill

4. _____ the phone rings in the middle of the night

5. _____ get to work late

6. _____ have a big breakfast

7. _____ not do my homework

Column B

a. my eyes get red

b. stay at work late

c. not answer it

d. get low grades on the tests

e. have no electricity

✓ f. feel shaky and nervous

g. have a lot of energy

Part II. Now, write habitual present sentences beginning with *If I* . . . .

1. _____*If I drink too much coffee, I feel shaky and nervous.*_____

2. _____

3. _____

4. _____

5. _____

6. _____

7. _____

▶ **Practice 16. Habitual present.** (Chart 11-5)
Answer the questions. Pay special attention to punctuation.

1. How do you feel if you're late for class?

   a. ___*If I'm late for class, I feel nervous.*___

   b. ___*I feel nervous if I'm late for class.*___

2. How do you feel after you eat too much?

   a. After _____

   _____

   b. _____

   after _____

3. What do you do if you get a headache?

   a. If _____

   b. _____ if _____

4. What do you do when your teacher talks too fast?

   a. When _____

   b. _____ when _____

▶ **Practice 17. Habitual present vs. future.** (Chart 11-5)
Circle *present habit* or *future* for each sentence.

1. When I'm tired, I take a nap.   ⟨present habit⟩   future

2. If I'm tired, I'm going to take a nap.   present habit   future

3. After the café closes, the manager will clean the
   kitchen.   present habit   future

4. After the café closes, the manager cleans the kitchen.   present habit   future

5. Before I get up, I listen to the news on the radio.   present habit   future

6. When Nancy moves to the city, she is going to sell
   her car.   present habit   future

7. Tim is going to check out of his hotel room before
   he has breakfast.   present habit   future

8. When Tim goes to the airport, he takes a taxi.   present habit   future

9. After Tim checks out of his hotel, he will call for
   a taxi.   present habit   future

▶ **Practice 18. Habitual present vs. future.** (Chart 11-5)
Complete the sentences with the words in parentheses. Use **be going to** for future.

1. My friends and I (*like*) _____*like*_____ to go swimming in the lake if the weather (*be*)
   _____*is*_____ warm.

2. We (*go*) _____ swimming tomorrow if the weather (*be*)
   _____ warm.

3. Before I (*go*) _____ to class today, I (*meet*) _____
   my friends for coffee.

4. Before I (*go*) _____ to my first class, I (*meet, usually*)
   _____ my friends in the cafeteria.

5. I (*buy*) _____ some stamps when I (*go*) _____
   to the post office this afternoon.

6. Jim (*be*) _____ often tired when he (*get*) _____ home from
   work. If he (*feel*) _____ tired, he (*exercise*) _____ for thirty
   minutes. After he (*exercise*) _____, he (*begin*) _____ to feel
   better.

7. If I (*be*) _____ tired tonight, I (*exercise, not*) _____.
   I need to work late at the office tonight.

8. When Mrs. Rose (*travel*) _____ by plane, she
   (*bring*) _____ her own snacks.

9. When she (*travel*) _____ to New York next
   week, she (*pack*) _____ enough food for lunch
   and dinner.

10. Jane is usually on time for appointments. When she (*be*) _____
    late for an appointment, she (*begin*) _____ to feel nervous.

11. Jane is late for work now. She is stuck in traffic. When she (*get*) _____ to
    work, she (*tell*) _____ her co-workers about the heavy traffic.

► **Practice 19.** *What + do.* (Chart 11-6)

Make questions for the given answers using a form of *do*.

1. _____*What are they doing*_____ now? They're taking a break.

2. _____ yesterday? They took a break.

3. _____ tomorrow? They're going to take a break.

4. _____ tomorrow? They will take a break.

5. _____ at 11:00 every day? They take a break.

6. _____ now? He's meeting with the teacher now.

7. _____ last week? We studied at the library.

8. _____ next week? Mara is going to quit her job.

9. _____ next week? I'm going to apply for Mara's
job.

10. _____? I work at a hotel. I'm an assistant
manager.

11. _____? Carlo is a chef at a five-star restaurant.

▶ **Practice 20. Asking about jobs.** (Chart 11-6)
Make questions for the given answers using a form of *do*.

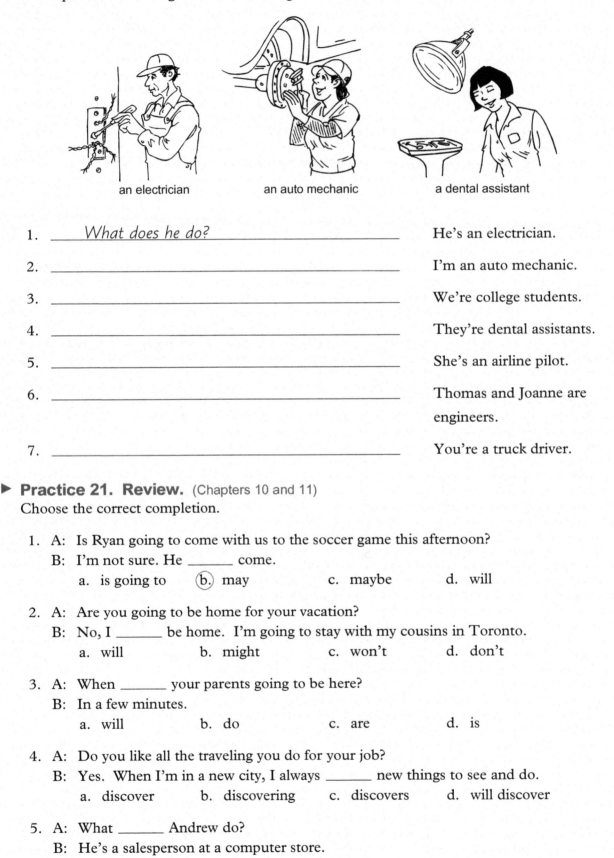

an electrician   an auto mechanic   a dental assistant

1. _____*What does he do?*_____ He's an electrician.

2. _____ I'm an auto mechanic.

3. _____ We're college students.

4. _____ They're dental assistants.

5. _____ She's an airline pilot.

6. _____ Thomas and Joanne are
                                              engineers.

7. _____ You're a truck driver.

▶ **Practice 21. Review.** (Chapters 10 and 11)
Choose the correct completion.

1. A: Is Ryan going to come with us to the soccer game this afternoon?
   B: I'm not sure. He _____ come.
      a. is going to   (b.) may   c. maybe   d. will

2. A: Are you going to be home for your vacation?
   B: No, I _____ be home. I'm going to stay with my cousins in Toronto.
      a. will   b. might   c. won't   d. don't

3. A: When _____ your parents going to be here?
   B: In a few minutes.
      a. will   b. do   c. are   d. is

4. A: Do you like all the traveling you do for your job?
   B: Yes. When I'm in a new city, I always _____ new things to see and do.
      a. discover   b. discovering   c. discovers   d. will discover

5. A: What _____ Andrew do?
   B: He's a salesperson at a computer store.
      a. is   b. did   c. will   d. does

6. A: When are you going to pick up the clothes at the dry cleaners?

   B: In a little while. I'm going to stop there before I _____ the kids at school.

      a. pick up   b. will pick up   c. picked up   d. am going to pick up

7. A: Why is the dog barking?

   B: I don't know. _____ someone is outside.

      a. May   b. Is   c. Maybe   d. Did

8. A: When Chen _____ to Taiwan next month, who will he stay with?

   B: I think his sister, but I'm not completely sure.

      a. will go   b. go   c. goes   d. going

▶ **Practice 22. Review.** (Chapters 8 → 11)
Complete each sentence with any appropriate form of the given verbs. Use **be going to** for future.

1. A: (*you, stay*) _____ here during

   vacation next week?

   B: No. I (*take*) _____ a trip to Montreal. I

   (*visit*) _____ my cousins.

   A: How long (*you, be*) _____ away?

   B: About five days.

2. A: Is Carol here?

   B: No, she (*be, not*) _____. She (*leave*)

   _____ a few minutes ago.

   A: (*she, be*) _____ back soon?

   B: I think so.

   A: Where (*she, go*) _____?

   B: She (*go*) _____ to the drugstore.

3. A: Why (*you, wear*) _____ a cast on your

   foot?

   B: I (*break*) _____ my ankle.

   A: How?

   B: I (*step*) _____ into a hole while I was running in the park.

   a cast

4. A: (*you, see*) _____ Romero tomorrow?

   B: No, I (*have, not*) _____ time.

A: (*you, see*) _____ him any time this week?

B: Maybe Friday.

A: Could you give him this book? I (*borrow*) _____ it a few months

ago and (*forget*) _____ to return it.

B: Sure.

▶ **Practice 23. Review.** (Chapters 8 → 11)
Complete the sentences with the words in parentheses. Use any appropriate verb form. For future, use **be going to**.

Part I.

Peter and Rachel are brother and sister. Right now their parents (be) _____
1

abroad on a trip, so they (stay) _____ with their grandmother. They (like)
2

_____ to stay with her. She (make, always) _____
3   4

wonderful food for them. And she (tell) _____ them stories every night before they (go)
5

_____ to bed.
6

Before Peter and Rachel (go) _____ to bed last night, they (ask)
7

_____ their grandmother to tell them a story. She (agree) _____. The
8   9

children (put) _____ on their pajamas, (brush) _____ their teeth, and
10   11

(sit) _____ with their grandmother in her big chair to listen to the story.
12

Part II.

GRANDMA: That's good. Sit here beside me and get comfortable.

CHILDREN: What (*you, tell*) _____ us about tonight, Grandma?
13

GRANDMA: Before I (*begin*) _____ the story, I (*give*) _____ each
14   15

of you a kiss on the forehead because I love you very much.

CHILDREN: We (*love*) _____ you too, Grandma.
16

GRANDMA: Tonight I (tell) _____₁₇_____ you a story about Rabbit and Eagle. Ready?

CHILDREN: Yes!

GRANDMA: Rabbit had light gray fur and a white tail. He lived with his family in a hole in a big, grassy field. Rabbit (be) _____₁₈_____ afraid of many things, but he (be) _____₁₉_____ especially afraid of Eagle. Eagle liked to eat rabbits for dinner. One day while Rabbit was eating grass in the field, he (see) _____₂₀_____ Eagle in the sky above him. Rabbit (be) _____₂₁_____ very afraid and (run) _____₂₂_____ home to his hole as fast as he could.

Rabbit (stay) _____₂₃_____ in his hole day after day because he (be) _____₂₄_____ afraid to go outside. He (get) _____₂₅_____ very hungry, but still he (stay) _____₂₆_____ in his hole. Finally, he (find) _____₂₇_____ the courage to go outside because he (need) _____₂₈_____ (eat) _____₂₉_____ .

Carefully and slowly, he (put) _____₃₀_____ his little pink nose outside the hole. He (smell, not) _____₃₁_____ any dangerous animals. And he (see, not) _____₃₂_____ Eagle anywhere, so he (hop) _____₃₃_____ out and (find) _____₃₄_____ some delicious new grass to eat. While he was eating the grass, he (see) _____₃₅_____ a shadow on the field and (look) _____₃₆_____ up. It was Eagle! Rabbit said, "Please don't eat me, Eagle! Please don't eat me!"

Part III.

GRANDMA: On this sunny afternoon, Eagle was on her way home to her nest when she (hear) _____₃₇_____ a faint sound below her. "What is that sound?" Eagle said to herself. She looked around, but she (see, not) _____₃₈_____ anything. She (decide) _____₃₉_____ to ignore the sound and go home. She was tired and (want) _____₄₀_____ (rest) _____₄₁_____ in her nest.

Then below her, Rabbit (*say*) _____ again in a very loud voice, "Please don't eat
                            42
me, Eagle! Please don't eat me!"

This time Eagle (*hear*) _____ Rabbit clearly. Eagle (*spot*) _____
                         43   44
Rabbit in the field, (*fly*) _____ down, and (*pick*) _____ Rabbit up in her
                         45   46
talons.

"Thank you, Rabbit," said Eagle. "I was hungry and (*know, not*) _____
                                                                 47
where I could find my dinner. It's a good thing you called to me." Then Eagle (*eat*)
_____ Rabbit for dinner.
    48

Part IV.

GRANDMA: There's a lesson to learn from this story, children. If you (*be*) _____
                                                                                49
afraid and expect bad things to happen, bad things will happen. The opposite is also true.

If you (*expect*) _____ good things to happen, good things will happen. (*you,*
                      50
understand) _____?
                           51

Now it's time for bed.

CHILDREN: Please tell us another story!

GRANDMA: Not tonight. I'm tired. After I (*have*) _____ a warm drink, I (*go*)
                                                    52
_____ to bed. All of us need (*get*) _____ a good night's sleep.
        53   54
Tomorrow (*be*) _____ a busy day.
                     55

CHILDREN: What (*we, do*) _____ tomorrow?
                                         56

GRANDMA: After we (*have*) _____ breakfast, we (*go*) _____
                                57   58
to the zoo at Woodland Park. When we (*be*) _____ at the zoo, we (*see*)
                                              59
_____ lots of wonderful animals. Then in the afternoon we
      60

(see) _____ a play at the Children's Theater. But before we (see) _____
          61   62

the play, we (have) _____ a picnic lunch in the park.
                                63

CHILDREN: Wow! We (have) _____ a wonderful day tomorrow!
                                         64

GRANDMA: Now off to bed! Goodnight, Rachel and Peter. Sleep tight.*

CHILDREN: Goodnight, Grandma. Thank you for the story!

---

* *Sleep tight* means "Sleep well. Have a good night's sleep."

Chapter 12
Modals, Part 1: Expressing Ability

▶ **Practice 1. Can.** (Chart 12-1)
Create your own chart by completing each sentence with the correct form of **can + speak**.

1. I _____can speak_____ some English.

2. You _____ some English.

3. He _____ some English.

4. She _____ some English.

5. We _____ some English.

6. They _____ some English.

7. Tim and I _____ some English.

8. You and your friend _____ some English.

9. My teacher _____ some English.

10. The Yangs _____ some English.

11. Mrs. Vu _____ some English.

▶ **Practice 2. Can or can't.** (Chart 12-1)
Choose the correct answer in each sentence.

1. Dogs (can / can't) swim.

2. Dogs (can / can't) climb trees.

3. Cars (can / can't) fly.

4. Machines (can / can't) talk.

5. People (can / can't) solve problems.

6. Animals (can / can't) communicate with other animals.

▶ **Practice 3. *Can* or *can't*.** (Chart 12-1)
Make sentences about what you and other people *can* and *can't* do. Use words from the box or your own words.

do algebra	play the guitar	sail a sailboat	read Chinese characters
fly an airplane	repair a computer	run fast	speak two languages fluently

1. I _____.

2. I _____.

3. I _____.

4. My best friend _____.

5. My best friend _____.

6. My (*a person in your family*) _____.

7. My (*a person in your family*) _____.

8. My teacher _____.

▶ **Practice 4. *Can* or *can't*.** (Charts 12-1 and 12-3)
Make questions and answers using the given information.

	Mia	George	Paul	Eva
drive a car	yes	yes	no	no
play the piano	no	yes	yes	yes
repair a bike	yes	no	yes	no
swim	yes	yes	yes	yes

1. Mia \ repair a bike ____*Can Mia repair a bike? Yes, she can.*____

2. George and Eva \ play the piano _____

3. George \ drive a car _____

4. Paul \ play the piano _____

5. Mia, George, and Paul \ swim _____

6. Paul and Eva \ drive a car _____

7. Eva and George \ repair a bike _____

8. Eva, Paul, and George \ play the piano _____

► **Practice 5. *Can* or *can't*.** (Charts 12-1 and 12-3)
Read the help-wanted ad and look at John's skills. Write interview questions and answers using the given information. Use *can* or *can't*.

JOB OPENING AT SMALL INTERNATIONAL HOTEL

Looking for person with the following: good typing and word-processing skills, excellent knowledge of English, friendly manner on the phone. Also needs to help guests with their suitcases and be available weekends.

John can:

_____✓_____ type

_____✓_____ do word processing

_____ speak English

_____ lift suitcases

_____✓_____ work weekends

Hotel Manager's Questions	John's Answers
1. ___Can you type?___	___Yes, I can.___
2. _____	_____
3. _____	_____
4. _____	_____
5. _____	_____

► **Practice 6. Information questions with *can*.** (Chart 12-3)
Match the question with the correct answer.

1. What can I get you? _____

2. Where can I register for class? _____

3. When can we leave? _____

4. Who can they talk to about their problem? _____

5. Where can I find the hotel manager? _____

a. The manager.

b. After class.

c. In the school administration office.

d. At the reservation desk.

e. Some coffee, please.

► **Practice 7. *Know how to*.** (Chart 12-4)
Rewrite the sentences using *know how to*.

1. Toni can make pizza.

   ___Toni knows how to make pizza.___

2. Martha can play chess.

   _____

3. Sonya and Thomas can speak Portuguese.

_____

4. Jack can't speak Russian.

_____

5. My brothers can't cook.

_____

6. I can't change a flat tire.

_____

7. We can't play musical instruments.

a flat tire

_____

8. Can you type?

_____

9. Can your children swim?

_____

10. Can Ari kick a soccer ball very far?

_____

▶ **Practice 8. Know how to.** (Chart 12-4)
Write sentences about what you and others **know how to** do or **don't know how to** do. Use the words from the list or your own words.

dance	drive a stick-shift car	milk a cow
cook rice	knit	sew clothes
do advanced math	make candy	use chopsticks

1. I _____.

2. I _____.

3. (*name of your best friend*) _____.

She knows how to knit.

4. My best friend and I _____ .

5. (*name of a cousin*) _____ .

6. (*name of a classmate*) _____ .

7. (*name of a classmate*) _____ .

▶ **Practice 9. *Could.*** (Chart 12-5)
Stefan and Heidi decided to live without electricity for one month. Write what they ***could*** and
couldn't do for that month.

✓ watch TV	spend time together	use electric heat
cook over a fire	use a computer	have heat from a fireplace
read books	turn on the lights	play board games

1. _____*They couldn't watch TV.*_____

2. _____

3. _____

4. _____

5. _____

6. _____

7. _____

8. _____

9. _____

► **Practice 10. Can or could.** (Charts 12-1 and 12-5)
Choose the correct answer in each sentence.

1. Yesterday we (*can't / couldn't*) go to the beach. It rained all day.

2. Please turn down the music! I (*can't / couldn't*) study.

3. (*Could / Can*) you speak English a few years ago?

4. I'm a fast typist. I (*can / could*) type 90 words-per-minute on my computer.

5. Sam (*could / can*) tell time when he was four years old.

6. (*Could / Can*) you finish the math test yesterday?

7. Our neighbors (*can't / couldn't*) control their dog. She needs dog-training classes.

► **Practice 11. Can and could.** (Charts 12-1 and 12-5)
Two months ago, Arturo fell off his bike and broke his leg. He was in a cast for six weeks. Now he is okay. Write what he **couldn't** do two months ago and **can** do now. Use the appropriate phrases from the box.

do homework	play soccer
✓ drive a car	ride a bike
go swimming	talk on the phone
listen to music	watch TV

1. Two months ago, _he couldn't drive a car._ Now, _he can drive a car._

2. Two months ago, _____ Now, _____

3. Two months ago, _____ Now, _____

4. Two months ago, _____ Now, _____

► **Practice 12. Can or could.** (Charts 12-1 and 12-5)
Complete the sentences with **can**, **can't**, **could**, or **couldn't**.

1. When I was a newborn baby, I _____couldn't_____ walk.

2. When I was a newborn baby, I _____ talk.

3. When I entered kindergarten, I _____ read and write my language.

4. A few years ago, I _____ speak a lot of English.

5. Now I _____ read and write some English.

6. I _____ understand native English speakers well.

7. I _____ always understand my English teacher.

▶ **Practice 13. Be able to.** (Chart 12-6)
Make sentences with the present, past, and future forms of **be able to**.

		Able to (Present)	*Able to* (Past)	*Able to* (Future)
1.	I can run.	*I am able to run.*	*I was able to run.*	*I will be able to run.*
2.	You can draw.	_____	_____	_____
3.	He can drive.	_____	_____	_____
4.	She can swim.	_____	_____	_____
5.	We can dance.	_____	_____	_____
6.	They can type.	_____	_____	_____

▶ **Practice 14. Be able to.** (Chart 12-6)
Make sentences with the present and past forms of **be able to**.

1. When I was a newborn baby, I _____ *wasn't able to* _____ walk.

2. When I was a newborn baby, I _____ talk.

3. When I entered kindergarten, I _____ read and write my language.

4. A few years ago, I _____ speak a lot of English.

5. Now I _____ read and write some English.

6. I _____ understand native English speakers well now.

7. I _____ understand my English teacher all the time.

▶ **Practice 15. Be able to.** (Chart 12-6)
Choose the sentence that is closest in meaning to the given sentence.

1. James can run very fast.
   a. He will be able to run very fast.
   b. He is able to run very fast.
   c. He was able to run very fast.

2. I will be able to have dinner with you.
   a. I can have dinner with you.
   b. I could have dinner with you.
   c. I was able to have dinner with you.

3. Jean couldn't finish her science project.

   a. She isn't able to finish her science project.

   b. She wasn't able to finish her science project.

   c. She won't be able to finish her science project.

4. My roommate wasn't able to come to the party.

   a. He won't be able to come to the party.

   b. He can't come to the party.

   c. He couldn't come to the party.

5. I can't help you later.

   a. I wasn't able to help you.

   b. I couldn't help you.

   c. I won't be able to help you.

▶ **Practice 16. *Be able to.*** (Chart 12-6)
Rewrite the boldfaced verbs with the correct form of *be able to*.

wasn't able to speak

Five years ago, Chang was in Australia. He **couldn't speak** any English. He had a difficult
₁

time communicating. He **couldn't ask** questions. People **couldn't give** him directions.
₂ ₃

Many times he got lost. He **couldn't visit** tourist sites he was interested in. He was frustrated
₄

because he **couldn't have** conversations with people.
₅

So Chang decided to study English. Four years later, he went back to Australia. He was

surprised he **could understand** so much. People **could have** long conversations with him.
₆ ₇

He **could learn** about local customs. He **could visit** interesting tourist areas. This time
₈ ₉

Chang had a great trip. Learning English made a big difference.

► **Practice 17. Can, can't, be able to, and know how to.** (Chart 12-6)
Choose all the grammatically correct verbs.

1. Alex _____ to program computers.
   a. can
   b. is able
   c. are able
   d. know how
   e. knows how

2. Mr. and Mrs. Cox _____ fix their car.
   a. can
   b. know how to
   c. knows how to
   d. isn't able to
   e. aren't able to

3. Jerry is _____ speak several languages.
   a. able to
   b. not able to
   c. can't
   d. know how to
   e. knows how to

4. Two of my friends don't _____ swim.
   a. can't
   b. aren't able to
   c. knows how to
   d. can
   e. know how to

5. Ellen doesn't _____ create movies on
   a computer.
   a. knows how to
   b. know how to
   c. can
   d. able to
   e. can't

► **Practice 18. Very or too.** (Chart 12-7)
Complete the sentences with *very* or *too*.

1. This leather coat is _____*too*_____ expensive. I can't buy it.

2. The tea is _____ hot, but I can drink it.

3. The shoe store is _____ big. There's a good selection.

4. The neighbors are _____ noisy. I want them
   to move.

5. These pants are _____ short. I'm not going to buy them.

6. My teacher talks _____ fast. It's good practice for me.

7. This car is _____ small. It won't use a lot of gas.

8. The Arctic Circle is _____ cold. I don't
   want to travel there.

► **Practice 19. *Very* or *too*.** (Chart 12-7)
Choose the best completion for each sentence.

1. Do you like this book?
   a. Yes, it's very interesting.　　　b. Yes, it's too interesting.

2. I can't watch this movie.
   a. It's too violent.　　　b. It's very violent.

3. You had no mistakes on your math test.
   a. Your knowledge of math is too good.　　　b. Your knowledge of math is very good.

4. We can do these math problems.
   a. They're too easy.　　　b. They're very easy.

5. This dress is too tight.
   a. I can't wear it.　　　b. I can wear it.

6. This puzzle looks very tricky.
   a. Let's see if we can figure it out.　　　b. It will be impossible to do.

7. Thomas is too friendly.
   a. I feel comfortable around him.　　　b. I feel uncomfortable around him.

8. Let's buy this mattress.
   a. It's very comfortable.　　　b. It's too comfortable.

► **Practice 20. *Very* or *too*.** (Chart 12-7)
Write answers to the questions.

1. What school subjects are very hard for you?

_____

2. What school subjects are too hard for you?

_____

3. What foods do you think are very spicy?

_____

4. What foods are too spicy for you?

_____

5. What cities have climates that are too hot for you?

_____

6. What cities have climates that are too cold for you?

_____

► **Practice 21. Review.** (Chapter 12)
Choose the correct completion for each sentence.

1. _____ play a musical instrument?
   a. Do you can   b. Can you   c. Do you be able to   d. Can you to

2. I _____ my homework. I was too tired.
   a. couldn't to finish   b. could finish   c. couldn't finish   d. couldn't finished

3. I don't know how _____ to the Palace Hotel from here.
   a. do I get   b. get   c. getting   d. to get

4. Gina _____ understand the speaker at the lecture last night.
   a. couldn't   b. doesn't able to   c. won't be able to   d. can't

5. My uncle can't _____ English.
   a. to speak   b. speaking   c. speaks   d. speak

6. The driving test was _____. I was so happy to pass it.
   a. very hard   b. too hard   c. very easy   d. too easy

7. Sorry, I _____ to get movie tickets. They were sold out.
   a. can't   b. didn't   c. couldn't   d. wasn't able

► **Practice 22. Verb review.** (Chapter 12)
Complete the sentences with the words in parentheses. Use any appropriate verb form.

Once upon a time there (be) _____ *a mouse named Young Mouse. He lived*
                                            1

near a river with his family and friends. Every day he and the other mice did the same things.

They (hunt) _____ *for food and* (take) _____ *care*
              2   3

of their mouse holes. In the evening they (listen) _____ *to stories around a*
                                                           4

fire. Young Mouse especially liked to listen to stories about the Far Away Land. He (dream)

_____ *about the Far Away Land. It sounded wonderful. One day he* (decide)
        5

_____ *to go there.*
        6

YOUNG MOUSE: Good-bye, Old Mouse. I'm leaving now.

OLD MOUSE: Why (*you, leave*) _____?
                                                    7

Where (*you, go*) _____?
                              8

YOUNG MOUSE: I (*go*) _____ to a new and different place. I (*go*)
                                9

_____ to the Far Away Land.
        10

OLD MOUSE: Why (*you, want*) _____ (*go*) _____ there?
                                          11   12

YOUNG MOUSE: I (*want*) _____ (*experience*) _____ all
                                  13   14

of life. I (*need*) _____ (*learn*) _____ about everything.
                        15   16

OLD MOUSE: You (can learn) _____ many things if you (stay)

17

_____ here with us. Please stay here with us.

18

YOUNG MOUSE: No, I (can stay, not) _____ here by the river for the rest

19

of my life. There (be) _____ too much to learn about in the world. I must

20

go to the Far Away Land.

OLD MOUSE: The trip to the Far Away Land is a long and dangerous journey. You (have)

_____ many problems before you (get) _____ there. You

21   22

(face) _____ many dangers.

23

YOUNG MOUSE: I understand that, but I need to find out about the Far Away Land. Good-

bye, Old Mouse. Good-bye, everyone! I (may see, never) _____ any of

24

you again, but I (try) _____ to return from the Far Away Land someday.

25

Good-bye!

So Young Mouse left to fulfill his dream of going to the Far Away Land. His first problem was the

river. At the river, he met a frog.

MAGIC FROG: Hello, Young Mouse. I'm Magic Frog. (you, need) _____

26

help?

YOUNG MOUSE: Yes. How (I, can cross) _____ this river? I (know, not)

27

_____ how to swim. If I (can cross, not) _____ this river,

28   29

I (be able, not) _____ to reach the Far Away Land.

30

MAGIC FROG: I (help) _____ you to cross the river. I (give)

31

_____ you the power of my legs so you (can jump) _____

32   33

across the river. I (give, also) _____ you a new name. Your new name

34

will be Jumping Mouse.

JUMPING MOUSE: Thank you, Magic Frog.

MAGIC FROG: You are a brave mouse, Jumping

Mouse, and you have a good heart. If you (lose,

not) _____ hope, you (reach)

35

_____ the Far Away Land.

36

With his powerful new legs, Jumping Mouse jumped across the

river. He traveled fast for many days across a wide grassland. One

day he met a buffalo. The buffalo was lying on the ground.

Modals, Part 1: Expressing Ability **219**

JUMPING MOUSE: Hello, Buffalo. My name is Jumping Mouse. Why (*you, lie*★)

_____ on the ground? (*you, be*) _____ ill?

    BUFFALO: Yes. I (*can see, not*) _____ . I (*drink*) _____

some poisoned water, and now I (*be*) _____ blind. I (*die*)

_____ soon because I (*can find, not*) _____ food and

water without my eyes.

    JUMPING MOUSE: When I started my journey, Magic Frog (*give*) _____

me her powerful legs so I could jump across the river. What (*I, can give*)

_____ you to help you? I know! I (*give*) _____ you my

sight so you can see to find food and water.

    BUFFALO: Are you really going to do that? Jumping Mouse, you are very kind! Ah!

Yes, I (*can see*) _____ again. Thank you! But now you (*can see, not*)

_____ . How (*you, find*) _____ the Far Away Land? I

know. Jump onto my back. I (*carry*) _____ you across this land to the foot

of the mountain.

    JUMPING MOUSE: Thank you, Buffalo.

So Jumping Mouse found a way to reach the mountain. When they reached the mountain,

Jumping Mouse and Buffalo parted.

    BUFFALO: I don't live in the mountains, so I (*can go, not*) _____ any

farther.

    JUMPING MOUSE: What (*I, do*) _____? I (*have*) _____

powerful legs, but I can't see.

★ The *-ing* form of *lie* is spelled *lying*.

BUFFALO: Keep your hope alive. You (*find*) _____ 54 a way to reach the Far Away Land.

Jumping Mouse was very afraid. He didn't know what to do. Suddenly he heard a wolf.

JUMPING MOUSE: Hello? Wolf? I (*can see, not*) _____ 55 you, but I (*can hear*) _____ 56 you.

WOLF: Yes, Jumping Mouse. I'm here, but I (*can help, not*) _____ 57 you because I (*die★*) _____ 58 .

JUMPING MOUSE: What's wrong? Why (*you, die*) _____ 59 ?

WOLF: I (*lose*) _____ 60 my sense of smell many weeks ago, so now I (*can find, not*) _____ 61 food. I (*starve*) _____ 62 to death.

JUMPING MOUSE: Oh, Wolf, I (*can help*) _____ 63 you. I (*give*) _____ 64 you my ability to smell.

WOLF: Oh, thank you, Jumping Mouse. Yes, I (*can smell*) _____ 65 again. Now I'll be able to find food. That is a wonderful gift! How (*I, can help*) _____ 66 you?

JUMPING MOUSE: I (*try*) _____ 67 to get to the Far Away Land. I (*need*) _____ 68 (*go*) _____ 69 to the top of the mountain.

WOLF: Come over here. I (*put*) _____ 70 you on my back and (*take*) _____ 71 you to the top of the mountain.

So Wolf carried Jumping Mouse to the top of the mountain. But then Wolf left.

Jumping Mouse was all alone. He (can see, not) _____ 72 *and he (can smell, not)* _____ 73 *, but he still had powerful legs. He almost (lose)* _____ 74 *hope. Then suddenly, he (hear)* _____ 75 *Magic Frog.*

★ The *-ing* form of *die* is spelled *dying.*

JUMPING MOUSE: Is that you, Magic Frog? Please help me. I'm all alone and afraid.

MAGIC FROG: Don't cry, Jumping Mouse. You have a generous, open heart. You

(*be, not*) _____ selfish. You help others. Your unselfishness caused you
₇₆

suffering during your journey, but you (*lose, never*) _____ hope. Now you
₇₇

are in the Far Away Land. Jump, Jumping Mouse. Use your powerful legs to jump high in the

air. Jump! Jump!

Jumping Mouse jumped as high as he could, up, up, up. He reached his arms out to his sides and

started to fly. He felt strong and powerful.

JUMPING MOUSE: I can fly! I can fly! I (*fly*) _____!
₇₈

MAGIC FROG: Jumping Mouse, I am going to give you a new name. Now your name is

Eagle!

So Jumping Mouse became the powerful Eagle and fulfilled his dream of reaching the Far Away

Land and experiencing all that life has to offer.

This fable is based on a Native American story and has been adapted from *The Story of Jumping Mouse* by John Steptoe; Lothrop, Lee & Shepard books, 1984.

Chapter 13

Modals, Part 2: Advice, Necessity, Requests, Suggestions

▶ **Practice 1. Should.** (Chart 13-1)
Create your own chart by completing each sentence with the correct form of **should + study**.

1. Mrs. Wang _____*should study*_____ more.

2. He _____ more.

3. We _____ more.

4. You _____ more.

5. She _____ more.

6. They _____ more.

7. I _____ more.

8. Nick and I _____ more.

9. The students _____ more.

▶ **Practice 2. Should.** (Chart 13-1)
Complete the sentences with **should** or **shouldn't**.

Sami wants to be on his high school soccer team.

1. He _____*should*_____ practice kicking a ball with his friends.

2. He _____ exercise a lot.

3. He _____ smoke cigarettes.

4. He _____ stop doing homework so he has more time for soccer.

5. He _____ practice running fast.

6. He _____ watch famous soccer games.

7. He _____ eat a lot of snack foods.

► **Practice 3. Should.** (Chart 13-1)
Write sentences with **should** or **shouldn't**.

Rose gets failing grades in school. She wants to get better grades.

1. She doesn't do her homework.

   She should do her homework.

2. She copies her roommate's homework.

   She shouldn't copy her roommate's homework.

3. She doesn't study for her tests.

   _____

4. She stays up late.

   _____

5. She daydreams in class.

   _____

6. She is absent from class a lot.

   _____

7. She doesn't take notes during lectures.

   _____

8. She doesn't take her books to school.

   _____

► **Practice 4. Should.** (Chart 13-1)
Give advice with **should** or **shouldn't**.

1. Sara's bedroom is very messy. She can't find her clothes.

   Sara _____ *should clean her room.* _____

2. The Browns play loud music at night. It wakes up the neighbors.

   The neighbors _____

3. Janet is a dance teacher. She has a backache.

   Janet _____

4. Bill has a sore tooth. It began to hurt four weeks ago.

   Bill _____

5. Ronnie isn't careful with his money. He spends too much and he's always broke.*

Ronnie _____

6. Mr. and Mrs. Brown are traveling to South America soon. They don't have visas.

They _____

▶ **Practice 5. *Have to* and *has to*.** (Chart 13-2)
Create your own chart by completing each sentence with the correct form of *have to/has to +*
leave.

1. I _____*have to leave*_____ soon.

2. We _____ soon.

3. They _____ soon.

4. You _____ soon.

5. He _____ soon.

6. She _____ soon.

7. My parents (not) _____ soon.

8. The children (not) _____ soon.

9. Mark (not) _____ soon.

10. Mark and I (not) _____ soon.

▶ **Practice 6. *Have to* and *has to*.** (Chart 13-2)
Complete the sentences with *has to* or *doesn't have to*.

Roger wants to be a pediatrician (children's doctor). What qualities does he have to have?

1. He _____*has to*_____ be smart.

2. He _____*doesn't have to*_____ be good-looking.

3. He _____ be patient.

4. He _____ speak several languages fluently.

5. He _____ be athletic.

6. He _____ like children.

7. He _____ like working with sick people.

---

*be broke = have no money.

▶ **Practice 7. *Have to* and *has to*.** (Chart 13-2)
Complete each sentence with *have to/has to* or *don't have to/doesn't have to*.

1. We _____ *have to* _____ leave now. Our class starts soon.

2. We _____ hurry. We're almost there.

3. A good teacher _____ begin on time.

4. The students _____ arrive on time. Late students get lower grades.

5. Students _____ arrive before 8:00. The school isn't open.

6. I _____ study hard. I want to go to medical school.

7. Jane _____ take difficult science classes. She wants to be an artist.

8. Teachers _____ correct a lot of homework. They collect it every day.

9. My teacher _____ correct a lot of papers. She has 50 students.

10. My friend's teacher has five students. She _____ correct a lot of papers.

▶ **Practice 8. *Had to* or *didn't have to*.** (Chart 13-2)
Read the information about Mr. Napoli. Then complete each sentence with *had to* or *didn't have to*.

Mr. Napoli is retired now. For thirty years, he owned a successful bakery. His bakery opened at 5:00 A.M. and closed at 7:00 P.M. What did he have to do? What didn't he have to do?

1. He _____ *had to* _____ work hard.

2. He _____ get up early.

3. His home was above the bakery. He _____ take the bus to work.

4. He _____ be friendly to his customers.

5. His wife took the children to school. He _____ take them.

6. He _____ work long hours.

7. His workers did the cleaning. He _____ clean up at night.

8. He _____ begin baking before 5:00 A.M.

▶ **Practice 9. *Had to* or *didn't have to*.** (Chart 13-2)
What chores did Nina have to do last week? Complete each sentence with ***had to*** or ***didn't have to***.

```
Nina's Chores (4/1— 4/7)
  Clean bedroom
  Fold laundry
  Feed pets
  Vacuum floors
```

1. She _____*had to*_____ clean her bedroom.

2. She _____ cook dinner for her family.

3. She _____ empty the garbage.

4. She _____ fold the laundry.

5. She _____ wash her clothes.

6. She _____ feed the pets.

7. She _____ sweep the floors.

8. She _____ vacuum the floors.

▶ **Practice 10. *Should*, *have to*, and *don't have to*.** (Charts 13-1 and 13-2)
Complete each sentence with ***should***, ***have to***, or ***don't have to***.

High school students in my country . . .

1. _____ work hard.

2. _____ go to school on Saturdays.

3. _____ stand up when the teacher comes in the room.

4. _____ clean the classroom after class.

5. _____ do homework every day.

6. _____ take extra classes after school or in the evening.

7. _____ memorize a lot of information.

8. _____ work together in small groups.

9. _____ be polite to other students.

10. _____ bring a dictionary to class.

11. _____ wear uniforms to school.

► **Practice 11. *Must* or *must not*.** (Chart 13-3)
Complete each sentence with *must* or *must not*.

Swimming Pool Rules

1. Swimmers _____*must*_____ take a shower before entering the pool.

2. Small children _____ be with a parent.

3. Non-swimmers _____ go in the deep end of the pool.

4. Non-swimmers _____ wear lifejackets.

5. Swimmers _____ dive in the shallow* end of the pool.

6. Non-swimmers _____ jump off the diving board.

► **Practice 12. *Must* or *must not*.** (Chart 13-3)
Complete each sentence with *must* or *must not*.

Beth is going to have surgery. What is her doctor going to tell her after the surgery?

1. She _____*must*_____ take her medicine.

2. She _____ go to work the next day.

3. She _____ rest.

4. She _____ lift heavy objects for several weeks.

5. She _____ call her doctor if she gets a fever.

6. She _____ stay quiet.

_____

shallow = opposite of *deep*.

▶ **Practice 13. *Must* or *should*.** (Charts 13-1 and 13-3)
Complete each sentence with *must* or *should*.

1. You _____*should*_____ make your bed every day. Your bedroom looks nicer when you make it.

2. You _____ take vitamins every day. They may help you stay healthy.

3. You _____ obey the speed limit. If you drive too fast, you will get a ticket.

4. You _____ bring your dictionary to writing class, but if you don't, you can use the teacher's.

5. If you want to go to a top university, you _____ have good grades.

6. You _____ watch old movies if you want to relax.

7. You _____ rest when you are tired.

8. You _____ stop in traffic when the light is red.

9. You _____ have an I.D. when you travel to another country.

▶ **Practice 14. *May I*, *Could I*, and *Can I*.** (Chart 13-4)
Make polite questions using *May I*, *Could I*, or *Can I please*.

1. You are at a restaurant. Your coffee is cold. You want hot coffee.

   _____*May I / Could I / Can I please have some hot coffee?*_____

2. You are in class. You want to look at your classmate's dictionary for a minute.

   _____

3. You are taking a test. You want to sharpen your pencil.

   _____

4. You are stuck in traffic with your friend. You want to borrow her cell phone.

   _____

5. You are in the library. You lost your library card. You need a new one.

   _____

▶ **Practice 15. *Could you* and *Would you*.** (Chart 13-5)
Write polite questions with *Could you* or *Would you please.*

1. You didn't hear your teacher's question. You want him/her to repeat it.

   Could / Would you please repeat the question?

2. You are a parent. You want your teenager to clean his bedroom.

   _____

3. You are a teenager. You want your parent to give you some money for a movie.

   _____

4. You are studying at home. You want your roommate to turn down the TV.

   _____

5. You are at a restaurant. The server brings you cream for your coffee and it is sour. You want some fresh cream.

   _____

6. You are at a park with your friends. You want someone to take a picture of all of you. You ask a person nearby.

   _____

▶ **Practice 16. Imperative sentences.** (Chart 13-6)
Choose the actions you usually do with each given activity.

1. Writing a check:
   a. Sign your name.
   b. Date the check.
   c. Fold the check and put it away.
   d. Call the bank after you write the check.

2. Making tea:
   a. Put oil in a pan.
   b. Boil water.
   c. Put a tea bag into a cup.
   d. Cool the tea with ice cubes.

3. Before an airplane takes off:
   a. Fasten your seat belt.
   b. Enter the cockpit and talk with the pilot.
   c. Put carry-on bags under your seat or in the overhead bin.
   d. Ask the flight attendant for a meal.

overhead bins
Please fasten your seat belts.

► **Practice 17. Imperative sentences.** (Chart 13-6)
Underline the imperative verbs in the following conversations.

1. MICHELLE: May I come in?

   PROFESSOR: Certainly. <u>Come</u> in. How can I help you?

   MICHELLE: I need to ask you a question about yesterday's lecture.

   PROFESSOR: Okay. What's the question?

2. STUDENT: Do we have any homework for tomorrow?

   TEACHER: Yes. Read pages 24 through 36, and answer the questions on page 37, in writing.

   STUDENT: Is that all?

   TEACHER: Yes.

3. HEIDI: Please close the window, Mike. It's a little chilly in here.

   MIKE: Okay. Is there anything else I can do for you before I leave?

   HEIDI: Could you turn off the light in the kitchen?

   MIKE: No problem. Anything else?

   HEIDI: Umm, please hand me the remote control for the TV. It's over there.

   MIKE: Sure. Here.

   HEIDI: Thanks.

   MIKE: I'll stop by again tomorrow. Take care of yourself. Take good care of that broken leg.

   HEIDI: Don't worry. I will. Thanks again.

► **Practice 18. Imperative sentences.** (Chart 13-6)
Describe how to make popcorn. Put the sentences in the correct order.

Making popcorn the old-fashioned way

_____ Stop shaking the pan when the popcorn stops popping.

_____ Put the popcorn in the pan.

_____ Shake the pan.

_____ Pour the popcorn into a bowl.

_____ Cover the pan with a lid.

_____ Pour melted butter over the popcorn.

_____ Heat the oil.

___1___ Put some oil in a pan.

_____ Salt the popcorn.

_____ Enjoy your snack!

► **Practice 19. Imperative sentences.** (Chart 13-6)
Use imperative sentences to write what you should and shouldn't do at school.

| ✓ sit | copy | do | work | answer | ✓ chew | talk |

School rules

1. _____Sit_____ quietly in class.

2. _____Don't chew_____ gum in class.

3. _____ to your friends when the teacher is talking.

4. _____ your homework.

5. _____ your classmates' homework.

6. _____ hard.

7. _____ the teacher's questions.

► **Practice 20. Imperative sentences.** (Chart 13-6)
Use imperative sentences to write about what you should and shouldn't do in the computer lab.

| ask | ✓ show | ✓ bring | follow | talk |
| turn off | use | play | download | |

Computer lab rules at school

1. _____Show_____ your ID to the lab director when you enter the lab.

2. _____Don't bring_____ food or drinks into the computer lab.

3. _____ the lab director's instructions.

4. _____ your cell phone.

5. _____ computer games.

6. _____ the computers for school work.

7. _____ in a quiet voice.

8. _____ the lab assistant for help if you are having trouble.

9. _____ music from the Internet.

► **Practice 21. Modal auxiliaries.** (Chart 13-7)
Add *to* where necessary. If *to* is not necessary, write Ø (nothing).

1. The sky is dark. It is going _____*to*_____ rain.

2. Would you please _____ speak more slowly?

3. You should _____ meet John. He's very interesting.

4. Do we have _____ have a test tomorrow?

5. Will you _____ join us for lunch?

6. Robert might not _____ work tomorrow. He doesn't feel well.

7. I'm not able _____ help you right now.

8. The neighbors shouldn't _____ have loud parties late at night.

9. We weren't able _____ get email yesterday.

10. Monica can't _____ talk much because she has a bad cough.

► **Practice 22. Modal review.** (Chart 13-8)
Choose the sentence that is closest in meaning.

1. We must leave.
   a. We should leave.
   (b.) We have to leave.
   c. We may leave.

2. I wasn't able to come.
   a. I couldn't come.
   b. I didn't have to come.
   c. I shouldn't come.

3. Mrs. Jones will pick us up tomorrow.
   a. Mrs. Jones may pick us up.
   b. Mrs. Jones is going to pick us up.
   c. Mrs. Jones could pick us up.

4. I won't be able to meet with you tomorrow.
   a. I don't want to meet with you.
   b. I don't have to meet with you.
   c. I can't meet with you.

5. Would you close the door, please?

    a. Should you close the door?

    b. Must you close the door?

    c. Could you close the door?

6. You should take a break.

    a. You have to take a break.

    b. You might take a break.

    c. It's a good idea for you to take a break.

7. Tom didn't have to work yesterday.

    a. Tom didn't need to work.

    b. Tom couldn't work.

    c. Tom didn't want to work.

8. It might be stormy tomorrow.

    a. It must be stormy.

    b. It may be stormy.

    c. It will be stormy.

▶ **Practice 23. Let's.** (Chart 13-9)
Write a response with **Let's**.

1. A: The sun is shining. It's going to be a warm day.

    B: _____Let's go to the park._____

2. A: We worked hard today.

    B: _____

3. A: Sandra's birthday is this weekend.

    B: _____

4. A: Breakfast is ready.

   B: _____

5. A: Mario's Pizzeria is having a special tonight: free pizza for kids.

   B: _____

▶ **Practice 24. Review.** (Chapter 13).
Choose the correct completion for each sentence.

1. It's very late and I have to get up early. I _____ go to bed.
   a. can   b. should   c. had to

2. We _____ up late last night. We had a lot of homework.
   a. have to stay   b. had to stayed   c. had to stay

3. It's a beautiful day. Let's _____ to the beach.
   a. going   b. to go   c. go

4. Please be quiet. I _____ the speaker very well.
   a. can't hear   b. am not hearing   c. couldn't hear

5. It's hot in here. _____ the window please?
   a. You will open   b. Could you open   c. Should you open

6. Excuse me. _____ me lift this box?
   a. Would you help   b. Would you to help   c. Would you helping

7. _____ leave now? We're having so much fun.
   a. Do we has to   b. Are we have to   c. Do we have to

8. Mia _____ pay for her groceries. She lost her wallet in the store.
   a. wasn't able   b. couldn't   c. can't to

9. The children are excited. It _____ snow tonight or tomorrow.
   a. can   b. must   c. might

10. You _____ take this medicine. You are very sick and you need it to get better.
    a. must   b. could   c. might

▶ **Practice 25. Review.** (Chapter 13)
Choose <u>all</u> the correct answers.

1. _____ help me carry this box?
   a. Would you
   b. Do you
   c. Could you
   d. Let's

2. Mario has a toothache. He _____ to call the dentist.

   a. have

   b. should

   c. needs

   d. must

3. Billy, you have no choice. You _____ clean your bedroom before you play with your friends.

   a. should

   b. have to

   c. had to

   d. must

4. When I was young, I _____ bend over and put my hands flat on the floor.

   a. am able

   b. could

   c. have

   d. was able to

5. It's really nice outside. _____ take a walk.

   a. We had to

   b. Let's

   c. Would we

   d. We should

6. A: Would you help me with the dishes?
   B: _____

   a. No problem.

   b. I'd be happy to.

   c. I'd be glad.

   d. Yes, of course.

7. _____ touch the pan. It's really hot.

   a. Not

   b. Don't

   c. Please

   d. Do not

Chapter 14
Nouns and Modifiers

▶ **Practice 1. Nouns and adjectives.** (Chart 14-1)
How are the words in the box usually used? Write each word in the correct column.

✓ tall	pens	boat	true
pretty	sad	store	happy
✓ clothes	hot	horse	truth

Adjectives	**Nouns**
tall	_clothes_
_____	_____
_____	_____
_____	_____
_____	_____
_____	_____

▶ **Practice 2. Nouns and adjectives.** (Chart 14-1)
Write all the words from the box that can go before each noun. You may use a word more than once.

camera	cell	chicken
delicious	English	grammar
old	sad	tasty

1. _____ soup

2. _____ phone

3. _____ teacher

► **Practice 3. Nouns and adjectives.** (Chart 14-1)
How is the underlined word used? Circle *adjective* or *noun*.

1. The <u>camera</u> store has photography classes. (adjective) noun
2. Do you have a digital <u>camera</u>? adjective noun
3. What are you going to order for <u>lunch</u>? adjective noun
4. Nancy's Café has a delicious <u>lunch</u> menu. adjective noun
5. I read an interesting <u>newspaper</u> article today about electric cars. adjective noun

HUMMMMM

6. Do you read the <u>newspaper</u> every day? adjective noun
7. We need to get some dog <u>food</u>. adjective noun
8. The <u>pet</u> store is having a sale. adjective noun

Pet Store

► **Practice 4. Nouns and adjectives.** (Chart 14-1)
Make two phrases for each given noun: **adjective + noun** and **noun + noun**. Use the words in the box.

accident	noisy	recipe	smelly
dangerous	old	sleeves	stairs

		Adjective + Noun	**Noun + Noun**
1.	traffic	*dangerous/noisy traffic*	*traffic accident*
2.	apartment	_____	_____
3.	sandwich	_____	_____
4.	shirt	_____	_____

► **Practice 5. Nouns and adjectives.** (Chart 14-1)
Use the information in the first part of the sentence to complete the sentence. Use **noun + noun** in the completion.

1. A house for a dog is called a ___*dog house*_____.

2. An article in a magazine is called a _____.

3. A card for business is called a _____.

4. An appointment with a dentist is called a _____.

5. Salad that has chicken in it is called _____.

6. A key for a house is called a _____.

7. A cord that is used with a computer is called a _____.

8. A carton for milk is called a _____.

9. A store that has clothes in it is called a _____.

10. A curtain for a shower is called a _____.

▶ **Practice 6. Nouns and adjectives.** (Chart 14-1)
Use the given words to make common **adjective + noun** or **noun + noun** phrases.

1. *birthday*

    a. present   _____*birthday present*_____

    b. happy   _____*happy birthday*_____

    c. cake   _____*birthday cake*_____

2. *kitchen*

    a. messy   _____

    b. cabinets   _____

    c. counter   _____

3. *bus*

    a. city   _____

    b. schedule   _____

    c. route   _____

4. *airplane*

   a. noise   _____

   b. movie   _____

   c. ticket   _____

5. *apartment*

   a. manager   _____

   b. one-bedroom   _____

   c. building   _____

6. *phone*

   a. number   _____

   b. broken   _____

   c. call   _____

7. *patient*

   a. hospital   _____

   b. sick   _____

   c. information   _____

▶ **Practice 7. Word order of adjectives.** (Chart 14-2)
Write the words in the correct order.

1. house
100-year-old
small

   a ____*small 100-year-old house*____

2. spicy
food
Mexican

   some _____

3. man
young
kind

   a _____

4. dirty
glass
brown

   a _____

5. tall
lovely
rose bush

   a _____

6. small   some _____
   paintings
   interesting
   old

7. film   a/an _____
   foreign
   new
   important

8. yellow   some _____
   flowers
   little

9. middle-aged a _____
   woman
   tall

10. cabinet   a/an _____
    wooden
    Chinese
    antique

▶ **Practice 8. Word order of adjectives.** (Chart 14-2)
Choose the correct completion.

1. We work in _____ office building.
   a. a large old   b. an old large

2. I spoke with a _____ man at the park today.
   a. Greek friendly   b. friendly Greek

3. I need some _____ socks.
   a. brown comfortable   b. comfortable brown

4. My sister makes _____ soup.
   a. vegetable delicious   b. delicious vegetable

5. The children found _____ box at the beach.
   a. an old metal   b. a metal old

6. My family loves _____ food.
   a. spicy Indian   b. Indian spicy

7. Robert gave his girlfriend _____ ring.
   a. an antique beautiful   b. a beautiful antique

8. We shared our _____ online.
   a. favorite pictures   b. pictures favorite

9. There is a _____ soccer field near our house.
   a. wonderful big grassy*   b. grassy big wonderful

▶ **Practice 9. Linking verbs + adjectives.** (Chart 14-3)
Check (✓) the sentences that have a linking verb. <u>Underline</u> the linking verb.

1. ___✓___ After it rains, the air <u>smells</u> very fresh.

2. _____ Your vacation plans sound interesting.

3. _____ The kids are playing happily in the backyard.

4. _____ They like to run and climb trees.

5. _____ Does the vegetable soup taste good?

6. _____ The roses smell wonderful.

7. _____ They look beautiful too.

8. _____ Jack looked for some flowers for his wife.

9. _____ Cindy went to bed early because she felt sick.

10. _____ Emily seems sad. Do you know why?

▶ **Practice 10. Linking verbs + adjectives.** (Chart 14-3)
Complete each sentence with an appropriate adjective.

1. There's a new movie about space at the theater. I really want to go. It sounds
   _____*interesting*_____.

2. Carl woke up at 3:00 A.M., and never went back to sleep. He looked
   _____ this morning.

3. Mmm. What are you baking? The kitchen smells _____.

4. I got 100% on all my tests. I feel _____.

5. Whew! Do you smell that smell? I think it's a skunk. It smells
   _____.

a skunk

6. I'm sorry, this chicken tastes _____. I can't
   eat it.

_____

*grassy = covered with grass.

7. The Smiths are having a beach party this weekend. It sounds _____.
   Do you want to go?

8. A few hours after dinner, Ellen and Bill got sick. They felt _____ for
   the rest of the evening.

▶ **Practice 11. Adverbs.** (Chart 14-4)
Write the adverb forms for the given adjectives.

1. quiet	_____*quietly*_____	8. careful	_____
2. clear	_____	9. quick	_____
3. neat	_____	10. slow	_____
4. correct	_____	11. late	_____
5. hard	_____	12. honest	_____
6. good	_____	13. fast	_____
7. early	_____	14. easy	_____

▶ **Practice 12. Adverbs.** (Chart 14-4)
Complete each sentence with the adverb form of the given adjective.

1. *clear*   Our teacher explains everything _____*clearly*_____.

2. *easy*   This is a simple car repair. I can do it _____.

3. *late*   Spiro came to class _____.

4. *safe*   The plane arrived at the airport _____.

5. *fast*   Mike talks too _____. I can't understand him.

6. *hard*   Ms. Chan is a hard worker. She worked _____ all her life.

7. *good*   I didn't understand my co-worker's instructions very
               _____.

8. *honest*   Andrew's reasons for missing work were hard to believe. Did you
               _____ believe them?

9. *soft*   When the students became loud, the teacher spoke _____.

10. *careless* The driver _____ threw a cigarette out the car window and
               started a forest fire.

▶ **Practice 13. Linking verbs, adjectives, and adverbs.** (Charts 14-3 and 14-4)
Complete the sentences with the adjective or adverb form of the given word. Remember, adjectives, not adverbs, follow linking verbs.

1. *nervous*   Bill looked _____nervous_____.

He began his speech _____nervously_____.

His hands shook _____nervously_____.

2. *beautiful*   Rita dressed _____ for the party.

She looked _____.

She wears _____ clothes.

3. *good*   The flowers smell _____.

They grow _____ in this sunny garden.

4. *good*   Does the food taste _____?

Robert is a _____ cook.

5. *interesting*   Your idea for the project sounds _____.

The project looks _____.

6. *bad*   Anita wrote a _____ check at the store and gave it to the clerk.

She had no money in the bank, but she didn't feel _____ about doing that.

7. *fast*   Tom drives _____.

He speaks _____ too.

▶ **Practice 14. Adjectives and adverbs.** (Charts 14-3 and 14-4)
Complete each sentence with the adjective or adverb form of the given word.

1. *clear*   The teacher speaks _____clearly_____. She gives _____clear_____ examples.

2. *correct*   You answered the question _____. That is the _____ answer.

3. *late*   I paid my phone bill _____. I don't like to make _____ payments.

4. *beautiful*   Look at the _____ pictures. The artist draws

     _____.

5. *honest*   Michael is an _____ child. He never lies. He answers

     questions _____.

6. *handsome*   Anton looked _____ on his wedding day. He is a

     _____ man.

7. *good*   Mmm. The food smells _____. I'm glad my roommate

     is a _____ cook.

8. *easy*   Isabelle writes _____ in English. Writing is an

     _____ subject for her.

9. *good*   The students swam _____. The team had a

     _____ competition.

10. *quick*   I need these copies _____. Is your copy machine

     _____?

11. *sweet*   Candy tastes very _____. I love

     _____ snacks.

12. *careless*   John is a _____ driver. Why does he drive so

     _____?

▶ **Practice 15. Adjective and adverb review.** (Charts 14-3 and 14-4)
Complete each sentence with the correct form of the given adjective or adverb.

1. *slow*   This is a _____*slow*_____ bus. I'm afraid we'll be late.

2. *slow*   There's a lot of traffic. The bus driver has to drive _____.

3. *hard*   The whole class studied _____ for the test.

4. *hard*   The teacher always gives _____ exams.

5. *clear*   The sky looks very _____ today.

6. *early*   The birds woke me up _____ this morning.

7. *fluent*   Jane speaks _____ French, but she can't speak English

     _____.

8. *neat*   Your homework looks very _____.

9. *careful*   It's clear that you do your work _____.

10. *good*   The teacher said our group gave a _____ presentation.

11. *good*   She said we worked together _____.

▶ **Practice 16. *All of, most of, some of,* and *almost all of.*** (Chart 14-5)
Match the picture with the sentence.

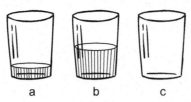

a   b   c

1. Meg drank most of the milk. Now the glass looks like ____*a*____.

2. Meg drank all of the milk. Now the glass looks like _____.

3. Meg drank some of the milk. Now the glass looks like _____ or _____.

4. Meg drank almost all of the milk. Now the glass looks like _____.

▶ **Practice 17. Understanding quantity expressions.** (Charts 14-5 and 14-6)
Choose the percentage that is closest in meaning to the quantity expression.

1. Almost all of the students are coming to the picnic.	(95%)	75%	100%
2. Most of the staff is coming to the picnic.	90%	100%	50%
3. All of the food for the picnic is ready.	90%	100%	95%
4. Some of the dishes are very spicy.	100%	60%	0%
5. Half of the class is bringing a friend.	50%	60%	40%
6. A lot of people in my class ride bikes to school.	75%	40%	25%
7. Some of the people in my class have motorcycles.	0%	99%	30%
8. Most of the teachers take the bus to school.	88%	65%	70%
9. All of the bus drivers are careful.	97%	90%	100%
10. Almost all of the drivers are friendly.	97%	100%	60%

▶ **Practice 18. Subject-verb agreement: expressions of quantity.** (Chart 14-6)
Choose the correct verb in each sentence.

1. All of your English work (*is* / *are*) correct.

2. All of your sentences (*is* / *are*) correct.

3. Some of your math work (*is* / *are*) correct.

4. Almost all of your science work (*is* / *are*) correct.

5. All of your facts (*is* / *are*) correct.

6. Most of my classes (*is* / *are*) hard.

7. Almost all of my classes (*is* / *are*) interesting.

8. Almost all of the class (*is* / *are*) ready.

9. Half of your homework (*is* / *are*) due.

10. Half of your assigments (*is* / *are*) due.

► **Practice 19. Agreement with quantity words.** (Chart 14-6)
Complete the sentences with *is* or *are*.

1. All of the work _____*is*_____ correct.

2. All of the answers _____ correct.

3. All of the information _____ correct.

4. All of the facts _____ correct.

5. Some of your homework _____ incorrect.

6. Some of the students _____ ready.

7. Almost all of the children _____ tired.

8. A lot of the class _____ tired.

9. A lot of the students _____ tired.

10. Half of the vocabulary _____ new for me.

11. Half of the words _____ new for me.

12. Most of the food _____ gone.

13. Some of the food _____ cold.

14. All of the apples _____ from our apple tree.

15. Almost all of the fruit _____ organic.

16. Most of the vegetables _____ fresh.

► **Practice 20. Review: expressions of quantity.** (Charts 14-5 and 14-6)
Choose the correct sentence in each group.

1. a. Some of the book are hard.
   b. Some of book is hard.
   c. Some of the book is hard.

2. a. Some of the money is gone.
   b. Some of money is gone.
   c. Some of the money are gone.

3. a. All of men have hats.
   b. All of the men have hats.
   c. All of the men has hats.

4. a. Most of the chairs is empty.
   b. Most of the chairs are empty.
   c. Most of chairs are empty.

5. a. Almost all of people are late.
   b. Almost all of the people are late.
   c. Almost all of the people is late.

6. a. Half of class is from Asia.
   b. Half of the class are from Asia.
   c. Half of the class is from Asia.

7. a. Half of the hotel rooms are ready.
   b. Half of hotel rooms are ready.
   c. Half of the hotel rooms is ready.

▶ **Practice 21. Subject-verb agreement with *every* and *all*.** (Chart 14-7)
Choose the correct completion for each sentence.

1. All of the _____ are ready to graduate.
   a. student   (b.) students

2. Every _____ in this room has worked hard.
   a. person   b. people

3. All of the _____ in the store are for sale.
   a. shirt   b. shirts

4. Are all of the _____ on sale too?
   a. sweater   b. sweaters

5. Every _____ at this party likes to dance.
   a. teenager   b. teenagers

6. Do all _____ like to dance?
   a. teenager   b. teenagers

7. Every _____ in the world wants loving parents.
   a. child   b. children

8. Do all _____ want to have children?
   a. parent   b. parents

▶ **Practice 22. Subject-verb agreement with *every* and *all*.** (Chart 14-7)
Choose the correct completion for each sentence.

1. All of the teachers _____ tests every week.
   a. gives   (b.) give

2. Everyone at this school _____ hard.
   a. studies   b. study

3. _____ all of the students in your class participate in discussions?
   a. Does   b. Do

4. _____ everyone in your class participate in discussions?
   a. Does   b. Do

5. Not everybody in the class _____ to give their opinion.
   a. likes   b. like

6. All of the people in line _____ concert tickets.
   a. is buying   b. are buying

7. Everything in these rooms _____ from South America.
   a. is   b. are

8. Every child at the party _____ a present to take home.
   a. get   b. gets

9. _____ everything look okay?
   a. Does   b. Do

10. Everything _____ okay.
    a. looks   b. look

▶ **Practice 23. Subject-verb agreement with *every* and *all*.** (Chart 14-7)
Check (✓) the incorrect sentences and correct them.

1. __✓__ Every ~~of the~~ teacher~~s~~ is on time.

2. _____ Every students is on time too.

3. _____ Everything in this room is very clean.

4. _____ Everything in the kitchen sink are dirty.

5. _____ Where does all of your friends live?

6. _____ Where was everyone when I called last night?

7. _____ Everybody in my family like dessert after dinner.

8. _____ Do everyone in your family likes dessert?

9. _____ Was everybody from your office at the wedding?

10. _____ Was all of the people at the wedding your friends?

11. _____ There are ten families in my apartment building. Everyone are friendly.

12. _____ Everything is okay.

► **Practice 24. Indefinite pronouns.** (Chart 14-8)
Complete the sentences with *something*, *someone*, *somebody*, *anything*, *anyone*, or *anybody*.

Statement	**Negative**

1. He ate _____ something _____ . He didn't eat _____ .

2. She met _____ / _____ . She didn't meet _anyone_ / _anybody_ .

Question

3. Did he eat _____ / _____ ?

4. Did she meet _____ / _____ / _____ / _____ ?

Statement	**Negative**

5. They bought _____ . They didn't buy _____ .

6. They spoke to _____ / _____ . They didn't speak to _____ / _____ .

Question

7. Did they buy _____ / _____ ?

8. Did they speak to _____ / _____ / _____ / _____ ?

► **Practice 25. Indefinite pronouns.** (Chart 14-8)
Choose all of the correct completions.

1. Did you talk to _____ at the pharmacy?
   a. somebody
   b. anything
   c. someone
   d. anyone
   e. anybody
   f. something

2. Did you see _____ outside?
   a. somebody
   b. anything
   c. someone
   d. anyone
   e. anybody
   f. something

3. I dropped off _____ at the airport.
   a. somebody
   b. anything
   c. someone
   d. anyone
   e. anybody
   f. something

4. Did you buy _____ at the mall?
   a. somebody
   b. anything
   c. someone
   d. anyone
   e. anybody
   f. something

Pharmacy

► **Practice 26. Indefinite pronouns.** (Chart 14-8)
Complete the sentences with **something**, **someone**, **somebody**, **anything**, **anyone**, or **anybody**. Use any word that fits.

1. I didn't buy _____*anything*_____ on sale at the grocery store.

2. I didn't talk to _____ at the grocery store.

3. I bought _____ for you at the mall.

4. I met _____ from high school at the train station.

5. Did you learn _____ at school today?

6. Did you know _____ at the party?

7. A: Close your eyes. I have _____
      special for you.

   B: Oh, no! I forgot it was our anniversary. I don't
      have _____ for you.

8. A: Did the doctor give you _____
      for your headaches?

   B: He did some tests. He didn't give me
      _____ yet.

9. A: I need to talk to _____ about my work schedule. Are you going to
      speak with _____ too?

   B: No, I'm not going to talk to _____.

10. A: I didn't see _____ from school on the bus today.

    B: A lot of people are absent. _____ got a cold, and now half of the
       class is sick.

11. A: Did you pick up _____ for dinner tonight?

    B: Sorry, I forgot. I didn't pick up _____.

12. A: I hear a loud noise. Maybe _____ is in the garage.

    B: I didn't hear _____. Are you sure?

    A: I'll look. Hmm. I don't see _____ or _____.

Chapter 15
Making Comparisons

▶ **Practice 1. Comparative form.** (Chart 15-1)
Write the comparative form for each adjective.

1. *young*   *younger than*

2. *wide*

3. *cheap*

4. *dark*

5. *smart*

6. *old*

7. *happy*

8. *important*

9. *difficult*

10. *expensive*

11. *easy*

12. *funny*

13. *good*

14. *far*

15. *fat*

16. *hot*

17. *thin*

18. *bad*

19. *pretty*

20. *famous*

► **Practice 2. Comparatives.** (Chart 15-1)
Complete the sentences. Use the comparative form of the given words.

1. *warm*   The weather today is _____*warmer than*_____ it was yesterday.

2. *funny*   This story is _____ that story.

3. *interesting* This book is _____ that book.

4. *smart*   Joe is _____ his brother.

5. *wide*   A highway is _____ an alley.

6. *large*   Your apartment is _____ mine.

7. *dark*   Ravi's hair is _____ Olaf's.

8. *good*   My wife's cooking is _____ mine.

9. *bad*   My cooking is _____ my wife's.

10. *confusing*   This story is _____ that story.

11. *far*   My house is _____ from downtown _____ your house is.

12. *good*   TV shows are _____ TV commercials.

13. *easy*   My English class is _____ my history class.

14. *beautiful*   A flower is _____ a weed.

a flower

a weed

► **Practice 3. Comparatives.** (Chart 15-1)
Compare the three places. Write comparative sentences using the given words. Give your own opinion.

the country   the city   the suburbs

Life in the . . .

1. *quiet*

    _____*Life in the country is quieter than life in the city.*_____

2. *expensive*

    _____

3. *relaxing*

_____

4. *busy*

_____

5. *convenient*

_____

6. *beautiful*

_____

7. *cheap*

_____

8. *nice*

_____

9. *safe*

_____

10. *good*

_____

▶ **Practice 4. Comparatives.** (Chart 15-1)
Compare the two culture classes using the given words. Give your own opinions.

Student Rating	
Culture 101 A	★★★★★
Culture 101 B	★★

CULTURE COURSES

Classes	101 A	101 B
Teaching style	discussions/games/movies	lecture
Student rating*	5/5	2/5
Homework	3 times/week	every day
Tests	3/term	every week
Average student grade	90%	75%

_____

*rating = 5 (excellent); 1 (bad).

1. interesting ____101 A is more interesting than 101 B.____

2. boring _____

3. hard _____

4. easy _____

5. popular _____

6. difficult _____

7. enjoyable _____

▶ **Practice 5. Comparative and superlative forms.** (Charts 15-1 and 15-2)
Write both the comparative form and superlative form of the given words.

	Comparative	Superlative
1. expensive	more expensive than	the most expensive
2. lazy		
3. clean		
4. old		
5. young		
6. new		
7. beautiful		
8. exciting		
9. nice		
10. quiet		
11. bad		
12. fat		
13. thin		
14. hot		
15. good		
16. cheap		
17. far		

► **Practice 6. Superlatives.** (Chart 15-2)
Complete the sentences using superlatives. Give your opinion.

1. *hard subject in high school*

   The ____*hardest subject in high school is calculus.*____

2. *beautiful city in the world*

   The _____

3. *interesting show on TV*

   The _____

4. *boring sport to watch*

   The _____

5. *easy language to learn*

   The _____

6. *talented movie star*

   The _____

7. *relaxing place to go for vacation*

   The _____

8. *good place to live*

   The _____

► **Practice 7. Superlatives.** (Chart 15-2)
Compare the three places to eat. Use the words from the box. Write superlative sentences using the given words. Give your own opinion.

> a fast-food restaurant
> a 5-star restaurant
> an Internet café

1. *expensive*____ *A 5-star restaurant is the most expensive.*____

2. *convenient* _____

3. *relaxing* _____

4. *busy* _____

5. *nice* _____

6. *interesting* _____

7. *popular* _____

8. *quiet* _____

9. *cheap* _____

10. *useful* _____

▶ **Practice 8. Review: comparatives and superlatives.** (Charts 15-1 and 15-2)
Write sentences using comparatives and superlatives. Use the given information.

Fluffy	Rex	Polly
15 lbs/7 kilos	70 lbs/32 kilos	1 ounce/.03 kilos
likes to sleep all day	likes to chase birds and hunt	likes to sing and look around
black and white fur	brown fur	blue and yellow feathers
2 years old	7 years old	10 years old

1. *lazy*   _____ *Fluffy is the laziest.* _____

_____ *Fluffy is lazier than Rex.* _____

2. *active*   _____

_____

3. *young*   _____

_____

4. *heavy*   _____

_____

5. *colorful*   _____

_____

6. *big* _____

_____

7. *old* _____

_____

8. *small* _____

_____

9. *light** _____

_____

▶ **Practice 9. *One of* + superlative + plural noun.** (Chart 15-3)
Complete each sentence with the correct form of the given adjective and noun.

1. *hot \ month*   August is one of _____*the hottest months*_____ in my
hometown.

2. *fast \ car*   A Ferrari is one of _____ in the
world.

3. *happy \ family*   Sam and Mia have one of _____
in our neighborhood.

4. *funny \ child*   Ricky is one of _____ in my class.

5. *good \ manager*   Louisa Hoff is one of _____ in
our office.

6. *tall \ woman*   Donna is one of _____ in our
class.

7. *old \ man*   Ken is one of _____ in our class.

8. *interesting \ person* Dan is one of _____ in our office.

9. *scary \ animal*   A tiger is one of _____ in the
world.

10. *easy \ language*   Is English one of _____ or one of
hard \ language   _____ to learn?

**light* = opposite of *heavy*.

► **Practice 10. *One of* + superlative + plural noun.** (Chart 15-3)
Make sentences with ***one of* + superlative**. Use the given adjectives and the sports from the box. Give your own opinion.

| baseball | golf | running | skydiving | swimming |
| boxing | karate | skiing | soccer | walking |

1. *easy sport to learn*   <u>*Running is one of the easiest sports to learn.*</u>

2. *dangerous* _____

3. *expensive* _____

4. *safe* _____

5. *difficult* _____

6. *interesting* _____

7. *good sport for your heart* _____

► **Practice 11. *One of* + superlative.** (Chart 15-3)
Make sentences with ***one of* + superlative**. Use the given words. Give your own opinion.

1. *small \ country*

    <u>*Liechtenstein is one of the smallest countries*</u> _____ in the world.

2. *big \ city*

_____.

3. *hard \ language to learn*

_____.

4. *interesting \ place to visit*

_____.

5. *pretty \ place to visit*

   _____.

6. *expensive \ city*

   _____ to visit.

7. *important \ person*

   _____ in the world.

▶ **Practice 12. Review: comparatives, superlatives, and *one of*.**
(Charts 15-1 → 15-3)
Complete the sentences with the correct form of the given words.

1. *big*   Asia is _____ *the biggest* _____ continent in the world.

2. *big*   North America is _____ South America.

3. *hot \ place*   The Sahara Desert is one of _____ in the
                       world.

4. *cold \ place*   The Arctic Circle is one of _____ in the
                       world.

5. *long*   The Nile is _____ the Amazon.

6. *large*   Is Canada _____ than
                       Russia?

7. *large*   Russia is _____ country
                       in the world.

8. *long*   The femur (thigh bone) is
                       _____ bone in our body.

9. *small*   _____ bone in our body
                       is in the ear. It is called the stirrup bone.

10. scary   Is a crocodile _____ an alligator, or are they
                       equally scary?

11. *scary*   What do you think is _____ animal in the
                       world?

12. *dangerous \ animal* The hippopotamus is one of _____ in the
                       world.

13. *expensive \ city* One of the _____ in the world is Tokyo.

14. *expensive*   Is Tokyo _____ than London?

► **Practice 13. Comparisons with adverbs.** (Charts 15-4 and 14-4)
Write the correct forms for the given adjectives.

Adjective	Adverb	Comparative	Superlative
1. quick	_quickly_	_more quickly_	_the most quickly_
2. clear			
3. slow			
4. beautiful			
5. neat			
6. careful			
7. fluent			
8. good			
9. hard			
10. early			
11. late			
12. fast			

► **Practice 14. Adverbs: comparatives and superlatives.** (Chart 15-4)
Complete the sentences with the correct form (comparative or superlative) of the given adverbs.

1. *beautifully*   The art students draw _____ more beautifully than _____ their instructor.

2. *carefully*   Rob drives _____ his brother.

3. *quickly*   Ted finished the test _____ of all.

4. *hard*   Who works _____ in your class?

5. *late*   The bride arrived at her wedding _____ the guests.

6. *early*   The groom arrived _____ of all.

7. *good*   Tina can swim _____ Tom.

8. *quickly*   Ana learns math _____ her classmates.

9. *slowly*   My grandfather walks _____ my grandmother.

10. *fluently*   Ben speaks English _____ of all the students.

11. *fast*   Ben learns languages _____ his classmates.

12. *good*   Sam can dive _____ of all.

▶ **Practice 15. Adjectives and adverbs: comparatives and superlatives.**
         (Charts 15-1, 15-2, 15-4, and 14-4)
Write the correct form of the given adjectives.

1. *heavy*   This suitcase is _____ *heavier than* _____ that one.

2. *dangerous*   A motorcycle is _____ a bike.

3. *dangerous*   Tom drives _____ Fred.

4. *dangerous*   Steven drives _____ of all.

5. *clear*   Pedro speaks _____ Ernesto.

6. *clear*   Our reading teacher is _____ our grammar teacher.

7. *clear*   She speaks _____ of all.

8. *hard*   Nina works _____ Ivan.

9. *hard*   Carlos works _____ of all.

10. *good*   My son can play the guitar _____ I can.

11. *good*   My mother can play the guitar _____ of all.

12. *good*   I like the guitar _____ the piano.

13. *long*   My husband's workdays are _____ his co-workers' workdays.

14. *long*   His workdays are _____ of all.

15. *neat*   Mrs. Bell's handwriting looks _____
                 Mr. Bell.

16. *neat*   Mrs. Bell dresses _____
                 Mr. Bell.

► **Practice 16. *The same (as), similar (to),* and *different (from).*** (Chart 15-5)
Complete the sentences with the correct preposition (*to, as, from*) or Ø.

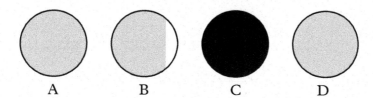

A   B   C   D

1. A and D are the same _____Ø_____.

2. A is the same _____ D.

3. A and C are different _____.

4. A and B are similar _____.

5. A is different _____ C.

6. A is similar _____ B.

7. B and D are similar _____.

8. C and D are different _____.

► **Practice 17. *The same (as), similar (to),* and *different (from).*** (Chart 15-5)
Complete the sentences using ***the same (as), similar (to),* or *different (from).***

1   2   3   4

1. 4 is _____*the same as*_____ 1.

2. 1 and 4 are _____*the same*_____.

3. 1 and 2 are _____.

4. 2 and 4 are _____.

5. 2 and 3 are _____.

6. 1 is _____ 2.

7. 2 is _____ 3.

8. 4 is _____ 2.

9. 1 and 3 are _____.

10. 3 is _____ 4.

▶ **Practice 18. The same (as), similar (to), and different (from).** (Chart 15-5)
Make sentences using the given words.

1. English \ Japanese

    a. (*different*) _____English and Japanese are different._____

    b. (*different from*) _____English is different from Japanese._____

2. trains \ buses

    a. (*similar*) _____

    b. (*similar to*) _____

3. your grammar book \ my grammar book

    a. (*the same as*) _____

    b. (*the same*) _____

4. women \ men

    a. (*different*) _____

    b. (*different from*) _____

▶ **Practice 19. Like and alike.** (Chart 15-6)
Complete the sentences with *like* or *alike*.

1. A pen is _____like_____ a pencil.

2. Fingers and toes are _____.

3. Hands and feet are _____.

4. Highways and freeways are _____.

5. A freeway is _____ a highway.

6. The Pacific Ocean and Atlantic Ocean are _____.

7. A mouse is _____ a rat.

8. A mouse isn't _____ a lion.

9. Are people around the world _____?

10. Are lakes and rivers _____ oceans?

11. French and Italian are _____ because they are both Romance languages.

12. French is _____ Italian. They both come from Latin.

▶ **Practice 20. *Like* and *alike*.** (Chart 15-6)
Complete the sentences with *like* or *alike* and a word from the box. Then explain why they are alike.

dark chocolate	milkshakes	physics
✓ doctors	newspapers	Thailand
knives		

1. *like*   Nurses _____ *are like doctors. They help people.* _____

2. *alike*   White chocolate _____

3. *like*   Magazines _____

4. *alike*   Scissors _____

5. *alike*   Malaysia _____

6. *like*   Ice-cream cones _____

7. *alike*   Chemistry _____

▶ **Practice 21. *The same as, similar (to), different (from), like,* and *alike*.**
               (Charts 15-5 and 15-6)
Choose all the completions that are grammatically correct and make sense.

1. Chapter 1 and Chapter 15 of this book are _____.
   a. different
   b. different from
   c. similar to
   d. like
   e. not the same

2. The color red is _____ the color orange.
   a. alike
   b. similar to
   c. similar
   d. like
   e. the same as

3. Lemons and limes taste _____.
   a. the same
   b. different
   c. different from
   d. alike
   e. similar

► **Practice 22. Review.** (Charts 15-1 → 15-6)

Part I. Read the story.

A Career Change

Martina is in college, but she is older than the other students. In fact, she is the oldest student in the class. This is her second time in college. The first time she went to college, she studied accounting. Now she is back in school because she wants to change careers.

She is interested in two fields: medicine and fire fighting. Martina likes to help people. Her mother was a nurse, and Martina learned a lot about taking care of people from her mother. Her brother is a firefighter, and she loves to hear stories about his work. She is thinking about three different careers: emergency room doctor, paramedic, or firefighter.

Martina wants an exciting job because she gets bored easily. She likes adventure and physical work. Firefighters have physically hard jobs. The work is also very dangerous. Martina likes the idea of going into burning buildings to rescue people. Of the three jobs, Martina thinks firefighting will be the most exciting.

Paramedic and emergency room work are similar. Both paramedics and doctors treat people in emergency situations. But Martina will need to spend much more time in school if she wants to be a doctor. If she chooses to become a paramedic, she can finish her studies more quickly.

The cost of education is important to her. The training for a doctor is the most expensive of the three careers. She will need scholarships or loans to pay for her education. Right now she has enough money for paramedic or firefighter training. But she knows she will earn more money later as a doctor.

She's not sure which job is the best for her. She knows she wants to help people, and she wants to do something exciting, so she is sure that she will choose one of these careers.

Part II. Check (✓) the true statements, according to the information in the story.

1. _____ The training for a paramedic is more expensive than the training for a doctor.

2. _____ Martina can become a paramedic more quickly than she can become a doctor.

3. _____ Firefighter training is cheaper than training for a doctor.

4. _____ An emergency room doctor works harder than a paramedic.

5. _____ The most exciting job for Martina will be firefighting.

6. _____ Doctors and paramedics do exactly the same work.

► **Practice 23. Using *but.*** (Chart 15-7)
Complete each sentence with the opposite adjective.

1. A sports car is fast, but a bike is _____*slow*_____ .

2. The sun is hot, but the moon is _____ .

3. Mr. Benton is an easy teacher, but Mrs. Benton is a _____ teacher.

4. Building a paper airplane is simple, but building a real airplane is

   _____ .

5. A giraffe has a long neck, but a rabbit has a _____ neck.

6. Real diamonds are expensive, but fake diamonds are _____ .

7. A hard pillow is uncomfortable, but a soft pillow is _____ .

8. Red is a warm color, but blue is a _____ color.

9. Feathers are light, but rocks are _____ .

10. The wheel is an old invention, but the car is a _____ invention.

► **Practice 24. Verbs after *but.*** (Chart 15-8)
Complete each sentence with an appropriate verb: affirmative or negative.

1. Fried foods are greasy, but boiled foods _____*aren't*_____ .

2. Cars can't fly, but planes _____ .

3. Kids often don't like vegetables, but adults generally _____ .

4. Warm baths feel relaxing, but cold baths _____ .

5. A warm bath feels relaxing, but a cold bath _____ .

6. The students were in class yesterday, but their teacher _____ .

7. Susan won't be at the party, but her husband _____ .

8. I don't like fish, but my husband _____ .

9. Ralph studied hard, but Daniel _____ .

10. Newborn babies sleep most of the day, but adults usually _____ .

11. Billy isn't a hard worker, but his brother _____ .

12. A few students in the class can understand the math problems, but I _____ .

13. Dr. Jones will work this weekend, but his partner _____ .

14. The English books aren't in the bookstore, but the science books _____.

15. Mark wasn't on time for class, but Gary _____.

16. Mark didn't arrive on time, but Gary _____.

17. Electric cars are quiet, but diesel cars _____.

▶ **Practice 25. Verbs after *but*.** (Chart 15-8)
Complete the sentences with your own words.

1. Birds have wings, but ____*cows don't*_____.

2. Dogs bark, but _____.

3. Fish can stay underwater for a long time, but _____.

4. Skunks don't smell good, but _____.

5. The weather in the desert is hot, but _____.

6. Tight shoes aren't comfortable, but _____.

7. Honey is sweet, but _____.

8. It (was/wasn't) cold yesterday, but today it _____.

9. I will be here tomorrow, but Evan _____.

10. The Smiths are going to celebrate their anniversary, but we _____.

▶ **Practice 26. Review.** (Chapter 15)
Choose the correct completion for each sentence.

1. Fingers and toes are _____.
   a. similar   b. like   c. the same   d. different from

2. The weather in Canada is _____ the weather in Mexico.
   a. coolest   b. cooler than   c. the coolest   d. more cool than

3. What is your _____ color?
   a. more favorite b. the most favorite c. favorite   d. more favorite than

4. Men are _____ women.
   a. different from b. different as   c. different   d. different to

5. We live _____ from town than you do.
   a. far   b. more far   c. farthest   d. farther

6. Is happiness _____ money?
   a. importanter than   c. important
   b. more important than   d. more important

7. The weather is cold today, but yesterday it _____.
   a. isn't   b. doesn't   c. wasn't   d. didn't

8. I have _____ you.
   a. a same shirt   b. same shirt   c. the same shirt as   d. same shirt as

9. The Atlantic Ocean isn't _____ ocean in the world.
   a. a biggest   b. the biggest   c. a big   d. bigger than

10. Alison and Jeff don't study in the library, but Kathy _____.
    a. does   b. doesn't   c. isn't   d. is

11. I thought the math test was hard, but my friends thought it was _____.
    a. easy   b. difficult   c. easier   d. hardest

12. I thought it was one of _____ of the year.
    a. the hard test   b. a hard tests   c. a hard test   d. the hardest tests

Appendix 1
Irregular Verbs

SIMPLE FORM	SIMPLE PAST	SIMPLE FORM	SIMPLE PAST
be	was, were	keep	kept
become	became	know	knew
begin	began	leave	left
bend	bent	lend	lent
bite	bit	lose	lost
blow	blew	make	made
break	broke	meet	met
bring	brought	pay	paid
build	built	put	put
buy	bought	read	read
catch	caught	ride	rode
choose	chose	ring	rang
come	came	run	ran
cost	cost	say	said
cut	cut	see	saw
do	did	sell	sold
draw	drew	send	sent
drink	drank	shake	shook
drive	drove	shut	shut
eat	ate	sing	sang
fall	fell	sit	sat
feed	fed	sleep	slept
feel	felt	speak	spoke
fight	fought	spend	spent
find	found	stand	stood
fly	flew	steal	stole
forget	forgot	swim	swam
get	got	take	took
give	gave	teach	taught
go	went	tear	tore
grow	grew	tell	told
hang	hung	think	thought
have	had	throw	threw
hear	heard	understand	understood
hide	hid	wake up	woke up
hit	hit	wear	wore
hold	held	win	won
hurt	hurt	write	wrote

Appendix 2
English Handwriting

English Handwriting					
PRINTING			CURSIVE		
Aa	Jj	Ss	Aa	Jj	Ss
Bb	Kk	Tt	Bb	Kk	Tt
Cc	Ll	Uu	Cc	Ll	Uu
Dd	Mm	Vv	Dd	Mm	Vv
Ee	Nn	Ww	Ee	Nn	Ww
Ff	Oo	Xx	Ff	Oo	Xx
Gg	Pp	Yy	Gg	Pp	Yy
Hh	Qq	Zz	Hh	Qq	Zz
Ii	Rr		Ii	Rr	

Vowels = *a, e, i, o, u*

Consonants = *b, c, d, f, g, h, j, k, l, m, n, p, q, r, s, t, v, w, x, y, z**

---

*The letter **z** is pronounced "zee" in American English and "zed" in British English.

Appendix 3
Numbers

CARDINAL NUMBERS		ORDINAL NUMBERS	
1	one	1st	first
2	two	2nd	second
3	three	3rd	third
4	four	4th	fourth
5	five	5th	fifth
6	six	6th	sixth
7	seven	7th	seventh
8	eight	8th	eighth
9	nine	9th	ninth
10	ten	10th	tenth
11	eleven	11th	eleventh
12	twelve	12th	twelfth
13	thirteen	13th	thirteenth
14	fourteen	14th	fourteenth
15	fifteen	15th	fifteenth
16	sixteen	16th	sixteenth
17	seventeen	17th	seventeenth
18	eighteen	18th	eighteenth
19	nineteen	19th	nineteenth
20	twenty	20th	twentieth
21	twenty-one	21st	twenty-first
22	twenty-two	22nd	twenty-second
23	twenty-three	23rd	twenty-third
24	twenty-four	24th	twenty-fourth
25	twenty-five	25th	twenty-fifth
26	twenty-six	26th	twenty-sixth
27	twenty-seven	27th	twenty-seventh
28	twenty-eight	28th	twenty-eighth
29	twenty-nine	29th	twenty-ninth
30	thirty	30th	thirtieth
40	forty	40th	fortieth
50	fifty	50th	fiftieth
60	sixty	60th	sixtieth
70	seventy	70th	seventieth
80	eighty	80th	eightieth
90	ninety	90th	ninetieth
100	one hundred	100th	one hundredth
200	two hundred	200th	two hundredth
1,000	one thousand	1,000th	one thousandth
10,000	ten thousand	10,000th	ten thousandth
100,000	one hundred thousand	100,000th	one hundred thousandth
1,000,000	one million	1,000,000th	one millionth

Appendix 4
Days/Months/Seasons

DAYS	ABBREVIATION	MONTHS	ABBREVIATION	SEASONS*
Monday	Mon.	January	Jan.	winter
Tuesday	Tues.	February	Feb.	spring
Wednesday	Wed.	March	Mar.	summer
Thursday	Thurs.	April	Apr.	fall or autumn
Friday	Fri.	May	May	
Saturday	Sat.	June	Jun.	
Sunday	Sun.	July	Jul.	
		August	Aug.	
		September	Sept.	
		October	Oct.	
		November	Nov.	
		December	Dec.	

*Seasons of the year are only capitalized when they begin a sentence.

WRITING DATES:

Month/Day/Year

10/31/41 = October 31, 1941
4/15/98 = April 15, 1998
7/4/1906 = July 4, 1906
7/4/07 = July 4, 2007

SAYING DATES:

Usual Written Form	Usual Spoken Form
January 1	January first / the first of January
March 2	March second / the second of March
May 3	May third / the third of May
June 4	June fourth / the fourth of June
August 5	August fifth / the fifth of August
October 10	October tenth / the tenth of October
November 27	November twenty-seventh / the twenty-seventh of November

Appendix 5

Two-Syllable Verbs: Spelling of -ED and -ING

VERB	SPEAKING STRESS			Some verbs have two syllables. In (a): *visit* has two syllables: *vis + it*. In the word *visit*, the stress is on the first syllable. In (b): the stress is on the second syllable in the word *admit*.
(a) visit	**VIS** • it			
(b) admit	ad • **MIT**			

VERB	STRESS	-ED FORM	-ING FORM	For two-syllable verbs that end in a vowel and a consonant:
(c) visit	**VIS** • it	visited	visiting	• The consonant is not doubled if the stress is on the first syllable, as in (c) and (d).
(d) open	**O** • pen	opened	opening	
(e) admit	ad • **MIT**	admitted	admitting	• The consonant is doubled if the stress is on the second syllable, as in (e) and (f).
(f) occur	oc • **CUR**	occurred	occurring	

<table>
<tr><td colspan="8" align="center">COMMON VERBS</td></tr>
<tr><td colspan="4">Stress on first syllable:</td><td colspan="4">Stress on second syllable:</td></tr>
<tr><td>VERB</td><td>STRESS</td><td>-ED FORM</td><td>-ING FORM</td><td>VERB</td><td>STRESS</td><td>-ED FORM</td><td>-ING FORM</td></tr>
<tr><td>answer</td><td>**AN** • swer</td><td>answered</td><td>answering</td><td>prefer</td><td>pre • **FER**</td><td>preferred</td><td>preferring</td></tr>
<tr><td>happen</td><td>**HAP** • pen</td><td>happened</td><td>happening</td><td>permit</td><td>per • **MIT**</td><td>permitted</td><td>permitting</td></tr>
<tr><td>listen</td><td>**LIS** • ten</td><td>listened</td><td>listening</td><td>refer</td><td>re • **FER**</td><td>referred</td><td>referring</td></tr>
<tr><td>offer</td><td>**OF** • fer</td><td>offered</td><td>offering</td><td>begin</td><td>be • **GIN**</td><td>(no -ed form)</td><td>beginning</td></tr>
<tr><td>enter</td><td>**EN** • ter</td><td>entered</td><td>entering</td><td></td><td></td><td></td><td></td></tr>
</table>

Index

Answer Key

CHAPTER 1

PRACTICE 1, p. 1.
2. She is late.
3. It is difficult.
4. He is sick.
5. She is also sick.
6. He is ready.
7. It is cold.
8. She is single.

PRACTICE 2, p. 1.
1. is
2. am
3. are
4. is
5. is
6. is
7. is
8. are
9. is
10. is

PRACTICE 3, p. 2.
3. B
4. B
5. A
6. A, B

PRACTICE 4, p. 2.
2. are
3. is
4. is
5. is
6. are
7. are
8. are
9. are
10. are

PRACTICE 5, p. 2.
3. She
4. He
5. She
6. They
7. We
8. We
9. She
10. You
11. They
12. They
13. She
14. He
15. We

PRACTICE 6, p. 3.
2. a
3. a
4. an
5. a
6. an
7. an
8. a
9. a
10. an

PRACTICE 7, p. 3.
2. a   yes
3. a   no
4. an   yes
5. a   yes
6. a   no
7. a   yes
8. a   yes

PRACTICE 8, p. 4.
2. dogs
3. languages
4. machines
5. countries
6. seasons
7. dictionaries

PRACTICE 9, p. 4.
3. Russian and Spanish are languages.
4. China is a country.
5. South America is a continent.
6. Dogs are animals.
7. Bangkok is a city.
8. Thailand is a country.

PRACTICE 10, p. 4.
3. Ø . . . Ø
4. Ø . . . Ø
5. s . . . s
6. Ø . . . Ø
7. Ø . . . s
8. Ø . . . Ø . . . s
9. Ø . . . Ø . . . s

PRACTICE 11, p. 5.
2. is
3. are
4. are
5. is
6. are
7. is
8. are
9. are
10. is
11. are

PRACTICE 12, p. 5.
2. am a student
3. are a student
4. are students
5. are students
6. is a student
7. are students
8. are students
9. are students
10. are students

PRACTICE 13, p. 6.
2. Africa is a continent.
3. Asia and Africa are continents.
4. Paris is a city.
5. Cairo is a city.
6. Paris and Cairo are cities.
7. Malaysia is a country.
8. Japan and Malaysia are countries.

PRACTICE 14, p. 6.
3. is a language
4. are languages
5. are countries
6. is a country
7. is an insect (also correct: an animal)
8. are insects (also correct: animals)
9. is a machine
10. are machines
11. is a city
12. are cities

PRACTICE 15, p. 7.
2. you're
3. he's
4. we're
5. it's
6. they're
7. she's

PRACTICE 16, p. 7.
2. are not
3. is not
4. is not
5. is not
6. is not
7. are not
8. are not
9. are not
10. are not
11. is not
12. are not

PRACTICE 17, p. 7.
2. is not   isn't OR she's not
3. am not   I'm not
4. is not   isn't OR he's not
5. is not   isn't
6. is not   isn't OR it's not
7. are not   aren't OR we're not
8. are not   aren't OR you're not
9. are not   aren't OR they're not

PRACTICE 18, p. 8.
2. is
3. is
4. isn't
5. are
6. aren't
7. is
8. are
9. aren't
10. isn't

PRACTICE 19, p. 8.
2. aren't . . . 're machines
3. is . . . isn't
4. aren't . . . 're seasons
5. isn't . . . 's a language
6. 'm not . . . 'm a student
7. 're . . . 're

PRACTICE 20, p. 8.
2. isn't
3. are
4. aren't
5. isn't . . . is
6. is/isn't . . . is/isn't
7. is/isn't . . . is/isn't
8. aren't . . . are
9. is . . . isn't
10. aren't . . . are

PRACTICE 21, p. 9.
2. A circle is round. It isn't square.
3. A piano is heavy. It isn't light.
4. Potato chips aren't sweet. They are salty.
5. The Sahara Desert is large. It isn't small.
6. The Nile River isn't short. It is long.
7. This exercise is/isn't easy. It is/isn't difficult.
8. My grammar book is/isn't new. It is/isn't old.
9. Electric cars are/aren't expensive. They are/aren't cheap.

PRACTICE 22, p. 10.
2. at; <u>at the train station</u>
3. from; <u>from Kuwait</u>
4. on; <u>on my desk</u>
5. in; <u>in her purse</u>
6. on; <u>on First Street</u>
7. next to; <u>next to the bank</u>
8. under; <u>under my desk</u>
9. between; <u>between my cheeks</u>
10. on; <u>on the third floor</u>
11. above; <u>above Mr. Kwan's apartment</u>

PRACTICE 23, p. 10.

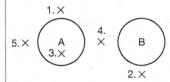

PRACTICE 24, p. 10.

Nouns	Adjectives	Prepositions
city	easy	at
country	empty	between
parents	happy	next to
sister	hungry	on
teacher	single	outside

PRACTICE 25, p. 11.
Sample answers:
2. a girl.
   at home.
   nice.
3. big.
   in Asia.
   a country.
4. on the desk.
   clear.
   a textbook.

PRACTICE 26, p. 11.

2. Canada is in North America.
3. France is next to Germany.
4. The downstairs of a building isn't above the upstairs.
5. Ice isn't hot.
6. Apples and oranges aren't vegetables.
7. Airplanes are fast.
8. Vegetables are healthy.
9. An alligator is dangerous.
10. Alligators aren't friendly.

PRACTICE 27, p. 12.

2. are
3. is
4. is
5. are
6. are
7. are

PRACTICE 28, p. 12.

2. is
3. is
4. am
5. is
6. is
7. am
8. is
9. am

CHAPTER 2

PRACTICE 1, p. 13.

2. c
3. b
4. b
5. a
6. c
7. c
8. c
9. b
10. c

PRACTICE 2, p. 13.

2. Is he a student?
3. Are they students?
4. Is she from New Zealand?
5. Are you ready?
6. Are we ready?
7. Is it ready?
8. Am I ready?

PRACTICE 3, p. 14.

2. Are bananas healthy?
3. Is Taka a nurse?
4. Are the kids at school?
5. Are you/we ready for the test?
6. Is Liz at school?
7. Are you tired?

PRACTICE 4, p. 14.

2. they are
3. they are
4. he is
5. they are
6. it is
7. she is
8. I am
9. we are
10. you are

PRACTICE 5, p. 15.

2. Is . . . is
3. Is . . . is
4. Is . . . is
5. Are . . . are
6. Is . . . is
7. Are . . . are
8. Are . . . are
9. Are . . . am
10. Are . . . are

PRACTICE 6, p. 15.

1. Is Paris a country? No, it isn't.
2. Are October and November months? Yes, they are.
3. Is soccer a season? No, it isn't.
4. Are fall and winter seasons? Yes, they are.

PRACTICE 7, p. 16.

2. isn't
3. Are Rosa and Dong . . . they are
4. Is Rosa . . . isn't
5. Is Dong . . . he is
6. Is Rosa . . . she is
7. Is Dong . . . isn't
8. Are Rosa and Dong . . . aren't

PRACTICE 8, p. 16.

1. A: Are you
2. A: Are you
   B: aren't . . . 're
   B: he isn't . . . 's

PRACTICE 9, p. 17.

2. b
3. a
4. b
5. a
6. b

PRACTICE 10, p. 17.

2. Is the teacher in the classroom?
3. Where are Pablo and Dina?
4. Are Pablo and Dina at home?
5. Is the map in the car?
6. Where is the store?
7. Are you outside?
8. Where are you?

PRACTICE 11, p. 18.

2. have
3. has
4. has
5. has
6. has
7. has
8. has
9. have
10. have
11. have

PRACTICE 12, p. 18.

2. has
3. have
4. have . . . has
5. has . . . has
6. have . . . have
7. has
8. have
9. has . . . has
10. has
11. have

PRACTICE 13, p. 19.

1. *My apartment*
   c. is
   d. is
   e. has
   f. is
   g. is
   h. has
   i. has
2. *My neighbor*
   a. is
   b. has
   c. is
   d. has
   e. has
   f. is
   g. is
   h. is
   i. has

PRACTICE 14, p. 19.
2. are . . . have
3. am . . . have
4. are . . . have
5. has . . . is

PRACTICE 15, p. 20.
2. has
3. has
4. have
5. has
6. have
7. has
8. is

PRACTICE 16, p. 20.
2. Your
3. My
4. Our
5. Your
6. Their
7. Their
8. His
9. Her
10. Their
11. Our
12. Our

PRACTICE 17, p. 21.
2. Her
3. His
4. Their
5. Her
6. Their

PRACTICE 18, p. 21.
2. have . . . Your
3. have . . . Their
4. have . . . Our
5. has . . . His
6. has . . . Her
7. has . . . His
8. have . . . Their
9. have . . . My
10. have . . . Their

PRACTICE 19, p. 22.
2. That
3. That
4. This
5. This
6. That
7. This
8. That

PRACTICE 20, p. 23.
2. These
3. Those
4. Those
5. These
6. Those

PRACTICE 21, p. 23.
1. These
2. Those
3. This
4. Those
5. That
6. These
7. This

PRACTICE 22, p. 23.
2. These . . . Those
3. This . . . That
4. These . . . That
5. This . . . That
6. These . . . Those
7. This . . . Those

PRACTICE 23, p. 24.
2. a
3. b
4. a
5. b
6. b

PRACTICE 24, p. 24.
2. What is that?
3. What are these?
4. Who are they?
5. What are those?
6. Who is that?

PRACTICE 25, p. 25.
2. This is Donna.
3. Yes, it is.
4. Yes, she is.
5. No, it isn't.
6. Yes, he is.
7. It's in Norway.
8. Yes, I am.
9. This is an insect.

PRACTICE 26, p. 25.
2. Their
3. her
4. their
5. His

PRACTICE 27, p. 26.
2. is
3. has
4. is
5. is
6. is
7. is
8. has
9. is
10. is
11. is
12. am
13. am
14. have
15. are

CHAPTER 3

PRACTICE 1, p. 27.
2. wake
3. wake
4. wakes
5. wake
6. wakes
7. wakes
8. wakes
9. wake
10. wakes
11. wakes
12. wake

PRACTICE 2, p. 27.
teaches, leaves, catches, comes, takes, begin, teaches, stays, drives, gets

PRACTICE 3, p. 28.
2. get
3. makes
4. cooks
5. leave
6. drive
7. listen to
8. work
9. arrive
10. come
11. take

PRACTICE 4, p. 28.

2. wake
3. eat
4. eats
5. leaves
6. take
7. cooks
8. falls
9. eat
10. fall
11. see
12. have

PRACTICE 5, p. 29.

2. I rarely eat breakfast.
3. The students seldom buy their lunch at school.
4. They usually bring lunch from home.
5. My husband and I often go out to a restaurant for dinner.
6. My husband sometimes drinks coffee with dinner.
7. We never have dessert.

PRACTICE 6, p. 29.

2. Roger seldom/rarely gets up late.
3. Mr. and Mrs. Phillips usually go to the movies on weekends.
4. I often clean my apartment.
5. My roommate never cleans our apartment.
6. The students always do their homework.
7. The teacher sometimes corrects papers on weekends.

PRACTICE 9, p. 31.

2. I pay my phone bill once a month.
3. I exercise once a day.
4. I visit my cousins twice a year.
5. Dr. Williams checks her email three times a day.
6. The Browns take a long vacation once a year.
7. Cyndi gives dinner parties twice a month.
8. Sam buys vegetables at the farmers' market twice a week.

PRACTICE 10, p. 32.

2. often . . . Ø
3. Ø . . . sometimes
4. Ø . . . rarely
5. rarely . . . Ø
6. Ø . . . usually
7. usually . . . Ø
8. never . . . Ø
9. never . . . Ø
10. Ø . . . always

PRACTICE 11, p. 32.

2. The students often help the teacher.
3. The classroom is always clean.
4. The parents usually visit the class.
5. The parents sometimes help the students with their work.
6. The parents are always helpful.
7. The classroom is seldom quiet.

PRACTICE 12, p. 33.

-s	-es
eats	finishes
listens	fixes
sleeps	kisses
talks	wishes

PRACTICE 13, p. 33.

2. teaches
3. mix
4. mixes
5. misses
6. miss
7. brush
8. brushes
9. wash
10. washes
10. cooks
12. reads
13. watches
14. begins
15. come
16. comes

PRACTICE 14, p. 34.

2. studies
3. study
4. studies
5. study
6. study
7. studies
8. study
9. studies
10. study

PRACTICE 15, p. 34.

-ies	-s
flies	enjoys
studies	pays
tries	plays
worries	says

PRACTICE 16, p. 34.

2. brushes
3. closes
4. fly
5. flies
6. stops
7. fixes
8. call . . . calls
9. studies
10. helps

PRACTICE 17, p. 35.

1. b. does homework at 10:00.
   c. goes to work at 11:00.
2. a. has class at 10:00.
   b. does homework at 11:00.
   c. goes to work at 2:00.
3. a. do homework at 9:00.
   b. have class at 11:00.
   c. go to work at 1:00.

PRACTICE 18, p. 36.

2. catches
3. gets
4. works
5. fixes
6. come
7. finishes
8. often meets
9. helps
10. usually have
11. goes
12. has
13. is often
14. enjoys

PRACTICE 19, p. 36.

2. Ø
3. Ø
4. -s
5. -s
6. Ø
7. -s
8. -s
9. Ø
10. Ø
11. -s
12. Ø
13. -s
14. -s
15. -s
16. Ø

PRACTICE 20, p. 37.
(Answers may vary.)

need	*want*
electricity	diamond jewelry
food	a digital camera
money	an expensive house
a place to live	a leather coat
water	a smartphone
	a sports car

PRACTICE 21, p. 37.

Part I.
Infinitives:
wants to have
needs to have
wants to do
needs to take
wants to skip
wants to have

Part II.
1. a, b
2. a, b, c
3. d, e

PRACTICE 22, p. 38.
2. to watch
3. to play
4. to talk to
5. to go . . . to cash
6. to do
7. to wash
8. to go . . . to buy
9. to marry
10. to take
11. to eat
12. to listen to
13. to swim
14. to pay

PRACTICE 23, p. 39.
1. don't eat
2. don't have . . . don't eat . . . aren't
3. doesn't have . . . doesn't eat . . . isn't
4. doesn't have . . . doesn't eat . . . isn't
5. doesn't have . . . doesn't eat . . . isn't
6. don't have . . . don't eat . . . aren't
7. don't have . . . don't eat . . . aren't

PRACTICE 24, p. 39.
2. You don't need more time.
3. They don't eat breakfast.
4. Yoshi doesn't like bananas.
5. Susan doesn't do her homework.
6. We don't save our money.
7. The printer doesn't work.
8. The coffee doesn't taste good.
9. Mr. and Mrs. Costa don't drive to work.

PRACTICE 25, p. 40.
3. doesn't have
4. breaks
5. don't grow
6. doesn't walk
7. cries
8. don't fly
9. don't have
10. helps
11. doesn't fix
12. fixes
13. don't like
14. chase
15. isn't
16. rains
17. doesn't rain
18. don't wash
19. washes

PRACTICE 26, p. 41.
Part I.
2. Mark watches TV.
3. Tom walks to school.
4. Tom, Janet, and Mark study grammar.
5. Janet goes shopping.

Part II.
7. Tom and Janet don't watch TV.
8. Mark doesn't skip lunch.
9. Janet doesn't eat dinner at home.
10. Tom and Mark don't eat dinner out.

PRACTICE 27, p. 41.
2. knows . . . doesn't know
3. want . . . don't want
4. isn't . . . doesn't want
5. doesn't drink . . . drinks
6. am not . . . don't have
7. doesn't belong . . . belongs
8. don't live . . . have
9. is . . . isn't . . . don't need
10. is . . . don't have
11. doesn't eat . . . isn't
12. read . . . don't watch
13. doesn't read . . . watches

PRACTICE 28, p. 42.
2. Do they study?
3. Does he know?
4. Does the doctor know?
5. Do we know?
6. Do I understand?
7. Do you understand?
8. Does the manager understand?
9. Does your roommate work?
10. Does the car work?
11. Does it work?
12. Do I care?
13. Does she care?

PRACTICE 29, p. 43.
1. b. Does he play soccer?
   d. Does he lift weights?
2. a. Does he run?
   b. Does he swim/play soccer?
   c. Does he lift weights?
3. a. Do they play soccer?
   b. Do they swim?
   c. Do they run?

PRACTICE 30, p. 44.
2. a	6. b
3. b	7. a
4. b	8. b
5. a	

PRACTICE 31, p. 44.
2. Does he fix . . . he doesn't
3. Do you fly . . . I don't
4. Do you teach . . . we don't
5. Do you clean . . . we don't
6. Do they design . . . they don't
7. Does she write . . . she doesn't
8. Do you work . . . I don't
9. Do they build . . . they don't
10. Does he play . . . he doesn't

PRACTICE 32, p. 45.

2. Is
3. Does
4. Do
5. Is
6. Do
7. Do
8. Do
9. Do
10. Are

PRACTICE 33, p. 46.

1. B: am
   A: Are
   B: am
   B: don't
2. A: Do
   B: do . . . is
3. A: Are
   B: am
   A: Do
   A: Do
   B: don't
4. A: Are
   A: Are
   A: are
   B: are
5. A: Is
   B: isn't
   A: is
   A: Is
   B: isn't
   A: is
6. A: are . . . Do
   B: Are
   A: aren't
   B: Are
   B: are

PRACTICE 34, p. 47.

1. Where
2. Where
3. What
4. What
5. Where
6. What
7. Where
8. What

PRACTICE 35, p. 47.

2. What does the teacher want?
3. Where does Dr. Varma stay?
4. Where do you catch the bus?
5. What does Lillian need?
6. What do the children want?
7. Where do the construction workers eat lunch?
8. Where are Victoria and Franco?
9. What does Mark bring his wife every week?
10. What do you need?

PRACTICE 36, p. 48.

2. Where does he work in the summer?
3. What does he look for?
4. Where does he stay?
5. Where does he work in the winter?
6. What does he teach?
7. Where does he live?
8. What does he love?

PRACTICE 37, p. 49.

3. When
4. What
5. Where
6. When
7. What
8. What
9. When
10. Where

PRACTICE 38, p. 49.

2. Do you get up early?
3. When does the bus come?
4. Does it come on time?
5. Where do you work?
6. When do you start work?
7. When do you leave work?
8. Do you like your job?
9. Is it interesting?
10. Are you a doctor?

PRACTICE 39, p. 50.

2. What does he teach?
   He teaches biology and chemistry.
3. Where does he teach chemistry?
   He teaches chemistry in the chemistry lab.
4. When is he in the chemistry lab?
   He's in the chemistry lab at 12:00.
5. Where does he teach biology?
   He teaches biology in the biology lab.
6. Is he in his office every day?
   No, he isn't.
7. Is he in his office at 1:00?
   Yes, he is.
8. Does he teach at 8:00?
   No, he doesn't.
9. When does he teach?
   He teaches at 9:00, 10:00, and 12:00.

PRACTICE 40, p. 51.

3. studies
4. don't have
5. doesn't clean
6. tastes
7. costs
8. know
9. don't want
10. A: look
    B: am not

PRACTICE 41, p. 51.

2. Where is she?
3. Are Susie and Johnny at home?
4. Where are they?
5. What time/When is dinner?
6. What does Jane have for dinner?

PRACTICE 42, p. 52.

2. b
3. a
4. c
5. c
6. c
7. a
8. b
9. b
10. c

CHAPTER 4

PRACTICE 2, p. 53.

2. is
3. am
4. is
5. is
6. are
7. are
8. is
9. are
10. are
11. are
12. is
13. is
14. are

PRACTICE 3, p. 54.
2. winning
3. joining
4. signing
5. flying
6. paying
7. studying
8. getting
9. waiting
10. writing

PRACTICE 4, p. 54.
2. coming
3. looking
4. taking
5. biting
6. hitting
7. hurting
8. clapping
9. keeping
10. camping

PRACTICE 5, p. 55.
2. are sitting
3. are talking
4. is doing
5. is reading
6. are kicking
7. is coming
8. are going

PRACTICE 6, p. 55.
Part I
3. He is working at his computer.
4. He is talking on the phone.
5. He isn't riding a horse.
6. He isn't buying food for dinner.
Part II
1. They are talking to patients.
2. They aren't washing cars.
3. They aren't watching movies.
4. They are working with doctors.
5. They are giving medicine to patients.

PRACTICE 8, p. 57.
2. Are you working?
3. Are they leaving?
4. Is she staying home?
5. Are we going to school?
6. Is the computer working?
7. Is it working?
8. Am I driving?
9. Is your friend coming?
10. Are the students laughing?
11. Is Mr. Kim sleeping?
12. Is Monica dreaming?

PRACTICE 9, p. 57.
2. A: Is he running
   B: he isn't . . . is driving
3. A: Are they studying
   B: they aren't . . . are swimming
4. A: Is she teaching
   B: she isn't . . . is shopping
5. A: Is she fishing
   B: she isn't . . . is sleeping
6. A: Are they working
   B: they aren't . . . are playing
7. A: Are you washing dishes
   B: I'm not . . . am reading a book.

PRACTICE 10, p. 58.
Part I
2. are working

3. is working
4. are working
5. is working
Part II
7. are not working
8. is not working
9. are not working
10. is not working
Part III
12. Is . . . working
13. Are . . . working
14. Are . . . working
15. Is . . . working

PRACTICE 11, p. 59.
Part I.
2. work
3. works
4. work
5. works
Part II.
7. do not work
8. does not work
9. do not work
10. does not work
12. Does . . . work
13. Do . . . work
14. Do . . . work
15. Does . . . work

PRACTICE 12, p. 60.
3. every day
4. every day
5. now
6. now
7. every day
8. now
9. now
10. every day

PRACTICE 13, p. 60.
Checked sentences: 2, 6, 8, 9

PRACTICE 14, p. 60.
2. am looking
3. are fishing
4. is sitting
5. are playing
6. are swimming
7. are jumping
9. walk
10. go
11. am working
12. work
13. write
14. am writing

PRACTICE 15, p. 61.
2. Are
3. Is
4. Are
5. Do
6. Is
7. Does
8. Do
9. Does
10. Do
11. Does
12. Do
13. Are
14. Do

PRACTICE 16, p. 61.
2. smell
3. is crying . . . wants
4. tastes . . . like
5. are running . . . likes . . . hates

PRACTICE 17, p. 62.
1. think
2. A: does Jan want
   B: needs . . . wants
3. A: Do you hear
   B: hear . . . don't see
4. A: loves
   B: don't believe . . . loves

PRACTICE 18, p. 62.
2. a
3. a
4. b
5. b
6. a
7. a
8. b
9. a

PRACTICE 19, p. 63.
2. is playing
3. is also listening
4. (is) looking
5. is wearing
6. is talking
7. is telling
8. isn't listening
9. doesn't hear
10. is listening

PRACTICE 20, p. 63.
2. hear
3. hear
4. listen to
5. A: look at
   B: look at . . . watch
6. A: Do you see
   B: see

PRACTICE 22, p. 64.
2. a
3. b
4. b
5. a

PRACTICE 23, p. 64.
1. B: am thinking about
   A: think that
2. A: think that
   B: don't think that . . . think that
3. A: am thinking about
   B: Are . . . thinking about
   B: think that
   A: think that

PRACTICE 24, p. 65.
1. rings . . . doesn't answer . . . doesn't want . . . believes
2. flies . . . is flying
3. A: Are you waiting
   B: am
   A: does the bus stop
   A: Is it usually
   B: rarely comes

4. A: does your teacher usually do
   B: think . . . corrects . . . has
   A: is she doing
   B: is talking
5. A: Do you know
   B: believe . . . is
   B: know

PRACTICE 25, p. 66.
1. is sitting
2. is looking at
3. is working
4. is studying
5. listening to
6. hears
7. isn't listening to
8. is thinking about
9. is memorizing
10. likes
11. thinks
12. understands
13. is
14. doesn't like
15. is cooking
16. cooks
17. is cutting
18. is rising
19. is standing
20. is taking off
21. is wearing
22. usually exercises
23. is thinking about
24. is
25. smells
26. wants
27. to watch
28. is
29. needs
30. to go
31. is eating
32. is
33. is sleeping
34. is dreaming about
35. is playing
36. doesn't see
37. is looking at
38. is singing
39. isn't listening to
40. hears
41. likes
42. to listen to

CHAPTER 5

PRACTICE 1, p. 68.
2. What time is it?
3. What's the date (today)?
4. What year is it?
5. What month is it?
6. What time is it?
7. What's the date (today)?

PRACTICE 2, p. 68.
2. b
3. b
4. a
5. b

PRACTICE 3, p. 69.
1. b. at
2. a. at
   b. in
   c. on
3. a. in
   b. at
   c. from . . . to
   d. on
   e. on
4. a. in
   b. on
   c. in
   d. at . . . in
   e. on
   f. in

PRACTICE 4, p. 70.
2. at
3. from . . . to
4. on
5. in
6. at
7. in
8. on
9. from . . . to

PRACTICE 5, p. 70.
Part I.
2. How's the weather / What's the weather like in Sydney?
3. How's the weather / What's the weather like in Seoul?
4. How's the weather / What's the weather like in Sydney?
5. How's the weather / What's the weather like in Moscow?

Part II.
7. no
8. no
9. no
10. yes
11. no

PRACTICE 6, p. 71.
1. like
2. How's
3. temperature
4. temperature
5. the weather

PRACTICE 7, p. 71.
2. a
3. b
4. a
5. a
6. b
7. a

PRACTICE 8, p. 71.
2. are
3. is
4. is
5. are
6. are
7. is
8. is
9. are

PRACTICE 9, p. 72.
2. There is one couch.
3. There is one table.
4. There are four books.
5. There is one lamp.
6. There are two pillows.

PRACTICE 10, p. 72.
2. Is   Yes, there is./No, there isn't.
3. Are   Yes, there are./No, there aren't.
4. Is   Yes, there is./No, there isn't.
5. Are   Yes, there are./No, there aren't.
6. Are   Yes, there are./No, there aren't.
7. Is   Yes, there is./No, there isn't.
8. Are   Yes, there are./No, there aren't.
9. Is   Yes, there is./No, there isn't.

PRACTICE 11, p. 73.
2. Is there a bus station?
3. Are there fast-food restaurants?
4. Are there movie theaters?
5. Is there a park?
6. Are there places to exercise?
7. Is there a visitor information office?

PRACTICE 12, p. 73.
2. girls
3. cars
4. words
5. minutes
6. seconds
7. stars
8. snowflakes

PRACTICE 13, p. 74.
2. How many states are there
3. How many colors are there
4. How many countries are there (3 countries = Canada, U.S., Mexico)
5. How many letters are there
6. How many main languages are there

PRACTICE 14, p. 74.
2. How many exercises are there in this chapter? There are 25.
3. How many pages are there in your dictionary? There are . . . .
4. How many students are there in your class? There are . . . .
5. How many males are there in your class? There are . . . .
6. How many females are there in your class? There are . . . .
7. How many teachers are there at your school? There are . . . .

PRACTICE 15, p. 75.
2. in
3. on
4. at
5. on
6. in
7. on
8. at

PRACTICE 16, p. 75.
1. in . . . in
2. in
3. in . . . in
4. at
5. at
6. at . . . at
7. in
8. in
9. in
10. in

PRACTICE 17, p. 75.
2. at
3. at
4. in
5. in
6. in
7. at
8. in
9. in
10. in

PRACTICE 18, p. 76.
2. in
3. in . . . at
4. at . . . in
5. in
6. at . . . at (*"in" is also possible.*)
7. in

PRACTICE 19, p. 76.
2. in front of
3. behind/in back of
4. on/on top of
5. next to/beside/near
6. above
7. under
8. between

PRACTICE 20, p. 77.
Sample answers:
2. On the floor.
3. On my desk.
4. On my book.
5. On my desk.
6. In my hand.

PRACTICE 21, p. 77.
2. would like
3. would like
4. would like
5. would like
6. would like
7. would like
8. would like
9. would like
10. would like
11. would like
12. would like

PRACTICE 22, p. 78.
2. like
3. likes
4. wants
5. like
6. want

PRACTICE 23, p. 78.
3. *no change*
4. Mark would like to get married this year.
5. He would like a pet this year too.
6. *no change*
7. What would he like first?

PRACTICE 24, p. 79.
Part I.
1. Mary is sleeping. She's dreaming about John.
2. John is sleeping. He's dreaming about Mary.
3. Mary and John are sleeping and dreaming (about each other).
4. I see an alarm clock, two pillows, John and Mary, and two beds.
5. Yes, she is. She's in her bedroom.
6. No, he isn't in class. He's in his bedroom.
7. He's lying down.

8. Yes, she's dreaming.
9. Yes, they are dreaming about each other.
10. Yes, they are in love.

Part II.
11. are . . . in
12. is . . . about . . . is . . . about . . . are . . . about
13. on
14. aren't
15. are . . . aren't
16. in
17. to

PRACTICE 25, p. 79.
2. a		8. c	
3. a		9. b	
4. c		10. b	
5. d		11. d	
6. d		12. d	
7. a		13. b	

CHAPTER 6

PRACTICE 1, p. 81.
Checked words: 5, 6, 7, 8, 9

PRACTICE 2, p. 81.
<u>store</u>, <u>list</u>, <u>eggs</u>, <u>bananas</u>, <u>rice</u>, <u>tea</u>, <u>cell</u>
(*Note: Mike and Judy are also nouns.*)

PRACTICE 3, p. 81.
2. <u>Snow</u>
3. <u>The sun</u>
4. <u>The children</u> . . . <u>their parents</u>
5. <u>Some people</u>
6. <u>Teenagers</u>

PRACTICE 4, p. 82.
3. patients . . . patients
4. milk . . . milk
5. drink . . . Ø (*Note: objects are nouns.*)
6. their mothers . . . mothers

PRACTICE 5, p. 82.
2. c. <u>soccer</u>
3. b. <u>eggs</u>
   c. <u>eggs</u>
4. a. <u>bones</u>
   b. <u>furniture</u>
5. b. <u>lunch</u>
6. a. <u>English</u>
   d. <u>English</u>
7. no objects of verbs
8. b. <u>Maria</u>

PRACTICE 6, p. 83.
Checked phrases:
3. <u>children</u>
4. <u>table</u>
7. <u>street</u>
9. <u>work</u>
10. <u>house</u>

PRACTICE 7, p. 83.
Checked sentences:
 2. a. <u>backpack</u>
    c. <u>snack</u>
 3. b. <u>library</u>
    d. <u>night</u>
 4. a. <u>students</u>
    c. <u>classroom</u>

PRACTICE 8, p. 84.
Nouns: car, chair, food, job, leg, rain, tree
Adjectives: bright, easy, fresh, nervous, poor, quiet, wet

PRACTICE 9, p. 84.
 2. old
 3. hard
 4. ugly
 5. old
 6. interesting
 7. slow
 8. short
 9. hard/difficult
10. quiet

PRACTICE 10, p. 85.
                          A
 2. It is very bright.
        N   A   A   N
 3. The rooms are large and have tall ceilings.
      N   A   N
 4. Her building is next to a Japanese restaurant.
     N   N
 5. I love food from other countries.
        A   A   A
 6. Mexican food is spicy and delicious.
                  A   N   N
 7. There is a wonderful cafe in my neighborhood.
      N   N
 8. My neighbors like to meet there for coffee.

PRACTICE 12, p. 85.
 2. Australia
 3. Canada
 4. China
 5. Egypt
 6. India
 7. Indonesia
 8. Italy
 9. Japan
10. Korea
11. Malaysia
12. Mexico
13. Russia
14. Saudi Arabia

PRACTICE 14, p. 86.
 2. He . . . her
 3. She . . . them
 4. He . . . them
 5. They . . . them
 6. They . . . him
 7. They . . . her
 8. They . . . them
 9. They . . . them

PRACTICE 15, p. 87.
 2. her
 3. them
 4. him
 5. me
 6. us
 7. him/it
 8. her/it
 9. she
10. he
11. they
12. he
13. you
14. you

PRACTICE 16, p. 87.
 2. it
 3. them
 4. him
 5. them
 6. them
 7. it
 8. her
 9. him

PRACTICE 17, p. 88.
 2. a
 3. b
 4. b
 5. a

PRACTICE 18, p. 88.
 2. They . . . them . . . They . . . it
 3. A: her
    B: She . . . her
 4. B: I . . . me
    A: he

PRACTICE 19, p. 89.
 3. Her . . . her
 4. His . . . him
 5. Our . . . us
 6. Their . . . them
 7. Her/Its . . . her/it
 8. His/Its . . . him/it
 9. Its/it

PRACTICE 20, p. 90.
 2. me
 3. him . . . his
 4. it
 5. you
 6. Our . . . our
 7. their

PRACTICE 21, p. 90.
 1. His . . . him
 2. their . . . They . . . them . . . their
 3. She . . . Her . . . her
 4. their . . . Their . . . their
 5. I . . . our . . . our . . . us

PRACTICE 22, p. 91.
 2. tomatoes
 3. zoos
 4. pen
 5. babies
 6. keys
 7. city
 8. wife
 9. dishes
10. thieves

PRACTICE 23, p. 91.

-s	-ies	-ves	-es
coins	babies	leaves	bushes
girls	cities	lives	glasses
shoes	ladies	thieves	potatoes
trays	parties	wives	taxes

PRACTICE 24, p. 91.

2. keys
3. classes
4. thieves
5. tests
6. Babies
7. boxes
8. radios
9. parties
10. cats
11. matches
12. textbooks
13. dictionaries
14. lives
15. tops
16. leaves
17. sandwiches

PRACTICE 25, p. 92.

2. mice
3. women
4. fish
5. feet
6. men
7. children
8. sheep

PRACTICE 26, p. 93.

Corrections for incorrect sentences:
3. My father **is** in the library.
4. **He** is a teacher.
5. My mother **is** a professor.
6. **She** is an excellent professor.
8. The university **has** many interesting and useful classes.

PRACTICE 27, p. 93.

2. b
3. a
4. d
5. d
6. c
7. b
8. c
9. a
10. d

PRACTICE 28, p. 94.

2. hers
3. ours
4. mine
5. yours
6. theirs
8. my
9. his
10. their
11. your
12. our

PRACTICE 29, p. 94.

2. one
3. more than one
4. more than one
5. one
6. one
7. more than one

PRACTICE 30, p. 95.

2. car . . . Bill
3. desk . . . the teacher
4. schedules . . . the students
5. truck . . . my parents
6. offices . . . the professors

PRACTICE 31, p. 95.

2. Dan's
3. teacher's
4. sister's
5. Smith's
6. pets'
7. neighbors'
8. mother's

PRACTICE 32, p. 96.

3. Ø
4. 's
5. Ø
6. Ø
7. 's

PRACTICE 33, p. 96.

2. Jane's
3. Mike's
4. Ruff's
5. Marie's
6. Belle's
7. John's
8. Jane's

PRACTICE 34, p. 97.

2. possessive
3. is
4. is
5. possessive
6. is
7. is
8. possessive

PRACTICE 35, p. 97.

2. a
3. a
4. b
5. a
6. b
7. b

PRACTICE 36, p. 97.

2. Whose glasses are these?
3. Whose toy is this?
4. Whose keys are these?
5. Whose shoes are these?
6. Whose shirt is this?
7. Whose cell phone is this?
8. Whose pens are these?

PRACTICE 37, p. 98.

2. Whose
3. Who's
4. Who's
5. Whose
6. Whose
7. Whose
8. Who's
9. Who's
10. Whose

PRACTICE 38, p. 98.

2. Whose children are those?
3. Who is next?
4. Whose shoes are in the middle of the floor?
5. Who is absent today?
6. Whose package is this?

PRACTICE 39, p. 99.

2. one
3. more than one
4. one
5. more than one
6. more than one
7. one
8. one
9. more than one

PRACTICE 40, p. 99.

3. girls' bikes
4. girl's bike
5. children's toys
6. students' passwords
7. woman's wage
8. women's wages
9. people's ideas
10. person's ideas
11. men's coats

PRACTICE 41, p. 100.

Corrections for incorrect sentences:
2. Several students' parents . . .
3. . . . my brother's friends (no apostrophe)
6. . . . other people's opinions
7. Women's opinions . . .
8. your husband (no apostrophe)

PRACTICE 42, p. 100.

2. d
3. b
4. a
5. c

6. c
7. a
8. d

CHAPTER 7

PRACTICE 1, p. 101.

2. P
3. S
4. S
5. P

6. S
7. P
8. S

PRACTICE 2, p. 101.

2. a, one
3. five, a lot of
4. five, a lot of

5. a, one
6. five, a lot of
7. an, one

PRACTICE 3, p. 101.

2. C
3. NC
4. NC
5. C

6. NC
7. NC
8. C

PRACTICE 4, p. 102.

2. a lot of, ten, twenty
3. a lot of
4. a lot of
5. a lot of, ten, twenty
6. a, one
7. a lot of, ten, twenty
8. a lot of

PRACTICE 5, p. 102.

1. Ø . . . -s . . . -s
2. Ø . . . Ø . . . -s . . . -s
3. Ø . . . Ø . . . Ø
4. Ø . . . Ø . . . -s . . . -s

PRACTICE 6, p. 102.

2. a, one
3. a lot of
4. a, one
5. an, one
6. a lot of

7. a lot of
8. a, one
9. a lot of
10. a lot of

PRACTICE 7, p. 102.

2. homework
3. music
4. vocabulary
5. information
6. advice

7. furniture
8. fruit
9. money
10. jewelry

PRACTICE 8, p. 103.

2. horses
3. cities
4. countries
5. monkeys
6. help
7. traffic
8. children
9. furniture

10. feet
11. fruit
12. potatoes
13. weather
14. work
15. advice
16. men
17. tools

PRACTICE 9, p. 104.

2. an
3. an
4. a
5. an
6. an

7. an
8. a
9. a
10. an

PRACTICE 10, p. 104.

3. Ø
4. an
5. a
6. an

7. an
8. Ø
9. Ø
10. Ø

PRACTICE 11, p. 105.

2. a
3. Ø
4. an
5. Ø
6. A
7. a
8. an . . . an

9. Ø
10. a
11. Ø
12. an
13. an
14. an . . . a

PRACTICE 12, p. 106.

a	*an*	*some*
dog	earache	advice
flower	elevator	eggs
letter	umbrella	furniture
suggestion		gardens
		mail
		packages
		umbrellas

PRACTICE 13, p. 106.

3. a — singular
4. some — plural
5. an — singular
6. some — plural
7. some — plural
8. some — plural
9. a — singular
10. some — plural

PRACTICE 14, p. 107.

2. some
3. Some
4. a
5. an
6. Some

7. a
8. some
9. some
10. an

PRACTICE 15, p. 107.

2. b
3. a, b
4. a, c

5. b
6. b

PRACTICE 16, p. 108.
2. a tube of toothpaste
3. a bar of soap
4. a bunch of bananas
5. a carton of milk
6. a jar of pickles
7. a box of candy
8. a bottle of olive oil
9. a can of corn

PRACTICE 17, p. 108.
2. paper
3. lettuce
4. bread, cheese, lettuce, paper
5. bread
6. bananas, lettuce
7. cereal, ice cream, rice
8. water
9. mayonnaise

PRACTICE 18, p. 109.
1. b. some
   c. some
   d. a
   e. an
   f. a
   g. some
   h. some
2. b. a
   c. some
   d. a
   e. a
   f. some
   g. some
   h. some

PRACTICE 19, p. 110.
2. many
3. much
4. much
5. much
6. much
7. much
8. much
9. many
10. many

PRACTICE 20, p. 110.
2. a few
3. a few
4. a little
5. a little
6. a few
7. a few
8. a few
9. a little
10. a few

PRACTICE 21, p. 110.
3. a few . . . s
4. a few . . . s
5. much . . . Ø . . . a little . . . Ø
6. many . . . s
7. a few . . . s . . . many . . . s

PRACTICE 22, p. 111.
2. How much cheese do we need?
3. How many eggs do we need?
4. How much flour do we need?
5. How much fruit do we need?
6. How much olive oil do we need?

PRACTICE 23, p. 111.
1. the
2. The
3. a . . . The . . . the
4. a . . . The . . . the
5. a . . . a . . . a . . . The . . . the
6. a . . . The
7. a . . . The
8. a . . . a

PRACTICE 24, p. 112.
2. specific
3. general
4. general
5. specific
6. specific
7. general
8. specific

PRACTICE 25, p. 112.
2. The
3. Ø
4. a
5. an
6. Ø
7. an
8. Ø
9. Ø . . . Ø
10. Ø . . . Ø . . . a
11. the
12. Ø . . . a

PRACTICE 26, p. 113.
2. b
3. b
4. a
5. b
6. a
7. a

PRACTICE 27, p. 113.
2. any
3. some
4. any
5. some, any
6. any
7. some
8. some
9. some, any
10. Some

PRACTICE 29, p. 114.
2. any
3. any
4. a
5. any
6. a
7. a
8. any
9. any
10. an
11. any

PRACTICE 30, p. 115.
4. any
5. any
6. any
7. a
8. any
9. any
10. any
11. a
12. any
13. a
14. any
15. any
16. a

PRACTICE 31, p. 115.
Draw a line through:
1. b, d, e
2. a, c, f
3. a, c

PRACTICE 32, p. 116.
2. Is there **much traffic** at 5:00 P.M.?
3. Are **you hungry**? Do you want some food?
4. My children come home every day with a lot of **homework**.
5. **Digital** cameras take wonderful pictures.
6. My eggs and coffee don't taste very good. **The** eggs are very salty, and **the** coffee is weak.
7. What do you like better for a snack: **oranges/an orange or orange** juice?

8. I wear dresses for work **and jeans** at home.
9. I'm going to **the** bank. I need money.
10. We need to get **some** furniture. Do you know **a** good furniture store?

CHAPTER 8

PRACTICE 1, p. 117.

2. were	7. were
3. was	8. were
4. were	9. was
5. was	10. were
6. was	

PRACTICE 2, p. 117.

2. were	7. was
3. was	8. were
4. was	9. was
5. was	10. were
6. was	

PRACTICE 3, p. 118.

2. weren't	7. wasn't
3. weren't	8. weren't
4. weren't	9. wasn't
5. wasn't	10. weren't
6. wasn't	11. weren't

PRACTICE 4, p. 118.

2. wasn't	6. weren't
3. weren't	7. wasn't
4. weren't	8. wasn't
5. wasn't	9. weren't

PRACTICE 5, p. 119.

Some possible answers:
2. wasn't at school. He was on vacation.
3. wasn't at work. She was out of town.
4. weren't at school. They were out of town.

PRACTICE 7, p. 119.

2. Was	7. Was
3. Was	8. Was
4. Were	9. Were
5. Were	10. Were
6. Was	

PRACTICE 8, p. 120.

2. A: Was Ellen at the library?
   B: No, she wasn't.
   A: Where was she?
   B: She was at the mall.
3. A: Were you at a party?
   B: No, I wasn't.
   A: Where were you?
   B: I was at home.
4. A: Was Thomas at the airport?
   B: No, he wasn't.
   A: Where was he?
   B: He was at the train station.
5. A: Were your kids at school?
   B: No, they weren't.
   A: Where were they?
   B: They were at the zoo.

6. A: Were Liz and you at the park?
   B: No, we weren't.
   A: Where were you?
   B: We were at the library.

PRACTICE 9, p. 121.

2. Were	6. Was
3. Were	7. Were
4. Was	8. Were
5. Was	

PRACTICE 10, p. 121.

2. studied	7. talked
3. walked	8. helped
4. worked	9. helped
5. smiled	10. listened
6. smiled	11. listened

PRACTICE 11, p. 122.

2. exercised at a gym.
3. cooked breakfast.
4. talked to friends on the phone.
5. watched TV.

PRACTICE 12, p. 122.

Group A.	*Group B.*
2. walked	16. arrived
3. washed	17. played
4. erased	18. signed
5. kissed	19. shaved
6. laughed	20. smiled
7. stopped	21. enjoyed
8. finished	22. closed
9. touched	23. rained
10. worked	24. sneezed
11. coughed	25. remembered
12. cooked	26. killed
13. asked	
14. helped	

Group C.
28. needed
29. counted
30. invited
31. visited
32. folded
33. waited
34. added

PRACTICE 13, p. 125.

1. liked	12. waited
2. closed	13. pointed
3. shaved	14. touched
4. loved	15. melted
5. hated	16. married
6. exercised	17. tried
7. planned	18. hurried
8. dropped	19. replied
9. clapped	20. dried
10. joined	21. stayed
11. shouted	22. delayed

PRACTICE 14, p. 126.

2. rained
3. helped
4. planned
5. dreamed
6. erased
7. closed
8. yawned
9. studied
10. worried
11. dropped

PRACTICE 15, p. 127.

2. learned
3. tasted
4. waited
5. stopped
6. carried
7. rubbed
8. stayed . . . cried
9. failed
10. smiled
11. clapped

PRACTICE 16, p. 128.

2. yesterday
3. last
4. last
5. last
6. last
7. yesterday
8. ago
9. ago
10. ago
11. yesterday
12. last

PRACTICE 17, p. 128.

2. Bonnie walked to the park yesterday/one day ago.
3. Tom was at home on vacation last week/one week ago.
4. Sam graduated from high school four years ago.
5. Jan worked 12 hours two days ago.
6. Thomas stayed with his parents two months ago.
7. We watched a DVD yesterday/last night/one day ago/ yesterday evening.

PRACTICE 18, p. 129.

2. ate
3. ate
4. ate
5. ate
6. ate
7. ate
8. did
9. did
10. did
11. did
12. slept
13. slept
14. slept
15. slept

PRACTICE 19, p. 129.

Present forms:
2. come
3. go
4. have
5. put
6. sleep
7. see
8. do
9. eat
10. write
11. sit
12. stand

PRACTICE 20, p. 130.

2. went
3. sat/slept/stood
4. saw
5. got
6. ate/had
7. saw
8. came/got/went
9. wrote
10. put, had

PRACTICE 22, p. 131.

2. didn't come
3. didn't come
4. didn't come
5. didn't come
6. didn't come
7. didn't play
8. didn't play
9. didn't answer
10. didn't see
11. didn't sleep
12. didn't do
13. wasn't
14. weren't

PRACTICE 24, p. 133.

Sample answers:
2. He didn't break a glass on the floor. He broke a plate.
3. He didn't eat a delicious breakfast. He had breakfast at school.
4. He didn't take the bus to school. He got/took his bike.
5. He didn't leave school late. He left school early.
6. He didn't take the bus home. He took a taxi.
7. He didn't pay the driver. His neighbor paid the driver/paid the fare.

PRACTICE 25, p. 134.

3. Does she play tennis?
4. Did she play tennis?
5. Does he walk to work?
6. Did he walk to work?
7. Does she work at home?
8. Did she work at home?
9. Do you like your new job?
10. Did you like your old job?

PRACTICE 26, p. 134.

2. Was
3. Did
4. Did
5. Were
6. Did
7. Was
8. Did
9. Were

PRACTICE 27, p. 134.

2. a. Do they help? — They don't help.
   b. Did they help? — They didn't help.
3. a. Does she listen? — She doesn't listen.
   b. Did she listen? — She didn't listen.
4. a. Does he work? — He doesn't work.
   b. Did he work? — He didn't work.
5. a. Does the baby cry? — The baby doesn't cry.
   b. Did the baby cry? — The baby didn't cry.
6. a. Are we sick? — We aren't sick.
   b. Were we sick? — We weren't sick.

PRACTICE 28, p. 135.

2. A: Is it cold today?
   B: No, it isn't.
3. A: Do you come to class every day?
   B: Yes, I do.
4. A: Was Roberto absent yesterday?
   B: Yes, he was.
5. A: Did Roberto stay home yesterday?
   B: Yes, he did.
6. A: Does Phillip change his passwords very often?
   B: No, he doesn't.
7. A: Is Mohammed in class today?
   B: No, he isn't.
8. A: Was he here yesterday?
   B: Yes, he was.
9. A: Did he come to class the day before yesterday?
   B: Yes, he did.
10. A: Does he usually come to class every day?
    B: Yes, he does.

PRACTICE 29, p. 136.

Present forms:

2. read
3. ride
4. run
5. drink
6. catch
7. drive
8. think
9. bring
10. teach

PRACTICE 30, p. 136.

2. taught
3. drove
4. bought
5. drank/bought
6. read
7. ran
8. thought
9. brought
10. caught

PRACTICE 31, p. 137.

Present forms:

2. speak
3. take
4. pay
5. wake up
6. break
7. send
8. sing
9. leave
10. meet
11. ring
12. hear

PRACTICE 32, p. 138.

2. heard
3. woke
4. took
5. met
6. left
7. rang
8. spoke . . . broke
9. sang
10. sent
11. paid

PRACTICE 33, p. 138.

Present forms:

2. say
3. find
4. lose
5. steal
6. hang
7. tell
8. begin
9. sell
10. tear

PRACTICE 34, p. 139.

2. tore
3. wore
4. told
5. hung
6. said . . . stole
7. lost
8. sold
9. found

PRACTICE 35, p. 140.

4. planned
5. joined
6. hoped
7. dropped
8. added
9. pointed
10. patted
11. shouted
12. replied
13. played
14. touched
15. ended
16. danced

PRACTICE 36, p. 140.

1. bought . . . picked up
2. caught . . . rode . . . got off . . . was
3. ate . . . drank . . . didn't eat
4. asked . . . thought
5. wanted . . . stayed
6. read . . . was
7. didn't pass . . . failed
8. drove . . . visited . . . camped . . . went . . . caught . . . didn't catch . . . enjoyed . . . was

PRACTICE 37, p. 141.

2. is walking
3. Does Tom walk
4. Do you walk
5. walked
6. saw
7. didn't see
8. Did you see
9. didn't walk . . . took
10. didn't walk

PRACTICE 38, p. 142.

1. went
2. isn't standing . . . is sitting
3. isn't . . . was
4. isn't raining . . . stopped
5. didn't go . . . went
6. went . . . didn't enjoy . . . wasn't
7. wrote . . . didn't spend
8. didn't come
9. went . . . are sleeping
10. were . . . started . . . didn't arrive
11. asked . . . didn't answer
12. went . . . bought . . . didn't buy
13. B: woke up . . . went . . . stole . . . took . . . got . . . tore . . . borrowed
    B: lost . . . found
14. want . . . need
15. A: didn't see . . . Were
    B: didn't feel . . . was . . . is
16. A: are you going
    B: called . . . picked . . . need
    B: know

CHAPTER 9

PRACTICE 1, p. 144.

2. A: When did he leave?
   B: He left on March 22.
3. A: Why did he go there?
   B: He went to visit family.
4. A: Where did Serena go?
   B: She went to the Canary Islands.
5. A: When/What time did she leave?
   B: She left at 6 AM.
6. A: Why did she go there?
   B: She went there for vacation.

PRACTICE 2, p. 145.

2. f
3. e
4. c
5. d
6. a

PRACTICE 3, p. 145.

2. When/What time did you leave the library?
3. Why did you leave the library?
4. Where did your friends and you go yesterday afternoon?
5. When did Sandra get back from Brazil?
6. Why was Bobby in bed?
7. Why was Bobby sick?
8. Where did you buy your sandals?

PRACTICE 4, p. 146.

2. Why didn't you ask the teacher?
3. Why didn't you bring the homework?
4. Why didn't you tell me the truth?
5. Why didn't you go to Sharon's party?
6. Why didn't you clean your bedroom?

PRACTICE 5, p. 146.

3. What did you study?
4. Did you study math?
5. What are they looking at?
6. Are they looking at a map?
7. What did you dream about last night?
8. Is she a new employee?
9. What does she tutor?
10. What did David talk about?
11. Did David talk about his country?
12. What are you thinking about?
13. What does *nothing in particular* mean?
14. What are you afraid of?

PRACTICE 6, p. 147.

2. a. Lea?
   b. the nurse check?
3. a. Felix help?
   b. the new assistant? Felix.
4. a. the advanced students?
   b. Professor Jones teach? The advanced students.
5. a. the police catch? The thief.
   b. the thief? The police.
6. a. a monster? Tommy.
   b. Tommy dream about? A monster.

PRACTICE 7, p. 148.

2. a. Who did the doctor examine?
   b. Who examined the patient?
3. a. Who called the supervisor?
   b. Who did Miriam call?
4. a. Who surprised the teacher?
   b. Who did the students surprise?
5. a. Who did Andrew and Catherine wait for?
   b. Who waited for Mrs. Allen?

PRACTICE 8, p. 149.

3. Who had a graduation party?
4. Who did Professor Brown invite?
5. Who had a New Year's party?
6. Who did Dr. Martin invite?

PRACTICE 9, p. 149.

2. Who did you talk to?
3. Who did you visit?
4. Who answered the question?
5. Who taught the English class?
6. Who helped you?
7. Who did you help?
8. Who carried the suitcases?
9. Who called?

PRACTICE 10, p. 150.

Present forms:
2. gives (he or she)
3. understand
4. hurt
5. spend
6. shut
7. lend
8. cut
9. hit
10. make
11. cost

PRACTICE 11, p. 150.

2. forgot
3. made
4. gave
5. understood
6. cut, hurt
7. cost
8. spent
9. gave, lent
10. hit, hurt
11. hurt

PRACTICE 12, p. 151.

2. feel
3. keep
4. swim
5. throw
6. draw
7. grow
8. fall
9. win
10. blow

PRACTICE 13, p. 152.

2. drew
3. fell
4. felt
5. threw
6. grew
7. kept
8. swam
9. knew
10. won

PRACTICE 14, p. 153.

Present forms:
2. bend
3. shake
4. become
5. feed
6. bite
7. hide
8. fight
9. build

PRACTICE 15, p. 154.

2. shook
3. fed
4. hid
5. bit, held, shook
6. became
7. fought
8. held
9. bent, bit

PRACTICE 16, p. 154.

Incomplete:
after they left
after several minutes
before school starts
after we finish dinner
Complete:
They left.
Before school starts, I help the teacher.
We ate at a restaurant.
We were at home.

PRACTICE 17, p. 155.

2. 2, 1
   After I looked in the freezer, I closed the freezer door.
   I closed the freezer door after I looked in the freezer.
3. 1, 2
   After I stood on the scale, the nurse wrote down my weight.
   The nurse wrote down my weight after I stood on the scale.

4. 2, 1
   After I put on my exercise clothes, I exercised.
   I exercised after I put on my exercise clothes.
5. 1, 2
   After the alarm rang at the fire station, the firefighters
   got in their truck.
   The firefighters got in their truck after the alarm rang
   at the fire station.

PRACTICE 18, p. 156.
2. 2, 1
   b, c
3. 2, 1
   a, d
4. 1, 2
   b, c

PRACTICE 19, p. 157.
2. a. When did the movie start?
   b. When the movie started,
3. a. When you were in high school,
   b. When were you in high school?
4. a. When it snowed,
   b. When did it snow?
5. a. When was Dave sick?
   b. When Dave was sick,

PRACTICE 20, p. 157.
3. When did you hear the good news?
4. When Mr. King died, we felt sad.
5. When were you here?
6. When did we meet?
7. When you arrived, we were happy to see you.
8. When Kevin was absent, the class had a test.
9. When the TV show ended, everyone clapped.
10. When was Mrs. Allen a teacher?

PRACTICE 21, p. 158.
2. a. When did you get sick?
   b. When you got sick, . . . (answers will vary)
3. a. When did the problem begin?
   b. When the problem began, . . .
4. a. When did they visit?
   b. When they visited, . . .

PRACTICE 22, p. 158.
2. were studying.
3. was studying.
4. was studying.
5. were studying.
6. were studying.
7. were not studying.
8. were not studying.
9. was not studying.
10. were not studying.
11. were not studying.
12. was not studying.

PRACTICE 23, p. 159.
3. are sitting
4. were sitting
5. is sitting
6. was sitting
7. are sitting
8. were sitting
9. is sitting
10. was sitting
11. are sitting
12. were sitting

PRACTICE 24, p. 159.
2. a. While I was talking to the teacher yesterday,
      another student interrupted me.
   b. Another student interrupted me while I was
      talking to the teacher yesterday.
3. a. A police officer stopped another driver for
      speeding while we were driving to work.
   b. While we were driving to work, a police officer
      stopped another driver for speeding.
4. a. While I was walking in the forest, a dead tree fell
      over.
   b. A dead tree fell over while I was walking in the
      forest.
5. a. While I was planting flowers in the garden, my
      dog began to bark at a squirrel.
      My dog began to bark at a squirrel while I was
      planting flowers in the garden.

PRACTICE 25, p. 160.
2. rang
3. didn't answer
4. wanted
5. noticed
6. was slowing
7. drove
8. saw

PRACTICE 26, p. 161.
2. were sitting
3. came
4. screamed
5. did your cousin do
6. yelled
7. Did your husband do
8. ran
9. was running
10. ran
11. began

PRACTICE 27, p. 161.
1. got
2. called . . . was taking
3. was eating . . . remembered
4. began . . . became
5. was driving . . . saw
6. was exercising . . . came
7. sent . . . was talking . . . told
8. heard . . . stopped

PRACTICE 28, p. 162.
1. a man sat down next to her. OR a man asked her
   about it.
2. he interrupted her. OR she tried to answer quickly.
3. he continued to talk.
4. he began to tell her about his health. OR he told her
   about his health.
5. she stood up. OR she excused herself.
6. he was talking to another passenger.

PRACTICE 29, p. 162.
2. When did Simone go to a conference?
3. Who went to a conference last month?
4. Who did you see?
5. Where did you see Ali?

6. What time/When did you see Ali?
7. What is the teacher talking about?
8. Why did the kids play in the pool?
9. Who called?
10. When did they call?
11. Who did you talk to?
12. Where were you last night?
13. What does ancient mean?
14. Where do you live?
15. What does Annie have in her pocket?

PRACTICE 30, p. 163.
Answers will vary.

PRACTICE 31, p. 164.
2. She caught a cold yesterday.
3. She found it on the teacher's desk.
4. Someone stole his wallet.
5. He ate too much for lunch.
6. It sold in three days.
7. It tore when she played outside.
8. She hung up after midnight.
9. Sam bent over and picked it up for her.
10. I caught a taxi.
11. Several students came to class without their homework.
12. I grew up there.

PRACTICE 32, p. 165.
2. broke	8. knew
3. told	9. met
4. spent	10. fell
5. made	11. lost
6. wore	12. stole
7. cost	

PRACTICE 33, p. 166.
2. sang	7. built
3. flew	8. put
4. left	9. fought
5. won	10. fed
6. shook	

PRACTICE 34, p. 167.
Part I.
1. was
2. saw
3. are
4. am doing
5. Would you like
6. sit
7. need
8. don't need (*Note: non-contracted forms are also correct.*)
9. are you doing
10. am getting
11. is
12. don't trust
13. do you want
14. want
15. had

Part II.
16. saw	25. aren't
17. love	26. was it
18. stopped	27. did the bee sting
19. reached	28. are you doing
20. came	29. are you holding
21. was	30. am holding
22. don't believe	31. tricked
23. don't believe	32. happened
24. are	

Part III.
33. got	42. dropped
34. wanted	43. fooled
35. to catch	44. tricked
36. caught	45. taught
37. looks	46. learned
38. don't believe	47. am
39. is	48. have
40. is coming	49. Would you like
41. don't see	

CHAPTER 10

PRACTICE 1, p. 170.
2. are going to be	7. is going to be
3. is going to be	8. are going to be
4. are going to be	9. is going to be
5. are going to be	10. are going to be
6. are going to be	

PRACTICE 2, p. 170.
1. B: am going to be
2. A: Is Albert going to fix
   B: am going to call
3. A: Are you going to apply
   B: am going to complete
4. A: Are Ed and Nancy going to join
   B: are going to meet

PRACTICE 3, p. 171.
She **is going to wake** up at 5:00. She **is going to have** a quick breakfast of toast and coffee. She **is going to catch** the 5:45 train to work. At 6:30, she **is going to have** a weekly meeting with her employees. For the rest of the morning, she **is going to be** at her desk. She **is going to answer** phone calls and emails, and she **is going to work** on project details. She **is going to answer** a lot of questions. She **is going to have** a big lunch at 11:00. In the afternoon, she **is going to visit** job sites. She **is going to meet** with builders and architects. She **is going to finish** by 7:00 and **is going to be** home by 8:00.

PRACTICE 4, p. 171.
2. am going to eat a big lunch.
3. am going to take some medicine.
4. am going to call the neighbors.
5. is going to do a search on the Internet.
6. are going to look for a bigger place.
7. is going to check the lost-and-found.
8. am going to take it back to the store.

PRACTICE 6, p. 173.

2. You are not going to eat.   Are you going to eat?
3. He is not going to eat.   Is he going to eat?
4. She is not going to eat.   Is she going to eat?
5. We are not going to eat.   Are we going to eat?
6. They are not going to eat.   Are they going to eat?
7. My friend is not going to eat.   Is my friend going to eat?
8. The students are not going to eat.   Are the students going to eat?

PRACTICE 7, p. 173.

1. B: are going to go
   A: Are you going to stay
   B: are going to come
2. A: is Sally going to work
   B: is not going to work . . . is going to take
3. A: Are the students going to have
   B: are going to have
4. A: Are Joan and Bob going to move
   B: is going to start
   A: Are they going to look for
   B: are not going to look for . . . are going to rent

PRACTICE 8, p. 174.

2. They are taking their teenage grandchildren with them.
3. They are staying in parks and campgrounds.
4. They are leaving from Vancouver in June.
5. They are arriving in Montreal in August.
6. Mr. and Mrs. Johnson are driving back home alone.
7. Their grandchildren are flying home because they don't want to miss the beginning of school.
8. Their parents are meeting them at the airport.

PRACTICE 9, p. 175.

2. F
3. P
4. F
5. P
6. F
7. P . . . P
8. F

PRACTICE 10, p. 175.

1. b. last   2. b. next
   c. last   c. next
   d. last   d. next
   e. yesterday   e. tomorrow
   f. ago   f. in
   g. last   g. next
   h. ago   h. in
   i. last   i. tomorrow
   j. yesterday   j. tomorrow

PRACTICE 11, p. 176.

2. ago   9. in
3. ago   10. yesterday
4. last   11. last
5. next   12. tomorrow
6. in   13. ago
7. yesterday   14. next
8. tomorrow

PRACTICE 12, p. 176.

6. a couple of years
9. a couple of weeks

PRACTICE 13, p. 177.

3. a few hours
4. a few days
6. a few years

PRACTICE 14, p. 177.

2. a. Susie married Paul a couple of months ago.
   b. Susie is going to marry Paul in a couple of months.
3. a. Dr. Nelson retired a few years ago.
   b. Dr. Nelson is going to retire in a few years.
4. a. Jack began a new job a couple of days ago.
   b. Jack is going to begin a new job in a couple of days.

PRACTICE 15, p. 178.

2. past   7. present
3. present   8. past
4. past   9. future
5. future   10. past
6. present   11. future

PRACTICE 16, p. 178.

2. this morning/today/right now
3. this morning/today
4. this morning/today
5. this morning/today/right now
6. this morning/today

PRACTICE 17, p. 179.

1. b. She overslept. OR She missed her math class.
2. a. She is going to sit in the kitchen.
   b. She is going to think about a solution.
3. She is sitting in her kitchen. OR She is thinking about going to school.

PRACTICE 18, p. 179.

2. will be   7. will be
3. will be   8. will be
4. will be   9. will be
5. will be   10. will be
6. will be

PRACTICE 21, p. 181.

2. You will need extra chairs for the party.
3. Hurry or we won't be on time for the movie.
4. Your brother and sister will help you with your science project.
5. The bus won't be on time today.
6. Watch out! You will cut yourself with that sharp knife.
7. Carlos and Olivia will graduate from nursing school with high grades.

PRACTICE 22, p. 181.

2. Will your friends live to be 100 years old?
3. Will your children live to be 100 years old?
4. Will we live on another planet?
5. Will my friends live on another planet?

6. Will some people live underwater?
7. Will I live underwater?
8. Will countries find a solution for poverty?

PRACTICE 23, p. 182.

2.	are going to go	will go
3.	are going to go	will go
4.	is going to go	will go
5.	are going to go	will go
6.	is not going to go	will not go
7.	am not going to go	will not go
8.	are not going to go	will not go
9.	Is she going to go	Will she go
10.	Are they going to go	Will they go
11.	Are you going to go	Will you go

PRACTICE 24, p. 183.
2. Will you need help tomorrow?
3. Did you need help yesterday?
4. Did Eva need help yesterday?
5. Will Eva need help tomorrow?
6. Does Eva need help now?
7. Do the students need help now?
8. Will the students need help tomorrow?
9. Did the students need help yesterday?

PRACTICE 25, p. 183.
2. eats
3. eats
4. has
5. cooked
6. was . . . loved
7. dropped . . . was . . . didn't burn
8. is going to invite (*be going to* = plan)
9. Is she going to cook/Will she cook
10. Is she going to make
11. isn't going to prepare/won't prepare
12. is going to surprise/will surprise

PRACTICE 26, p. 184.
2. Are you going to be/Will you be sick tomorrow?
3. Were you sick yesterday?
4. Was Steve sick yesterday?
5. Is Steve going to be/Will Steve be sick tomorrow?
6. Is Steve sick now?
7. Are your kids sick now?
8. Are your kids going to be/Will your kids be sick tomorrow?
9. Were your kids sick yesterday?

PRACTICE 27, p. 185.
1. am . . . will be/am going to be . . . was . . . will be/am going to be
2. A: were you . . . Were you
   B: wasn't . . . was
   A: was . . . were you
   B: were
   A: was
3. A: Is the post office
   B: isn't . . . is
   A: Are
   B: aren't . . . are

PRACTICE 28, p. 185.

2. Are	6. Do
3. Do	7. Do
4. Do	8. Are
5. Are	9. Do

PRACTICE 29, p. 186.

2. Did	5. Did
3. Were	6. Did
4. Were	7. Did
	8. Were

PRACTICE 30, p. 186.

	Every day/Now	Yesterday	Tomorrow
1.	drink / am drinking	drank	am going to drink / will drink
2.	work / are working	worked	are going to work / will work
3.	is / is	was	is going to be / will be
4.	help / are helping	helped	are going to help / will help
5.	doesn't come / isn't coming	didn't come	isn't going to come / won't come
6.	doesn't do / isn't doing	didn't do	isn't going to do / won't do
7.	Do they exercise / Are they exercising	Did they exercise	Are they going to exercise / Will they exercise
8.	Is he / Is he	Was he	Is he going to be / Will he be
9.	isn't / isn't	wasn't	isn't going to be / won't be

PRACTICE 31, p. 187.
1. left
2. A: are you going to wear
   B: am going to wear . . . will be/is going to be
3. A: Did she tell . . . did she tell
   B: told
4. I am making . . . is getting
5. A: Are you going to study
   B: don't have
   B: gave . . . is giving
6. A: Are you going to be/Will you be
   B: is going to have
   B: broke . . . didn't heal
7. A: said
   B: didn't understand
8. A: is
   B: is meeting
9. had . . . ran . . . slammed . . . missed
10. A: Are you going to call
    B: forget

PRACTICE 32, p. 189.

1. lived	8. will give
2. were	9. took
3. didn't have	10. was
4. decided	11. are
5. took	12. don't have
6. met	13. threw
7. will buy	14. saw

15. climbed
16. found
17. will eat
18. Are you going to give
19. is
20. fell
21. was
22. didn't want
23. went
24. never caught
25. ran
26. died
27. lived

CHAPTER 11

PRACTICE 1, p. 190.
2. sure
3. sure
4. unsure
5. unsure
6. sure
7. unsure
8. unsure
9. sure

PRACTICE 3, p. 191.
2. a. You might need to see a doctor soon.
   b. Maybe you will need to see a doctor soon.
3. a. We may play basketball after school.
   b. We might play basketball after school.
4. a. Maybe our class will go to a movie together.
   b. Our class may go to a movie together.

PRACTICE 4, p. 191.
2. a
3. b
4. a
5. b
6. a, b
7. b

PRACTICE 5, p. 192.
2. They may come.   They might come.
3. She might not study.   She may not study.
4. We might not need help. We may not need help.
5. I might not need help. I may not need help
6. He may understand.   Maybe he will understand.
7. You may understand.   Maybe you will understand.
8. They may understand.   Maybe they will understand.

PRACTICE 6, p. 192.
2. It may snow next week./It might snow next week./ Maybe it will snow next week.
3. We may go ice-skating on the lake./We might go ice-skating on the lake./Maybe we will go ice-skating on the lake.
4. The kids will play in the snow.
5. The snow won't melt for several days.

PRACTICE 7, p. 193.
2. a, b, d
3. a, b, c
4. b, d

PRACTICE 8, p. 193.
2. 2, 1
   a. Before I turn in my homework, I am going to check my answers.
   b. After I check my answers, I am going to turn in my homework.

3. 2, 1
   a. After I clear off the table, I am going to wash the dishes.
   b. Before I wash the dishes, I am going to clear off the table.
4. 1, 2
   a. After I get my umbrella, I am going to go out in the rain.
   Before I go out in the rain, I am going to get my umbrella.
5. 2, 1
   a. After I go to the departure gate, I am going to board the airplane.
   b. Before I board the airplane, I am going to go to the departure gate.

PRACTICE 9, p. 194.
2. he goes to school, he is going to eat breakfast.
3. he gets to school, he is going to go to his classroom.
4. he has lunch in the cafeteria, he is going to talk to his friends.
5. he cooks dinner for his roommates, he is going to pick up food at the grocery store.
6. he goes to bed, he is going to do his homework.
7. he falls asleep, he is going to have good dreams.

PRACTICE 10, p. 195.
2. have . . . am going to go
3. see . . . are going to make
4. takes . . . is going to practice
5. takes . . . is going to feel
6. gets . . . is going to be

PRACTICE 11, p. 195.
2. goes . . . is going to study
3. enjoys . . . will take
4. will apply . . . does
5. attends . . . is going to study
6. completes . . . is going to work

PRACTICE 12, p. 196.
2. rains . . . am not going to/will not spend
3. gets . . . are going to/will be
4. are going to/will get . . . does not do
5. gets . . . is going to/will earn
6. doesn't get . . . is going to/will delay
7. feels . . . is not going to/will not come
8. is going to/will call . . . misses
9. needs . . . are going to/will help
10. are going to/will make . . . does not need

PRACTICE 13, p. 196.
3. talks
4. is going to/will meet
5. agree
6. is going to/will buy
7. says
8. is going to/will surprise
9. does not say
10. is going to/will save

PRACTICE 14, p. 197.

2. Will he get to work on time? Yes, he will.
3. Will he stay awake at work? Yes, he will.
4. Will he delete emails before he reads them? No, he won't.
5. Will he answer his phone? Yes, he will.
6. Will he help his co-workers when they ask? Yes, he will?
7. Will he tell his co-workers he is too busy? No, he won't.
8. Will his father and co-workers be happy? Yes, they will.

PRACTICE 15, p. 198.

Part I.

2. a
3. e
4. c
5. b
6. g
7. d

Part II.

2. If I cry, my eyes get red.
3. If I don't pay my electric bill, I have no electricity.
4. If the phone rings in the middle of the night, I don't answer it.
5. If I get to work late, I stay at work late.
6. If I have a big breakfast, I have a lot of energy.
7. If I don't do my homework, I get low grades on the tests.

PRACTICE 17, p. 199.

2. future
3. future
4. present habit
5. present habit
6. future
7. future
8. present habit
9. future

PRACTICE 18, p. 200.

2. are going to go . . . is
3. go . . . am going to meet
4. go . . . usually meet
5. am going to buy . . . go
6. is . . . gets . . . feels . . . exercises . . . exercises . . . begins
7. am . . . am not going to exercise
8. travels . . . brings
9. travels . . . is going to pack
10. is . . . begins
11. gets . . . is going to tell

PRACTICE 19, p. 201.

2. What did they do
3. What are they going to do
4. What will they do
5. What do they do
6. What is he doing
7. What did you (we) do
8. What is she going to do
9. What are you going to do
10. What do you do
11. What does he do

PRACTICE 20, p. 202.

2. What do you do?
3. What do you (we) do?
4. What do they do?
5. What does she do?
6. What do they do?
7. What do I do?

PRACTICE 21, p. 202.

2. c
3. c
4. a
5. d
6. a
7. c
8. c

PRACTICE 22, p. 203.

1. A: Are you going to stay
   B: am going to take . . . am going to visit
   A: are you going to be
2. A: isn't . . . left
   A: Is she going to be
   A: did she go
   B: went
3. A: are you wearing
   B: broke
   B: stepped
4. A: Are you going to see
   B: am not going to have
   A: Are you going to see
   A: borrowed . . . forgot

PRACTICE 23, p. 204.

1. are
2. are staying
3. like
4. always makes
5. tells
6. go
7. went
8. asked
9. agreed
10. put
11. brushed
12. sat
13. are you going to tell
14. begin
15. am going to give
16. love
17. am going to tell
18. was
19. was
20. saw
21. was
22. ran
23. stayed
24. was
25. got
26. stayed
27. found
28. needed
29. to eat
30. put
31. didn't smell
32. didn't see
33. hopped
34. found
35. saw
36. looked
37. heard
38. didn't see
39. decided
40. wanted
41. to rest
42. said
43. heard
44. spotted
45. flew
46. picked
47. didn't know
48. ate
49. are
50. expect
51. Do you understand
52. have
53. am going to go
54. to get
55. is/is going to be
56. are we going to do
57. have
58. are going to go
59. are
60. are going to see
61. are going to see
62. see
63. are going to have
64. are going to have

CHAPTER 12

PRACTICE 1, p. 208.
2. can speak
3. can speak
4. can speak
5. can speak
6. can speak
7. can speak
8. can speak
9. can speak
10. can speak
11. can speak

PRACTICE 2, p. 208.
2. can't
3. can't
4. can
5. can
6. can

PRACTICE 4, p. 209.
2. Can George and Eva play the piano? Yes, they can.
3. Can George drive a car? Yes, he can.
4. Can Paul play the piano? Yes, he can.
5. Can Mia, George, and Paul swim? Yes, they can.
6. Can Paul and Eva drive a car? No, they can't.
7. Can Eva and George repair a bike? No, they can't.
8. Can Eva, Paul, and George play the piano? Yes, they can.

PRACTICE 5, p. 210.
2. Can you do work processing? Yes, I can.
3. Can you speak English? No, I can't.
4. Can you lift suitcases? No, I can't.
5. Can you work weekends? Yes, I can.

PRACTICE 6, p. 210.
1. e
2. c
3. b
4. a
5. d

PRACTICE 7, p. 210.
2. Martha knows how to play chess.
3. Sonya and Thomas know how to speak Portuguese.
4. Jack doesn't know how to speak Russian.
5. My brothers don't know how to cook.
6. I don't know how to change a flat tire.
7. We don't know how to play musical instruments.
8. Do you know how to type?
9. Do your children know how to swim?
10. Does Ari know how to kick a soccer ball very far?

PRACTICE 9, p. 212.
2. They could cook over a fire.
3. They could read books.
4. They could spend time together.
5. They couldn't use a computer.
6. They couldn't turn on the lights.
7. They couldn't use electric heat.
8. They could have heat from a fireplace.
9. They could play board games.

PRACTICE 10, p. 213.
1. couldn't
2. can't
3. Could
4. can
5. could
6. Could
7. can't

PRACTICE 11, p. 213.
2. he couldn't go swimming.
   he can go swimming.
3. he couldn't play soccer.
   he can play soccer.
4. he couldn't ride a bike.
   he can ride a bike.

PRACTICE 13, p. 214.
2. You are able to draw. You were able to draw. You will be able to draw.
3. He is able to drive. He was able to drive. He will be able to drive.
4. She is able to swim. She was able to swim. She will be able to swim.
5. We are able to dance. We were able to dance. We will be able to dance.
6. They are able to type. They were able to type. They will be able to type.

PRACTICE 15, p. 214.
2. a
3. b
4. c
5. c

PRACTICE 16, p. 215.
2. wasn't able to ask
3. weren't able to give
4. wasn't able to visit
5. wasn't able to have
6. was able to understand
7. were able to have
8. was able to learn
9. was able to visit

PRACTICE 17, p. 216.
1. b, e
2. a, b, e
3. a, b
4. e
5. b

PRACTICE 18, p. 216.
2. very
3. very
4. too
5. too
6. very
7. very
8. too

PRACTICE 19, p. 217.
2. a
3. b
4. b
5. a
6. a
7. b
8. a

PRACTICE 21, p. 218.
1. b
2. c
3. d
4. a
5. d
6. a
7. d

PRACTICE 22, p. 218.
1. was
2. hunted
3. took
4. listened
5. dreamed/dreamt
6. decided
7. are you leaving
8. are you going
9. am going
10. am going
11. do you want
12. to go
13. want
14. to experience
15. need
16. to learn
17. can learn
18. stay
19. can't stay
20. is
21. will have*
22. get
23. will face
24. may never see
25. will try
26. Do you need
27. can I cross
28. don't know
29. can't cross
30. won't be able
31. will help
32. will give
33. can jump
34. will also give
35. don't lose
36. will reach
37. are you lying
38. Are you
39. can't see
40. drank
41. am
42. will die
43. can't find
44. gave
45. can I give
46. will give
47. can see
48. can't see
49. will you find
50. will carry
51. can't go
52. will I do
53. have
54. will find
55. can't see
56. can hear
57. can't help
58. am dying
59. are you dying
60. lost
61. can't find
62. am starving/will starve
63. can help
64. will give
65. can smell
66. can I help
67. am trying
68. need
69. to go
70. will put
71. (will) take
72. couldn't see
73. couldn't smell
74. lost
75. heard
76. aren't
77. never lost
78. am flying

be going to is also possible for the *will* answers.

CHAPTER 13

PRACTICE 1, p. 223.
2. should study
3. should study
4. should study
5. should study
6. should study
7. should study
8. should study
9. should study

PRACTICE 2, p. 223.
2. should
3. shouldn't
4. shouldn't
5. should
6. should
7. shouldn't

PRACTICE 3, p. 224.
3. She should study for her tests.
4. She shouldn't stay up late.
5. She shouldn't daydream in class.
6. She shouldn't be absent from class a lot.
7. She should take notes during lectures.
8. She should take her books to school.

PRACTICE 4, p. 224.
Sample answers:
2. should talk to the Browns.
3. should rest.
4. should call the dentist.
5. should save his money.
6. should get visas.

PRACTICE 5, p. 225.
2. have to leave
3. have to leave
4. have to leave
5. has to leave
6. has to leave
7. don't have to leave
8. don't have to leave
9. doesn't have to leave
10. don't have to leave

PRACTICE 6, p. 225.
3. has to
4. doesn't have to
5. doesn't have to
6. has to
7. has to

PRACTICE 7, p. 226.
2. don't have to
3. has to
4. have to
5. don't have to
6. have to
7. doesn't have to
8. have to
9. has to
10. doesn't have to

PRACTICE 8, p. 226.
2. had to
3. didn't have to
4. had to
5. didn't have to
6. had to
7. didn't have to
8. had to

PRACTICE 9, p. 227.
2. didn't have to
3. didn't have to
4. had to
5. didn't have to
6. had to
7. didn't have to
8. had to

PRACTICE 11, p. 228.

2. must
3. must not
4. must

5. must not
6. must not

PRACTICE 12, p. 228.

2. must not
3. must
4. must not

5. must
6. must

PRACTICE 13, p. 229.

2. should
3. must
4. should
5. must

6. should
7. should
8. must
9. must

PRACTICE 14, p. 229.

Sample answers:

2. May/Could/Can I look at your dictionary for a minute?
3. May/Could/Can I please sharpen my pencil?
4. May/Could/Can I please borrow your cell phone?
5. May/Could/Can I please get a new library card?

PRACTICE 15, p. 230.

Sample answers:

2. Could/Would you please clean your bedroom?
3. Could/Would you please give me some money for a movie?
4. Could/Would you please turn down the TV?
5. Could/Would you please bring me some fresh cream?
6. Could/Would you please take a picture of us?

PRACTICE 16, p. 230.

1. a, b
2. b, c
3. a, c

PRACTICE 17, p. 231.

2. STUDENT: Do we have any homework for tomorrow?
   TEACHER: Yes. <u>Read</u> pages 24 through 36, and <u>answer</u> the questions on page 37, in writing.
   STUDENT: Is that all?
   TEACHER: Yes.
3. HEIDI: Please <u>close</u> the window, Mike. It's a little chilly in here.
   MIKE: Okay. Is there anything else I can do for you before I leave?
   HEIDI: Could you turn off the light in the kitchen?
   MIKE: No problem. Anything else?
   HEIDI: Umm, please <u>hand</u> me the remote control for the TV. It's over there.
   MIKE: Sure. Here.
   HEIDI: Thanks.
   MIKE: I'll stop by again tomorrow. <u>Take</u> care of yourself. <u>Take</u> good care of that broken leg.
   HEIDI: <u>Don't worry</u>. I will. Thanks again

PRACTICE 18, p. 231.

Answers may vary:

1. Put some oil in a pan.
2. Heat the oil.
3. Put the popcorn in the pan.
4. Cover the pan with a lid.
5. Shake the pan.
6. Stop shaking the pan when the popcorn stops popping.
7. Pour the popcorn into a bowl.
8. Pour melted butter over the popcorn.
9. Salt the popcorn.
10. Enjoy your snack!

PRACTICE 19, p. 232.

3. Don't talk
4. Do
5. Don't copy
6. Work
7. Answer

PRACTICE 20, p. 232.

3. Follow
4. Turn off
5. Don't play
6. Use
7. Talk
8. Ask
9. Don't download

PRACTICE 21, p. 233.

2. Ø
3. Ø
4. to
5. Ø
6. Ø

7. to
8. Ø
9. to
10. Ø

PRACTICE 22, p. 233.

2. a
3. b
4. c
5. c

6. c
7. a
8. b

PRACTICE 23, p. 234.

Sample answers:

2. Let's relax.
3. Let's have a party for her.
4. Let's eat.
5. Let's go there for dinner.

PRACTICE 24, p. 235.

2. c
3. c
4. a
5. b
6. a

7. c
8. b
9. c
10. a

PRACTICE 25, p. 235.

1. a, c
2. c
3. b, d
4. b, d
5. b, d
6. a, b, d
7. b, d

CHAPTER 14

PRACTICE 1, p. 237.

Adjectives	Nouns
tall	clothes
pretty	pens
sad	boat
hot	store
true	horse
happy	truth

PRACTICE 2, p. 237.
1. delicious, old, chicken, tasty
2. camera, old, cell
3. old, English, sad, grammar

PRACTICE 3, p. 238.
2. noun
3. noun
4. adjective
5. adjective
6. noun
7. noun
8. adjective

PRACTICE 4, p. 238.
Adjective + Noun
2. dangerous, old, noisy, smelly apartment
3. old, smelly sandwich
4. old, smelly shirt

Noun + Noun
2. apartment stairs
3. sandwich recipe
4. shirt sleeves

PRACTICE 5, p. 238.
2. magazine article
3. business card
4. dentist appointment
5. chicken salad
6. house key
7. computer cord
8. milk carton
9. clothes store
10. shower curtain

PRACTICE 6, p. 239.
2. a. messy kitchen
   b. kitchen cabinets
   c. kitchen counter
3. a. city bus
   b. bus schedule
   c. bus route
4. a. airplane noise
   b. airplane movie
   c. airplane ticket
5. a. apartment manager
   b. one-bedroom apartment
   c. apartment building
6. a. phone number
   b. broken phone
   c. phone call

7. a. hospital patient
   b. sick patient
   c. patient information

PRACTICE 7, p. 240.
2. spicy Mexican food
3. kind young man
4. dirty brown glass
5. lovely tall rose bush
6. interesting small old paintings
7. important new foreign film
8. little yellow flowers
9. tall middle-aged woman
10. antique Chinese wooden cabinet

Exercise 8, p. 241.

2. b		6. a	
3. b		7. b	
4. b		8. a	
5. a		9. a	

PRACTICE 9, p. 242.
2. <u>sound</u>
5. <u>taste</u>
6. <u>smell</u>
7. <u>look</u>
9. <u>felt</u>
10. <u>seems</u>

PRACTICE 10, p. 242.
Sample answers:

2. tired		5. terrible
3. good		6. bad
4. great		7. fun
		8. terrible

PRACTICE 11, p. 243.

2. clearly		9. quickly
3. neatly		10. slowly
4. correctly		11. late
5. hard		12. honestly
6. well		13. fast
7. early		14. easily
8. carefully		

PRACTICE 12, p. 243.

2. easily		7. well
3. late		8. honestly
4. safely		9. softly
5. fast		10. carelessly
6. hard		

PRACTICE 13, p. 244.
2. beautifully . . . beautiful . . . beautiful
3. good . . . well
4. good . . . good
5. interesting . . . interesting
6. bad . . . bad
7. fast . . . fast

PRACTICE 14, p. 244.
2. correctly . . . correct
3. late . . . late

4. beautiful . . . beautifully
5. honest . . . honestly
6. handsome . . . handsome
7. good . . . good
8. easily . . . easy
9. well . . . good
10. quickly . . . quick
11. sweet . . . sweet
12. careless . . . carelessly

PRACTICE 15, p. 245.
2. slowly
3. hard
4. hard
5. clear
6. early
7. fluent . . . fluently
8. neat
9. carefully
10. good
11. well

PRACTICE 16, p. 246.
2. c
3. b . . . a
4. a

PRACTICE 17, p. 246.
2. 90%
3. 100%
4. 60%
5. 50%
6. 75%
7. 30%
8. 88%
9. 100%
10. 97%

PRACTICE 18, p. 246.
2. are
3. is
4. is
5. are
6. are
7. are
8. is
9. is
10. are

PRACTICE 19, p. 247.
2. are
3. is
4. are
5. is
6. are
7. are
8. is
9. are
10. is
11. are
12. is
13. is
14. are
15. is
16. are

PRACTICE 20, p. 247.
1. c
2. a
3. b
4. b
5. b
6. c
7. a

PRACTICE 21, p. 248.
2. a
3. b
4. b
5. a
6. b
7. a
8. b

PRACTICE 22, p. 248.
2. a
3. b
4. a
5. a
6. b
7. a
8. b
9. a
10. a

PRACTICE 23, p. 249.
2. Every **student** is . . .
4. . . . sink **is** dirty.
5. Where **do** all . . .
7. . . . family like**s**
8. **Does** everyone . . .
10. **Were** all . . .
11. . . . Everyone **is** . . .

PRACTICE 24, p. 250.
1. anything
2. someone/somebody
3. something/anything
4. someone/somebody/anyone/anybody
5. something . . . anything
6. someone/somebody . . . anyone/anybody
7. something/anything
8. someone/somebody/anyone/anybody

PRACTICE 25, p. 250.
1. a, c, d, e
2. a, b, c, d, e, f
3. a, c, f
4. b, f

PRACTICE 26, p. 251.
2. anyone/anybody
3. something
4. someone/somebody
5. anything/something
6. anyone/anybody/someone/somebody
7. A: something
   B: anything
8. A: anything/something
   B: anything
9. A: someone/somebody . . . someone/somebody/
   anyone/anybody
   B: anyone/anybody
10. A: anyone/anybody
    B: Someone/Somebody
11. A: something/anything
    B: anything
12. A: someone/somebody (OR: something = possibly an
    animal)
    B: anyone/anything
    A: anyone . . . anything

CHAPTER 15

PRACTICE 1, p. 252.
2. wider than
3. cheaper than
4. darker than
5. smarter than
6. older than
7. happier than
8. more important than
9. more difficult than
10. more expensive than
11. easier than
12. funnier than
13. better than
14. farther/further than
15. fatter than

16. hotter than
17. thinner than
18. worse than
19. prettier than
20. more famous than

PRACTICE 2, p. 253.
2. funnier than
3. more interesting than
4. smarter than
5. wider than
6. larger than
7. darker than
8. better than
9. worse than
10. more confusing than
11. farther/further . . . than
12. better than
13. easier than
14. more beautiful than

PRACTICE 3, p. 253.
Sample answers:
2. Life in the city is more expensive than life in the country.
3. Life in the suburbs is more relaxing than life in the city.
4. Life in the city is busier than life in the country.
5. Life in the suburbs is more convenient than life in the country.
6. Life in the country is more beautiful than life in the suburbs.
7. Life in the country is cheaper than life in the city.
8. Life in the country is nicer than life in the city.
9. Life in the suburbs is safer than life in the city.
10. Life in the country is better than life in the city.

PRACTICE 4, p. 254.
2. 101B is more boring than 101A.
3. 101B is harder than 101A.
4. 101A is easier than 101B.
5. 101A is more popular than 101B.
6. 101B is more difficult than 101A.
7. 101A is more enjoyable than 101B.

PRACTICE 5, p. 255.
2. lazier than . . . the laziest
3. cleaner than . . . the cleanest
4. older than . . . the oldest
5. younger than . . . the youngest
6. newer than . . . the newest
7. more beautiful than . . . the most beautiful
8. more exciting than . . . the most exciting
9. nicer than . . . the nicest
10. quieter than . . . the quietest
11. worse than . . . the worst
12. fatter than . . . the fattest
13. thinner than . . . the thinnest
14. hotter than . . . the hottest
15. better than . . . the best
16. cheaper than . . . the cheapest
17. farther/further than . . . the farthest/the furthest

PRACTICE 6, p. 256.
2. The most beautiful city in the world is . . .
3. The most interesting show on TV is . . .
4. The most boring sport to watch is . . .

5. The easiest language to learn is . . .
6. The most talented movie star is . . .
7. The most relaxing place to go for vacation is . . .
8. The best place to live is . . .

PRACTICE 7, p. 256.
Sample answers:
1. A 5-star restaurant is the most expensive.
2. A fast-food restaurant is the most convenient.
3. A 5-star restaurant is the most relaxing.
4. A fast-food restaurant is the busiest.
5. A 5-star restaurant is the nicest.
6. An Internet café is the most interesting.
7. A fast-food restaurant is the most popular.
8. An Internet café is the quietest.
9. A fast-food restaurant is the cheapest.
10. An Internet café is the most useful.

PRACTICE 8, p. 257.
Sample answers:
2. Rex is the most active.
   Rex is more active than Polly.
3. Fluffy is the youngest.
   Fluffy is younger than Rex.
4. Rex is the heaviest.
   Rex is heavier than Polly.
5. Polly is the most colorful.
   Polly is more colorful than Fluffy.
6. Rex is the biggest.
   Rex is bigger than Polly.
7. Polly is the oldest.
   Polly is older than Fluffy.
8. Polly is the smallest.
   Polly is smaller than Rex.
9. Polly is the lightest.
   Polly is lighter than Rex.

PRACTICE 9, p. 258.
2. the fastest cars
3. the happiest famil**ies**
4. the funniest child**ren**
5. the best managers
6. the tallest women
7. the oldest men
8. the most interesting **people**
9. the scariest animal**s**
10. the easiest language**s** . . . the hardest language**s**

PRACTICE 10, p. 259.
2. . . . is one of the most dangerous sport**s**.
3. . . . is one of the most expensive sport**s**.
4. . . . is one of the safest sport**s**.
5. . . . is one of the most difficult sport**s**.
6. . . . is one of the most interesting sport**s**.
7. . . . is one of the best sport**s** for your heart.

PRACTICE 11, p. 259.
2. . . . is one of the biggest cit**ies**.
3. . . . is one of the hardest language**s** to learn.
4. . . . is one of the most interesting place**s** to visit.
5. . . . is one of the prettiest place**s** to visit.
6. . . . is one of the most expensive cit**ies**
7. . . . is one of the most important **people**

PRACTICE 12, p. 260.

2. bigger than
3. the hottest places
4. the coldest places
5. longer than
6. larger
7. the largest
8. the longest
9. The smallest
10. scarier than
11. the scariest
12. the most dangerous animal**s**
13. the most expensive cit**ies**
14. more expensive

PRACTICE 13, p. 261.

	Adjective	Adverb	Comparative	Superlative
2.	clear	clearly	more clearly	the most clearly
3.	slow	slowly	more slowly	the most slowly
4.	beautiful	beautifully	more beautifully	the most beautifully
5.	neat	neatly	more neatly	the most neatly
6.	careful	carefully	more carefully	the most carefully
7.	fluent	fluently	more fluently	the most fluently
8.	good	well	better	the best
9.	hard	hard	harder	the hardest
10.	early	early	earlier	the earliest
11.	late	late	later	the latest
12.	fast	fast	faster	the fastest

PRACTICE 14, p. 261.

2. more carefully than
3. the most quickly
4. the hardest
5. later than
6. the earliest
7. better than
8. more quickly than
9. more slowly than
10. the most fluently
11. faster than
12. the best

PRACTICE 15, p. 262.

2. more dangerous than
3. more dangerously than
4. the most dangerously
5. more clearly than
6. clearer than
7. the most clearly
8. harder than
9. the hardest
10. better than
11. the best
12. better than
13. longer than
14. the longest
15. neater than
16. more neatly than

PRACTICE 16, p. 263.

2. as
3. Ø
4. Ø
5. from
6. to
7. Ø
8. Ø

PRACTICE 17, p. 263.

3. similar
4. similar
5. different
6. similar to
7. different from
8. similar to
9. different
10. different from

PRACTICE 18, p. 264.

2. Trains and buses are similar.
   Trains are similar to buses.
3. Your grammar book is the same as my grammar book.
   Your grammar book and my grammar book are the same.
4. Women and men are different.
   Women are different from men.

PRACTICE 19, p. 264.

2. alike
3. alike
4. alike
5. like
6. alike
7. like
8. like
9. alike
10. like
11. alike
12. like

PRACTICE 20, p. 265.

Sample answers:

2. White chocolate and dark chocolate are alike. They are sweet.
3. Magazines are like newspapers. They have articles.
4. Scissors and knives are alike. They are sharp.
5. Malaysia and Thailand are alike. They are hot.
6. Ice-cream cones are like milkshakes. They are delicious.
7. Chemistry and physics are alike. They are difficult.

PRACTICE 21, p. 265.

1. a, e
2. b, d
3. b (Some people may also say e.)

PRACTICE 22, p. 266.

Checked statements: 2, 3, 5

PRACTICE 23, p. 267.

Sample answers:

2. cold
3. hard
4. complicated
5. short
6. cheap/inexpensive
7. comfortable
8. cool
9. heavy
10. new

PRACTICE 24, p. 267.

2. can
3. do
4. don't
5. doesn't
6. wasn't
7. will
8. does
9. didn't
10. don't
11. is
12. can't
13. won't
14. are
15. was
16. did
17. aren't

PRACTICE 25, p. 268.

Sample answers:

2. cats don't
3. people can't
4. flowers do
5. the weather in the mountains isn't.
6. loose shoes are
7. lemons aren't
8. was/wasn't . . . is/isn't
9. won't
10. aren't

PRACTICE 26, p. 268.

2. b
3. c
4. a
5. d
6. b
7. c
8. c
9. b
10. a
11. a
12. d

NOTES

NOTES

NOTES

NOTES

NOTES

NOTES

NOTES